Praise for *Deliberate Cruelty*

"Juicy true crime."

—*New York Journal of Books*

"The tragic collision of two lives—Truman Capote's and socialite-murderess Ann Woodward's—makes for riveting reading in Roseanne Montillo's memorable account of two social-climbing strivers and the lives they touched."

—Meryl Gordon, author of *Bunny Mellon* and *Mrs. Astor Regrets*

"When the life of Ann Woodward, self-made socialite from Kansas, collided with that of Truman Capote, genius jester at the court of the beautiful people, the result was a twentieth-century morality tale of enduring fascination, rooted in a particular kind of American dream—the one that seeks entry into the sleek, exigent world of Manhattan's Upper East Side. Roseanne Montillo tells the story supremely well, with a cool relentlessness reminiscent of Zola."

—Laura Thompson, author of *The Heiresses*

"The brash and beautiful Ann Woodward's escape from a hardscrabble past and her ambitious rise from model and showgirl to the upper tiers of New York's high society is a both a rags-to-riches story and a cautionary tale—just the kind of story literary provocateur Truman Capote adored. In crafting the side-by-side tales of two arriviste strivers born of humble roots, Roseanne Montillo has given us a thrilling, tragic, Gatsbyesque saga. A wild romp of a story, boldly and beautifully told."

—Neal Thompson, author of *The First Kennedys*
and *A Curious Man*

"An enticing plot and colorful characters."

—*Avenue*

Also by Roseanne Montillo

Atomic Women

Fire on the Track

The Wilderness of Ruin

The Lady and Her Monsters

DELIBERATE CRUELTY

TRUMAN CAPOTE,
THE MILLIONAIRE'S WIFE,
AND THE MURDER
OF THE CENTURY

ROSEANNE MONTILLO

ATRIA PAPERBACK
New York · London · Toronto · Sydney · New Delhi

ATRIA
PAPERBACK

An Imprint of Simon & Schuster, Inc.
1230 Avenue of the Americas
New York, NY 10020

First Atria Paperback edition June 2023

ATRIA PAPERBACK and colophon are trademarks of Simon & Schuster, Inc.

For information about special discounts for bulk purchases, please
contact Simon & Schuster Special Sales at 1-866-506-1949 or
business@simonandschuster.com.

The Simon & Schuster Speakers Bureau can bring authors to your live event. For
more information or to book an event, contact the Simon & Schuster Speakers
Bureau at 1-866-248-3049 or visit our website at www.simonspeakers.com.

Interior design by Dana Sloan

Manufactured in the United States of America

1 3 5 7 9 10 8 6 4 2

Library of Congress Cataloging-in-Publication Data is available.

ISBN 978-1-9821-5373-1
ISBN 978-1-9821-5374-8 (pbk)
ISBN 978-1-9821-5375-5 (ebook)

For T. "S." P.

There is only one unpardonable sin—deliberate cruelty.

—TRUMAN CAPOTE, *THE THANKSGIVING VISITOR*

DELIBERATE CRUELTY

PROLOGUE

⌒⌯⌒

If Ann Woodward had resolved to live a quiet life in Europe, where she could mourn her late husband, Billy Woodward, far from the madding crowd of the American press, the town of Saint Moritz, high in the Swiss Alps, was certainly an unusual place to retreat to. Renowned for its winter sports, popular as a spa hamlet, and exclusive as a community where entertainers, celebrities, and assorted socialites gathered, Saint Moritz was a lesser European sun around which various society moons revolved. While summer tourism was popular, it was in winter that this small city shined. Luminaries descended in head-to-toe furs in the daytime and flashy jewels at night, their diamonds and bangles competing with the glittering snow. In the fall of 1956, Ann Woodward was once again the center of attention as she sat down for dinner at one of Europe's most elite restaurants.

Back in the United States, those familiar with Ann Woodward—and lately there were few who had not heard of her, whether over lunch at the Colony on New York's Upper East Side, or on the front pages of tabloids—believed that she had been banished to Europe by

1

her formidable mother-in-law, Elsie Woodward, and was now likely leading a lonely life, without family or friends, much less a lover, with plenty of time to reflect on the transgressions that had forced her into exile.

But as Truman Capote watched her from a table across the restaurant, he saw that she was not the solitary widow they expected. Capote was not only surprised to see her in this particular location, but astonished to see her in the company of a man, which was a cause for raised eyebrows, considering that she had entered widowhood by her own hand not so very long ago. But Ann Woodward did not seem rattled by the patrons staring with obvious disdain as she exchanged languorous looks with her companion.

Truman recognized the man she was with: Claus von Bülow. A noted womanizer, the tall and handsome von Bülow had committed himself to the effort of charming a long list of social contacts and prided himself on his cultivation of illustrious connections—much as Ann herself had done during her early years in New York. Ann found in von Bülow an amusing companion, younger than herself, a man with a past as colorful as her own, if not more so. The rumors surrounding him were dark: that he was a necrophile; that he had killed his mother and stashed her body on ice; that somehow, he was still embroiled in espionage; that as a youth he had attended Hermann Göring's wedding. Von Bülow could rebut most of the gossip if he ever found himself in the mood to explain, which was rare. Most of the time he shrugged away the stories with a smirk, which made him even more beguiling to many.

In later years, long after Ann Woodward had come and gone from his life, Claus von Bülow would be indicted for the attempted murder of his wife, Sunny, whom he married in June 1966, and who would spend twenty-seven years and eleven months in a coma after it was suspected Claus von Bülow attempted to kill her by injecting her with sedatives and insulin. The position he would find himself in was not unlike Ann Woodward's, and further solidified his bizarre connection to her.

Truman Capote had, of course, heard all about Billy Woodward's murder when it happened back on Long Island. On November 15, 1955, not two weeks after Billy's death, Truman had written to his friend the photographer Cecil Beaton that "Ann Woodward continues to occupy the front pages—but those who discuss it have had to move to *L'Aiglan* since Mr. Soulé closed the *Pavillion*. *L'Aiglan* has upped its prices." But Capote most often frequented Henri Soulé's restaurant La Côte Basque, which had opened in the late 1950s and was located just across the street from the Saint Regis Hotel in New York City. There, Truman's eyes often widened in mischief and delight when he and his friends told the most cutting jokes and dished the other diners, including Ann Woodward, who was not only a patron but also lately a topic of discussion.

Truman Capote found Ann Woodward interesting. Indecorous, perhaps. Certainly audacious for showing herself in public so soon after being accused of killing her husband, and with a man who appeared to be a lover. He continued to stare, but at a certain point he was compelled to get up from his table and walk toward Ann Woodward. He must have also had a suspicion that the encounter, however short, would annoy her, if not downright distress her, which likely increased his delight at his own mischief. As he arrived at the table, Ann immediately got up from her chair, angry that she should have been disturbed during her meal. A short conversation followed, during which, apparently, Ann called Truman "a little fag."

That was not the first time that Truman Capote had been insulted for his sexual orientation, nor would it be the last. But with the insult coming from Ann Woodward, an accused killer, he took more offense to the jab than he usually did. He returned the slur by wagging his finger at her and calling her "Mrs. Bang Bang," a moniker that would stick to her for the rest of her days. After leaving Saint Moritz, he would repeat the story of how he had met the notorious Ann Woodward whenever the opportunity presented itself, embellishing his tale and relishing each detail.

Ann Woodward eventually came to learn that Truman was constantly talking about her. She grew to despise the man she referred to as a "little toad," but she also should have known he was dangerous. He once confessed, "I am about as tall as a shotgun, and just as nasty." He was especially keen to hurt those who hurt him. An insult to his sexuality would sharpen his wit. In later years, Truman's friend Lee Radziwill echoed Ann Woodward's words when Truman Capote was in a spat with his novelist rival Gore Vidal. "What does it matter?" Radziwill told the reporter Liz Smith. "They are just a couple of fags."

When Truman learned of that conversation and was asked about it during a televised interview, he smiled sardonically and said, "I'll tell you something about fags, especially southern fags. We is mean. A southern fag is meaner than the meanest rattler. . . . We just can't keep our mouth shut."

In the years that followed their encounter in the restaurant in Saint Moritz, the lives of Ann Woodward and Truman Capote would occasionally converge. Ann would drift, a wan figure, on the outskirts of the social world that had once admitted her, however reluctantly. Truman, a literary bad boy who built on his early success and went on to write what he called the "nonfiction novel" *In Cold Blood*, became more and more of an ornamental fixture, gadfly, commentator, walker, and chronicler of the New York social world that centered on La Côte Basque and shunned Ann. Though one was the striking socialite whose life had gone wrong with the killing of her husband and the other was a small-town southern homosexual of literary brilliance, the two were not that different. Both had overcome hardscrabble, unsteady, fraught childhoods. Both had cajoled, clawed, and charmed their way into the elite circles they sought to enter. Both were vulnerable and mean. Both were familiar with violence. And the violence that caused the death of Billy Woodward would, as recounted by Truman Capote in 1975, incite fresh violence that would ultimately destroy them both. What began with insults in Saint Moritz would end in death for one and ignominy for the other.

ONE

❧

Ann Woodward always enjoyed the drive past the millionaires' mansions along Long Island's Gold Coast. It eased the low hum of her anxiety, when she contemplated how far she'd come. Born on a desolate farm in Kansas, having fought profound hardship to gain a foothold in New York society, she was now, at age forty, Mrs. Richard William Woodward Jr., the wife of one of America's richest men. She tightened her hand over her little clutch purse, where she had stashed her jewel-encrusted necklace and bracelets after the evening's party. What a life she had made for herself.

It was now one o'clock on the morning of Sunday, October 30, 1955, and a steady drizzle fell as they sped along. Lightning flashed in the distance, and fog shrouded the majestic Gold Coast estates. But she knew they were there in all their glory, set on acres of well-groomed grounds staked with signs warning trespassers to beware of dogs and guards. As Billy steered the curves at a frightening velocity, Ann let go of the purse and held tightly to the door handle of the car. They had ridden to the party in Billy's black Ford Thunderbird, a car Ann enjoyed driving herself, although Billy's favorite vehicle was what he called his "Studillac," a customized hardtop Studebaker. It was not a car that went unnoticed, just as Billy wanted it, and they had driven it from New York City to Long Island that weekend. Not so long ago he had brought the Studillac to the horse races in Saratoga, where Ian Fleming, the writer of the James Bond books, was staying. The car had so impressed Fleming that he would dedicate his book *Diamonds Are Forever* to Billy: "To the memory of W.W. J.R., at Saratoga, 1954 and 1955."

They were almost home. Ann had named their estate the Playhouse. It was a two-story frame house of wood and stucco set on forty-three-acres of striking gardens maintained by well-paid landscapers. The front of the house faced west, while the main entrance was the circular drive on Berry Hill Road.

The party had been given by George and Edith Baker in honor of Wallis Simpson, the Duchess of Windsor, at Peacock Point, their estate owned in Locust Valley, an unincorporated area in Oyster Bay. Billy had known the Bakers for decades, having spent his childhood carousing with their son and his best friend, Grenville "Bean" Baker.

There had been only sixty guests and at least that many bottles of wine and champagne. While the waiters carried serving plates full of canapes and other minuscule bites, the Bakers' silver, china, and crystal caught the light and glittered, dazzling the guests. Ann had been a guest at the Bakers' before. She knew the type of canapes the family preferred, and which crystal they used for such functions.

When Ann had first arrived at the party, she took a long drag from her cigarette and surveyed the room. The air was perfumed by candles that had been doused in Chanel Number 5. Ann had started doing this for her own parties, spending freely on white candles and Chanel. When she'd first married Billy, in 1943, attending these soirees had felt like a privilege, but by now it had become routine. Sometimes she was even hit hard with a wave of sadness, and so made sure to fortify herself with a few special capsules of tranquilizers before appearing on the scene. She didn't know where that sadness came from; or better, she did, although she refused to talk about it with her analyst.

Everywhere she looked were people she'd come to know, admire, and wonder about: the politicians, the doctors, the bankers, and those (like her husband) who had simply inherited their wealth. There were Mr. and Mrs. Phipps, and Mr. and Mrs. Frost, the Sanfords, of course—they wouldn't miss this for the world. And Mr. and Mrs. Guest—a party would not be a party without them. And the Blackwells, the Reeds, and the Slaters; and so many others. The Bakers and the Duchess of Windsor had attracted a who's who of Manhattan and Long Island society. They owned homes on the North Shore, brownstones in the city, villas on the islands, and castles in Europe. These individuals had everything Ann had long coveted: money, privilege, taste, beauty, and the freedom to move about as they desired. They gave off a commanding aura, as if everything were their birthright. She admired the gems dangling from their ears and the diamonds strung on their necks. Ann was wearing a long strand of pearls that coyly dipped and disappeared inside her bosom. She'd adjusted her cleavage and made sure the necklace fell just right between her breasts, which she had dusted with a translucent powder that sparkled under the light. Her light blue-gray silk evening gown rustled as she walked, which she liked.

Ann was still seething from an argument with Billy during the ride over. Their alcohol-fueled fights had become routine and often public, so she was grateful that this time their spat had stayed in the privacy of their car and had not spilled over to the party itself. Across the room, she saw Billy staring back at her—she suspected they weren't done quarreling yet.

Ann watched him chat gregariously with his friends and flirt with the women guests. Her husband had been born into this world and moved through it with ease; she did not. Growing up, she had never felt sheepish about joining a conversation, but ever since marrying into the Woodward family twelve years earlier, she had found the social conversations to be of a different, more contentious and intimidating caliber. Everyone's manners, affectations, and even laughter appeared to be choreographed. Elsie Woodward, her mother-in-law, had warned her repeatedly about embarrassing or disrespecting the family, as if she expected such things of her. Many people thought Ann was a simpleton: a Kansas farm girl, a God-knows-what in Kansas City, a showgirl in a club in New York City. But in truth, when she was a little girl, a school test had revealed an outstanding fact—her IQ was at 139, a level of very superior intelligence. The Woodwards and their friends were unaware of that number; nor did they suspect it. And Ann did not feel compelled to share with them.

Bolstered by champagne, Ann finally joined the discussions with her husband and the rest of the attendees. The main topic this evening was the recent string of robberies plaguing their neighborhoods in Oyster Bay Cove. The perpetrator had already hit several homes, and Ann feared that theirs would be next. She wondered aloud how she'd react if it were to happen. At some point during the discussion Ann got the feeling the guests were enjoying seeing her so unnerved. These people never seemed to worry about losing their wealth to robbers lurking in the dark or to fate. When Ann was growing up, her mother, Ethel, would hide her crumpled five-dollar bills inside a little fabric pouch pinned to a blouse several sizes too big for her. The contents of that pouch were all Ethel had ever possessed, and had she lost it, she would not have known how to survive. Ann had smiled, but as she always did, she had felt that the gap between herself and these people was unbridgeable, as much as she tried to close it. Nothing helped her anxiety, not even downing several gulps of imported bubbly or popping an extra capsule from the jewel-encased pillbox inside her clutch.

Finally, after several hours and a short conversation with the Duchess of Windsor, they'd left the party. By the time they arrived home, Ann was eager to turn in for the night and forget all the chatter of the burglaries.

Not an hour later, around two in the morning, Ann awoke to the growling of her poodle. She removed the silk sleeping mask from her eyes. As she adjusted to the darkness around her, Ann heard a crash. Her children were sleeping upstairs, but her husband was across the hall; they hadn't shared a bed in months. Had Billy heard something too?

Despite the pills she had ingested before going to bed, Ann felt a headache coming on and cursed the drinks she had had at the party. She always felt fuzzy after a night of entertainment and tried to stay in bed as long as she could the next day. Now she struggled to get up from bed and then grabbed the shotgun she kept next to her.

She crept across her room, heading for the door. Later, she would recall the chill of her bare feet on the floor, the silk nightclothes barely covering her, the bed jacket unbuttoned across her chest. When she got to the door, she turned the knob and opened it slowly. There, at the far end of the darkened hallway, she made out the silhouette of a man. She didn't say a word, barely inhaled as she slowly brought the gun to eye level, aimed, and shot twice, hitting her mark, the figure crashing to the floor.

Or that is the story that she would tell the police, her mother-in-law, and all who asked during the rest of her life. Many would doubt her, including Truman Capote. Many people suspected she had deliberately shot her husband.

TWO

꧁ ❧ ꧂

The young William Woodward Jr. often appeared in the society pages, showing off a smiling face and a full shock of black hair, in stories declaring him "the most eligible bachelor in America." He seemed to exude good breeding and wealth, the prince of a New York banking family who hobnobbed with the British royals. In fact, the Woodwards themselves were often considered an American dynasty. Not surprisingly, Billy—as William Woodward Jr. was known to friends—would eventually succeed his father as the director of the Hanover National Bank; he would also inherit the Belair Stud and Farm, the oldest horse farm in the United States, known for raising some of the finest Thoroughbreds in the country, including several Kentucky Derby winners and the legendary stallion Nashua.

Outwardly, Billy seemed to be manor born, enjoying the money, homes, private education, parties, privilege, friends, and the promise he was heir to. But the reality was that his acquaintances didn't believe he possessed much of a backbone, his life ruled by his domineering mother, Elsie Woodward. His best friend, Bean Baker, suspected that

Billy was still a virgin well into his twenties, and likely a homosexual. Others around him, thinking likewise, looked for evidence of both. He took no interest in the women his family and friends introduced him to, and he appeared to be more intrigued by the young men he came in contact with.

From his earliest days, Billy spoke with the flair and finesse that his parents had imbued in him, as if indeed he came from European aristocracy. For the better part of his youth he'd concluded that his father owned the world and everybody who lived in it, and he did not let anyone forget that. At school, he reminded those around him of his pedigree and last name, and his family's banking empire always found its way into the conversation. So did the horses they raised and raced. It made sense to Billy that his father was never around the house or enjoying the company of his family. It was not because the senior Woodward preferred to spend his time with his horses or go off to the races, or because he was bedding his mistresses. It was because his father was supervising the world and the people who populated it, and doing so took most of his time and effort.

Billy's four sisters, all older than him, had decided Billy was born to be their plaything. This was especially true for Elizabeth "Libby" Woodward, who was fourteen at the time of his birth. The girls often argued with Billy's nannies over the privilege of changing his diapers, bathing him, or taking him outside for a walk in his fancy pram. Elsie Woodward, the matriarch of the family, didn't mind. Immediately after the birth of her youngest child, she had developed strong headaches and a serious passion for afternoon naps, and so she left the rearing of her offspring to the strong European governesses and nannies, or to her own daughters. In later decades, toward the end of her life, Elsie Woodward admitted that being a mother was not her favorite activity.

Billy Woodward grew up pampered, indulged, and entitled. There was only one individual who could put him in his place and make him feel inadequate: his father. Billy always felt something was amiss when he compared himself with his father, that he was lacking in some fashion, and he tried his best to overcome that feeling of deficiency. However, in time Billy Woodward realized that, rather than competing with his father to better resemble him, he yearned to do more than what both of his parents had planned for him.

Eager to show that he could become something of his own making, without touting his last name or his family background, he joined the navy, where he was awarded a Purple Heart during World War II for surviving a torpedo attack that sank his ship and killed several of his shipmates. Battle had left him reckless; he had at last become interested in women and wanted to be known as a playboy. Most of all, he didn't want to follow convention the way his sisters had, marrying a prim, parent-approved debutante. So, in March 1943, Billy took what he thought was the daring step of marrying Ann Eden Crowell.

～

The new Mrs. Woodward was not like any woman Billy's mother would have chosen for him. Ann was loud, mouthy, brassy. She wore her hair big, blond, and mussed, much like movie stars might have in their more tousled, come-hither moments; and at twenty-eight, she was five years older than Billy. Friends of the Woodwards murmured that she lacked grace and charm. Billy appreciated that Ann didn't try to impress him or his family, partly because she knew she would never be fully accepted into his circle.

Ann Eden Crowell was born Angeline Luceic Crowell in 1915 on a small and dilapidated farm in Pittsburg, Kansas, to an ambitious mother and a lazy father. Early on, she rechristened herself Ann Eden, finding the name more fitting for the actress she desired to be. She inherited from her mother, Ethel Smiley Crowell, a habit of never standing still. Ann could recall her mother bustling around the farm, feeding the animals, picking up the eggs, snapping butter beans, making preserves, knitting sweaters, taking care of not only her own family but also her in-laws. Later, Ethel would display the same level of energy when she decided to go back to school, the drudgery of a life on the farm no longer enough for her.

Soon after Ethel's marriage to Jesse-Claude Crowell, their farm in Mexico, Missouri, failed. They heard from friends that opportunities were much better in Kansas, particularly near the small town of Pittsburg, so they left the security of the home they knew. Kansas weather appeared to suffer from mood swings, and the Crowells received the brunt of its viciousness wherever they went. There were the droughts to contend with, and the hot winds to add to their woes; the prairie fires sparked alive during the night and crackled for hours on end, while in the fall the torrential rains overwhelmed them with mud. The winter blizzards made certain to bury them entirely in January and February, and biblical swarms of locusts and rattlesnakes beset them in the summer. The depression they felt, especially Ethel's, often made their conditions much worse. Then Jesse-Claude suffered an accident while working on the farm and broke his back. He could no longer be employed full time, and the family had to rely on Ethel to provide for all of them.

One morning, Ann's four-year-old brother, Jesse-Claude Jr., awoke with a chill that shook him for hours; he was burning with fever. Ethel pressed cool compresses over his forehead to bring down the temperature, but his fever raged on. A doctor prescribed medicine that seemed to work, but in the middle of the night he began to vomit and choked to death during a fit. Ethel became inconsolable and, unable to care for Ann, sent the girl to live with her grandmother. By the time summer arrived, only months later, a doctor advised Jesse-Claude to send Ethel away from the farm. That move marked the beginning of Ann's parents' slow separation, as Ann began to be shuffled among relatives. By the time she was a teenager, Ann had lived in eight different homes with her mother, grandmother, and aunts.

Long after she had graduated to a life of abundance, Ann Woodward would remember the wide, empty parcels of land dotted by long-stemmed blue flowers and tall prairie grass; the soft gray Kansas sky that seemed to go on forever; and the barking of wild dogs at night, which sent a thrill through her. But more than anything, Ann would remember the shack her family had lived in, a one-story barrack abandoned by the previous owner whose own dreams of finding fortune had not materialized. There was no running water; instead, Ethel had fetched buckets of it from a well. An outdoor shed had served as a latrine.

Years later, Ann told one of her friends that when she slipped into her silk nightgown and the oversize bed she shared with Billy Woodward, she tried her best not to think back to the straw mattress she had slept on, or to the insects that had crawled over her skin. But her memories were so tenacious, so vivid, she would wake up with a start, the terror so real, that her legs would shake. Only a handful of pills, swallowed with a few beers in the comfort of her bedroom, allowed her to rest.

THREE

⚜

After the death of her son, Ethel returned to school, and by the end of 1919 she was looking forward to graduating with a bachelor's degree in science and hoping to embark on a teaching career. She believed her luck was turning. Instead, when she returned home after the semester, her husband, Jesse-Claude, admitted to her that the bank was about to repossess the farm. He had already packed their belongings and was moving the family to Hugoton in western Kansas, where he could work a few hours a day on a cattle ranch.

Ethel did not enjoy western Kansas, an isolated and downcast spot where she worried the family would never thrive. Despite her waves of depression, she helped Jesse-Claude plant corn and wheat into sandy earth she suspected would never return their efforts. She taught her daughter to read and write, enrolled in correspondence courses, sewed new dresses for Ann and mended clothes for herself and her husband, then patched her husband's shoes before preparing for the next day's work, which would be the same thing over again.

Ethel was not the only one who disliked Kansas. The early pioneers hadn't been too keen on the state either. They called it "the great American desert." However, by the middle of the nineteenth century, the population had begun to grow. Parcels of land were cheap to purchase, and those who had a dream of owning a piece could buy a few acres for a reasonable price, build a house, and raise a family. They came from back east, and from foreign countries, where they had heard that the American prairie lands offered the chance to become rich. They left behind families to venture across the ocean and found that in the Midwest the streets were not paved with gold but with dust and backbreaking labor that filled the hours.

But Jesse-Claude was not as ambitious as any of the pioneers or immigrants before him. He chose to stay in Kansas and try his hands at almost anything yet succeeded at nothing concrete, which seemed to Ethel another sign of his unwillingness to see that the state offered them little opportunity.

❧

Ethel had always believed in self-improvement, and she urged her husband to learn a trade. As the automobile became more commonplace, Ethel pushed Jesse-Claude to learn about the vehicles and get a job working on them. He refused. Ethel's drive to learn more by taking extra correspondence courses had always irked him. Her suggestion that he advance his station irritated him even further. In June 1920 Ethel graduated with a bachelor of science degree in social science from the University of Kansas and received an offer to become principal of a tiny schoolhouse more than two hours away. She could not bring Ann to live with her; married women were not allowed to teach, and Ethel lied and told school officials that she was a widow. She rented a small room in the home of a family whose youngest son attended her classes, and wrote Ann long, detailed letters, describing her tight little bed and worn blanket, the chair she used as a night-stand, her clothes folded inside her suitcase.

Ann did not see her mother again until the end of the school year, when Ethel returned home. Ethel made it clear that she was home for only a short while; she was off to the University of Kansas in Lawrence, some four hundred miles away, to study toward her master's degree. She was home to visit her family, as well as to pack a few additional items before leaving again, she told them.

But rather than going forward with her master's studies, she reappeared home in the fall and found a job teaching in a town called Liberal, where, to the dismay of her husband and several acquaintances, she drove thirty-two miles each way in order to work. The small frontier town was a disheveled collection of homes, rendered even more isolated by the harsh winters that blasted it with several feet of snow. However, stunning those who knew her, Ethel refused to give up her position. While she sometimes taught in what others considered primitive lodgings, Ethel took it all in stride.

Jesse-Claude was becoming increasingly resentful of his wife's escapades. To him, and to those around him, these daily commutes appeared more like a woman going off to an amorous rendezvous rather than to a job.

When Ann was almost five years old, Jesse-Claude sent her to live with her aunt Lydia, who was also a teacher near Pittsburg, Kansas. He asked Ethel to return to help him on the farm again; she did return, but only long enough to pack up Ann to live with her. Ethel had found lodging for herself and Ann in a small cabin near the town of Johnson, population three hundred. The high school there was a three-room space above the post office, which was where she would teach. She sent Jesse-Claude half of her monthly income and tried to visit him every two or three months, taking Ann with her to see her father.

Johnson was a small, close-knit town. It did not take long for those living there to hear about the tempestuous marriage between Ethel and Jesse-Claude. Neighbors considered Ethel to be morally bankrupt, because she had no husband in tow—and others were jealous of her for precisely the same reason.

When Jesse-Claude finally asked Ethel for a divorce, no one was surprised. The couple divided the livestock, household items, and farm equipment, arguing only over their daughter's future. Jesse-Claude asked for permanent custody, alleging Ethel was unsuited to care for the child. He tried to discredit Ethel as a mother, saying she was unfit because of the hours she kept; he also still believed some illicit affairs were taking place, although many testified that this was not true. Accusations flew back and forth, and bitter and ugly words were exchanged. After a few months, Jesse-Claude gave up his fight, saying Ethel had become too attached to Ann after the death of their boy, and he had no desire to hurt her. In reality, he'd been caught having an affair with a neighbor, which Ethel had threatened to expose. They divorced in November 1923, when Ann was eight years old. Ann remained with Ethel. Ethel's relatives were not pleased by this turn of events. This was the first divorce in the family, and the way she was conducting her life seemed to shame them.

After the divorce, Ethel accepted a teaching job at a high school in Pittsburg, Kansas, where her family lived. Having her parents' and sisters' support while raising a child would prove helpful. And for Ann, being near relatives would give her a measure of support when her mother was too busy or despondent to care for her. Ethel was still suffering bouts of depression over the death of her son, and Ann did not want to bother her mother during those periods: not with her schoolwork, or with anything else.

∽

After three years in Pittsburg, Ethel had enough money to purchase a small house. However, her relatives, including her mother and her sisters, were still troubled that she had divorced her husband and was, as they saw it, denying her daughter a father figure. Most of all, they resented the stain that Ethel was inflicting on the family. Ethel enrolled her daughter at the local elementary school, where Ann made few friends with children who spoke little English, those newly arrived from other countries, mostly from Italy.

Jesse-Claude left for Detroit to find work. The pay for his labor in Michigan was meager, and he barely had enough money left over from his railroad paycheck to spare any for himself, let alone to help out Ethel and Ann. Afraid that somehow he would return to claim their daughter, Ethel began to feed Ann a litany of lies, asserting that Jesse-Claude was a poor father, that he refused to extend them an allowance to buy their groceries or new clothes for her. Jesse-Claude often wrote long letters to his daughter, which Ethel intercepted and shredded before Ann could read them. And when he visited Kansas in an attempt to see his daughter, Ethel kept Jesse-Claude far away from Ann. Ann never spoke to her father again. Jesse-Claude eventually became a trolley car conductor in Detroit. Through the next many years, he came to believe that Angie—he still called his daughter by a diminutive of her birth name—had made it to Hollywood, where she changed her name and became the actress known as Eve Arden.

When Ann was eleven, she announced to her mother that one day she would be in the movies. She began to parade back and forth in front of a mirror, staring at herself, reciting lines from school plays and poems she had learned years earlier as a much younger child. She would stroll into the kitchen, assume the seductive pose she'd seen in a movie or a magazine (much to her mother's displeasure), and assure Ethel that they would no longer be poor once she got to California and became the next Clara Bow. It was her dream, she told her mother; nothing would stop her.

∾

During the evenings, Ethel began giving lessons on the history of Kansas and the United States at Pittsburg's First Christian Church. Attendees filled the pews, eagerly listening to Ethel, who wore a long dress with her hair flowing freely behind her, as she lectured enthusiastically.

The lectures proved popular. In 1926, Percy Victor Jordan attended one of Ethel's evening talks. Jordan was amused by the thirty-year-old teacher, and when she finished her talk, he waited his turn to speak to her. When they finally chatted, he told her that he lived nearby in the home of a widow with his seventeen-year-old son, Charles.

Percy Victor liked Ethel, a woman younger than himself, and Ethel enjoyed their flirtatious banter. Only Ann was indifferent to him. Even at her young age, she could tell where this relationship was heading, and she feared that her mother would put this man's needs ahead of hers. She tried to keep her distance from the man, something her mother did not appreciate, as Ethel and Percy Victor were becoming closer and closer. Ann and Ethel fought more viciously as time wore on, and occasionally Ethel even slapped Ann when she expressed her opinion about having this new beau around the house.

Rather than fighting with her mother, Ann started to smile, showing off those very same beautiful but saccharine smiles she had learned from her favorite movie stars, such as Joan Crawford and Norma Shearer, in the magazines she was fond of, *Modern Screen* or *Picture Play*. The kind of seductive and flirtatious smiles she believed would get her anything and that one day would lead her all the way to Hollywood but in fact would take her to the top of East Coast society.

One morning, when Ann was twelve, she woke up to the sound of an empty house. There was no racket coming from the kitchen, or the smell of breakfast. Eventually she found a note from Ethel, explaining she had asked Percy Victor to get married and he had agreed. Ann was stunned, but also frightened that her mother would never come back. Her body trembling, she hurried back to bed, where she remained for the rest of the day, missing school.

But Ethel did return, with Percy Victor and his son, Charles. Ann tried to play the part of dutiful daughter, but she resented having to share her mother. Ann secretly prayed the marriage would end, and soon she began to see signs that it would. Percy Victor was fastidious about the way things should be done around the house, how the washing should be folded, the food cooked, the house dusted, the plants watered, the furniture arranged to fit his liking and the needs of his son. He also told Ethel to stop giving her history lessons at the church. Ethel was becoming too popular, he told her, and he didn't like so many people focusing attention on her. Moreover, he didn't approve of her continuing her studies toward her master's degree at the University of Kansas, even if the classes were done by mail. At that moment she was enrolled in several psychology and criminology classes, and Percy Victor believed those subjects were inappropriate for a woman. He was starting to wonder about the mind of a woman who was interested in such matters. Ethel was devastated that he should ask her to give up her studies, but also angry. It seemed that her new husband was no better than her previous; both were men who feared the progress women made. However, given that it was so early in the marriage, Ethel agreed to do as asked, hoping that as time passed Percy Victor would change his mind.

But the arguments over her education continued, and one night he left the house with Ethel angrily shouting after him. Ann, who had been listening to their altercation from above the staircase, now ran after her mother, frightened by what she might do. Ann hated to admit it, but she was happy Percy Victor would finally be gone from their lives; the marriage was only weeks old, but she hoped they would never see him again.

Ethel was thrilled by Percy Victor's departure, not to mention that of his teenage son, Charles, a sulky boy who'd never seemed at ease around the house. Ethel packed several suitcases, gathered Ann's schoolbooks and supplies, and drove nearly 150 miles to Lawrence to continue working on her degree. Ann found herself once again enrolled in a new school, where she knew no one; her solitude allowed her to sharpen her imaginary life even further. Ethel dispatched a letter to her mother in Pittsburg, urging her not to tell Percy Victor where she and Ann were living.

A little more than a month later, Ethel and Ann were awakened at dawn by heavy knocks on the door. Ethel rushed to open it, then quickly closed it. She hurried to Ann's room, telling her to dress swiftly and go outside to play for a few minutes. When Ann returned to the house, Percy Victor was standing in the middle of the room while Ethel packed their belongings. The three of them went back to Pittsburg.

This time, Ethel decided to be more secretive about her affairs. She was determined to continue her correspondence courses toward her master's degree, intending not to tell her husband until the following May, when she graduated. She did well for a while, hiding her books and homework so that no one could find them, until one night when Ethel was studying for her final exam and Percy Victor strolled into the room before she had expected him home. Not surprisingly, he became furious. Ann could hear the argument from her bedroom, including his threats: he would leave her, he told her, if she did not drop out of school. Ann rushed out of her room and headed down the corridor to see Ethel strike her husband with her fists again and again.

In the summer of 1927, Ethel tried to convince Percy Victor to let her return to graduate school. She had only a few courses left to finish and then her final exams to study for. Or if she didn't go back to school, maybe she could teach her history courses in the community again, she argued. He refused. He reiterated that her only job was to be his wife, to care for the house and both of their children. Watching all of this unfolding, Ann wondered how long her mother would tolerate his behavior.

One night, Ethel and Percy Victor had a loud argument that drove him away from the house. Ethel then picked up her belongings again, along with Ann's, and went back to Lawrence. This time Ethel finished the course load for her degree and enrolled Ann in eighth grade. Ann didn't particularly care either way. By now she didn't see the point to trying to be friendly to anyone. She enjoyed her reclusiveness and avoided children of all ages; she was certain that it wouldn't be too long before her mother moved them again.

By the summer, Ethel had determined that she'd be better off finding new opportunities away from Lawrence and especially away from Pittsburg. She no longer wanted to deal with her family, who would further humiliate her because of her latest breakup with her second husband. Ethel knew they would try to convince her to return to Percy Victor, just as they had tried to convince her to reconcile with Jesse-Claude. Ethel could imagine what her two sisters would think of her. She no longer had a mind to listen to their nagging, much less to explain her newest problem: she was pregnant.

She went back to Pittsburg that July to visit a doctor regarding her pregnancy, and to file for divorce. She did not have much money, and, in an act that would repeat itself over and over thereafter, she skipped on the doctor's bill. Before moving away permanently from Pittsburg, she spent some time with her mother. Despite the heat, Ethel rarely left her mother's house, in order to avoid rude glances and intruding questions. And as she had expected, her mother begged her to return to Percy Victor. Ethel refused. She would move to Kansas City in order to begin again. Her mother believed her aspiration absurd. She thought Ethel should go back to her husband, especially now that a baby was on the way. To silence her mother, Ethel explained that her husband had infected her with a sexually transmitted disease he had acquired when he had cheated on her with a prostitute. It wasn't true, but that little lie helped her put an end to the subject of marital reconciliation.

While still in Pittsburg Ethel went into labor early. After hours of pain, she delivered a little girl, who was stillborn, whom she named Mary Elizabeth Jordan. Ethel was possessed by the same sadness she had when she had lost her Jesse-Claude Jr. For Ann too, the experience brought back her brother's death. Being a little older now, she wondered how much comfort she could provide her mother, if any.

Nonetheless, they found a measure of happiness when Ethel and Percy Victor's divorce was finalized. Ethel and Ann were able to move on with their lives, free of a controlling man who had brought little more than tumult and misery.

FOUR

⟨✦⟩

Having earned her degree, Ethel was certain she could find a job teaching in a prestigious institution in Kansas City and give her child the stability that had so far eluded them. This was a philosophy she would pass on to her child: that life could always be better somewhere else; that you could always pack up and start over in a different town, a different city. In the nineteenth century, pioneers had a saying regarding Kansas: "In God we trusted, in Kansas we busted." Maybe it was true. Making a living and surviving in Kansas was not for the faint of heart, much less for a twice-divorced woman raising a child on her own. Now Ethel was leaving Kansas behind for Missouri, and looking forward to better opportunities.

When Ethel moved to Kansas City with Ann, she brought with her not only her diplomas and experience, but also several letters of recommendation, all praising her skills, her character, and her dedication to her pupils. But these proved useless in the new city. In Kansas City, teaching jobs went to people with connections, either personal or political, and she had none.

Ethel scoured the newspapers for decent jobs, but there seemed to be none. Not a year after their arrival in Kansas City, the stock market crashed, and millions nationwide became unemployed in the Great Depression. Ann discovered that these newspapers also gave rapturous coverage to the glamorous lives of celebrities and debutantes, their expensive vacations in Europe and on private islands, and their nightly rounds of nightclubs in New York, Los Angeles, and abroad. Take life lightly, those stories and pictures seemed to say. This too shall pass. "It was a good time in New York," said Angelo Zuccotti, who worked at El Morocco, one of the most famous and fashionable nightclubs in the city. "In those days it was fashionable not to have responsibilities. People would stay out until 4 A.M. and then go to Reuben's for breakfast." Many Americans yearned to be a part of this elite world, and those with a dream eventually headed not only to Hollywood but also New York. Rudy Stanish, who also worked at El Morocco, confirmed what everybody believed: "It mattered as much to be a part of Café Society as it did to be alive."

Ann Crowell, growing up poor and with a mother strapped for money, studied those articles closely.

❧

Rather than the teaching jobs Ethel had imagined and expected in Kansas City, she ended up in jobs she felt were beneath her. Her life, and in turn that of her child, was going nowhere. Soon she began plotting a new way to support herself and her growing daughter: operating a taxi service. You needed to have only some available money to purchase a vehicle or two. Ethel found herself still possessing a small cache of savings, which she used to buy a few cars, her preference being the Chrysler DeSoto, and then hired a handful of drivers. Although it was not the direction she had wanted her life to take, it was a means to make a living. She started the Westport Taxi and Livery Service out of her home at 813 West Thirty-Ninth Street.

No woman in Kansas City had ever engaged in such an endeavor. Ethel hung up a handmade sign outside her rental place, leased four additional DeSotos, and hired more drivers to work for her, men who would not have found employment anywhere else. They rode around the city with knives and handguns in their pockets. They often got drunk and stole fares from her. Roaming the city looking for passengers, they dealt with pimps, madams, gangsters, and bootleggers. Ethel also knew there was plenty of social resentment directed her way. Women were expected to have a man by their side, not to build a business and hire employees to work for them, especially these types of men. But if anything, she now felt emboldened.

Ethel repeatedly warned her daughter about the men who worked for her. Ann, a restless teenager, listened. She kept to herself, hiding in the little office, where she did her homework and barely conversed with the drivers. However, she overheard her mother's often contentious interactions with her employees and wanted to respond to them with a word or two of her own. But she never did, still young enough to be afraid.

Many of Ethel's drivers loathed working for a woman, retaliating by loudly exchanging dirty jokes, or sniping about Ethel's figure and face. Ethel had the gaunt look and sickly pallor of someone who worked too much and slept too little. In fact, it seemed that Ethel barely closed her eyes for a rest before it was time to wake up again.

Ann heard the insults and hated the drivers for their words, yet she also grew to despise her mother. She often looked at her drab surroundings and wondered why Ethel couldn't do any better. But more deeply, Ann felt pity for Ethel, and for herself. Ann knew that her mother was physically exhausted and emotionally drained. Ethel had no time for rest, much less for leisure. Every hour of every day was dedicated to the grubby, backbreaking work of making money. But Ethel was always coming up short. Ann realized that, more than anything else, she did not want to end up like her mother.

In 1931 the laws changed: the new ordinances required taxi companies to be licensed by the state. And to make matters worse, several of Ethel's drivers stole her cabs and drove them to Jefferson City, registering them and Ethel's company name under their own. The Westport Livery, along with the existing roster of telephone numbers, became theirs, as if the company had always belonged to them. Ethel had to register a new company name and number, starting all over yet again.

❧

Now, as her teenage years unfolded, Ann dreaded her future. She still attended school, but unlike many of her peers, afterward she went straight to the taxi service, which had become her waking-hours home. She didn't want to spend her days in the taxi shack, eating cold sandwiches and resting her head on an oil-stained cot beneath an itchy blanket. Behind the shack stood the Roanoke Movie Theatre, and the back door of the taxi company opened into the theater's men's room, causing the smell of urine to permeate the air at all hours. Ann loathed everything about her situation, and she felt that in her mother's taxi company, and in Kansas City itself, she would be lost forever.

It was only at the movies that Ann felt a measure of escape. As she watched her favorite stars, especially Joan Crawford, she imagined that her own life could unfurl similarly to theirs. It seemed that her life and Joan's life followed a similar pattern: born into wretched poverty and destitution, the women were somehow picked from obscurity to go on and inhabit lives full of adventure, fame, glamour, and, especially, exuberant financial security.

The economic impact of the Great Depression struck women more disastrously than men. Their prospects became even more limited. However, a Joan Crawford movie, such as *Grand Hotel*, lured women into imagining an alternate vision of themselves. By her own sheer will, Crawford had risen from an impoverished background to become a movie star. She had started her career as a background dancer in a traveling theatrical company before becoming a chorus girl on Broadway. That was followed by a movie contract with Metro-Goldwyn-Mayer. Her determination had brought her to Hollywood and allowed her to become the very embodiment of personal grit, fortitude, and tenacity. Women, most especially young and impressionable ones, drew inspiration from her: with sheer willpower, it seemed, anything could be accomplished.

Ann thought that if it could happen on the screen, if it could happen to Joan Crawford and in the roles that she played, it could happen to her. The line between the fictional world of the movies and the life she lived seemed so thin that it could be bridged at any moment. She just needed a chance. She had never taken acting lessons or studied acting but was part of the drama class at her school. And now she wanted to improve her skills and expand her talents, eventually even beyond Kansas City.

Ann watched as her mother continued to work and started to worry about losing her own looks and her health. Ethel had also developed a permanent racking cough that often made her vomit. Ann did not want to see her own dreams die the way her mother's had. She wanted to go to Hollywood, or to New York. Ginger Rogers had come from Kansas City, she informed her few friends, as had William Powell. As she entered her final months of high school, her grades were so high that she received admission to a small college in Illinois, which she saw as a way to escape. But she had no way of paying for the tuition, nor could she ask her mother for the money. She had to stay in Kansas City, working with Ethel in the taxi company. As Ann graduated from high school, she feared she was becoming just another hapless, hopeless girl on the margins of American society.

∽

Ann's beauty was impossible to ignore. She lightened her already blond hair with peroxide in the style of Hollywood actresses. Her green-blue eyes sparkled. By the time she turned twenty-two, her curves had filled out and so had her seductive manners. She arched her neck and looked flirtatiously at her mother's employees in just the way she'd learned from magazines. She had also permanently changed her name. "Angeline" seemed too provincial; "Ann Eden," she believed, sounded more refined and aristocratic. Her mother was aghast.

Ann walked around the taxi office as if sauntering down a fashion runway; she reacted to men's jokes even when she didn't need to, letting out a tinkling laugh that rang in their ears. She smiled indulgently at them—too indulgently, her mother felt. Ethel came to fear that, one day, one of them might take her up on whatever she was offering. But she was just practicing, Ann told Ethel with a twinkle in her eye; though for what, she never explained.

Ann also started working in a nearby department store. During one of her shifts, an executive from its main division asked Ann if she had any interest in posing for its print advertisements. She immediately accepted, seeing it as a type of audition—and indeed, it turned out to be one. Another executive in the main office came across her photographs and said he would send them to a colleague and friend, John Robert Powers, the owner of a large and well-known modeling agency in New York. Ann's heart leaped. Maybe the future she was yearning for was finally opening up to her. And right away a plan began to form in her mind. Unwilling to wait for Powers to write back, she decided that somehow, she'd have to get to New York herself, because once she was there, her life would change. So would her mother's, thanks to her. Sparked by the possibility of Powers's interest, Ann withdrew her savings and bought a used car in order to drive to New York City. In the big city, she reckoned, she would establish a new identity, becoming everything she wanted to be. She didn't realize it, but in that moment, she sounded very much like her mother had years before, during their drive to Kansas City, hoping to fulfill her own dreams of becoming someone else.

Ethel felt her daughter's plan was mad. She remained adamant that Ann was making a mistake, but she could not make her daughter change her mind. Ethel had done the same thing when she'd left behind both of her husbands, as well as her previous life, to move to the city in order to look for a new teaching job. Of course, matters had not turned out the way she had planned. But there was no way of determining whether the same thing would happen to Ann, that fortune would not shine on her daughter. As they said goodbye, Ethel removed a pouch from her blouse and handed Ann four hundred dollars in crumpled five-dollar bills. Ann hugged her tightly, then, pocketing the money her mother had given her, peeled right out of the taxi lot. She was determined to place as much distance as she could between her old life and her new one. She did not give Kansas City a backward glance.

FIVE

❧

Truman Streckfus Persons resembled Ann Woodward more than he cared to admit, and their lives ran on parallel tracks from beginning to end. He was born in New Orleans, Louisiana, in 1924, and had been christened Truman after his paternal grandfather, his middle name coming from the Mississippi River steamship line that had once employed his father, Archulus "Arch" Persons. His mother, Lillie Mae Faulk, had taken poorly to motherhood, handing him off whenever she could to the spinster cousins who had given her shelter when her own parents had died. Truman was raised in various locations across the South before settling with relatives in Monroeville, Alabama.

Even in childhood, Lillie Mae was considered a great beauty, one of those dramatic and magnetic characters the South created and celebrated. And Truman had inherited her pale coloring, as well as her height; she stood only a whisper above five feet. Even when he was fully grown, Truman was just a mere inch or two taller than his mother. Lillie Mae was imbued with an enthusiastic spirit, a blend of attitudes and characteristics that appealed to the men she tried to seduce, but that often repelled the women in her circle, most especially her women relatives. For Lillie Mae, much as for Ann Woodward, the starlets of an emerging Hollywood became the perfect women to mimic, with Clara Bow eventually as her absolute idol. Their moves, their way of talking and walking, their gestures, all became demeanors to embrace if not copy. Her postures, behaviors, and modes of dressing were calculated to attract a man's attention. As her sister Marie later said, Lillie Mae walked as if she had "a twitch in her buttocks that mesmerized the boys in school."

As a teenager, Lillie Mae participated in local beauty contests and managed to win a few regional ones that were sponsored by brands like Lux soap. Ultimately, she won the title of Miss Alabama. Her son later embellished that win, not only granting her her rightful participation in the Miss America contest, but awarding her the title.

When Truman's parents married, on August 23, 1923, Arch Persons was almost twenty-six years old, while Lillie Mae was sixteen. The near-decade difference between the two proved insurmountable. Their issues were many, similar to those that plague other young couples; but most of all, their lack of money was the main topic of contention. Lillie Mae's desire had always been to live a grand life. She had dreamed it for herself and imagined that Arch would be the one to provide all that she expected. But it turned out that he was useless.

Lillie Mae had never planned on spending her life in tiny Monroeville. She had convinced herself that her birthright was high society, and misfortune had caused her to land at its fringes. It was because of the death of her parents that she had been forced to get used to far less than was her worth. Now she was ready to go after everything she deserved. Her ambition was for something bigger and better, either in New Orleans or in New York City.

There was something tragically beautiful in Lillie Mae's story. A gorgeous orphan living in a small town in Alabama with her spinster cousins, spending countless hours dreaming of ways to escape toward a better life in the big city and, against all odds, succeeding in making it there. Hers was the type of story her son would one day draw inspiration from and write tales about. But it was the in-between stuff, all those fine gritty details that made up what happened during the years between Alabama and New York, that was most compelling to her child.

Lillie Mae's desire to escape Monroeville came to fruition in 1923, in the form of Arch Persons, when the twenty-five-year-old showed up in front of her house to ask her for a date. The good sense and work ethic that existed in the prominent and monied Persons family seemed to have eluded Arch. He was thin and wore thick glasses, hardly the type of man friends and relatives knew usually caught Lillie Mae's eye. But in all probability, she thought he could afford the kind of life she was searching for. Arch's two brothers had settled in the business world, and his parents were notorious for being wealthy. Arch Persons, however, was considered the black sheep in his family, the one they all worried about. While he had studied law, he had never practiced and now lived on an allowance provided by his mother, although Mrs. Persons was growing tired of supporting him and lately had been urging her son to find himself a steady job. However, early in their relationship, Lillie Mae didn't know any of this.

When he met Lillie Mae, Arch Persons had a head full of elaborate schemes and million-dollar ideas. Lillie Mae found him thrilling and enterprising, she said. She learned the sad truth soon after the honeymoon: Arch Persons wasn't himself rich, not even well off, and all the plans he made were just that: plans, pipe dreams, ideas that had no backbone and were unlikely to be actualized. Arch barely made do with the allowance from his mother, and he often pleased himself by eating canned food at every meal. These were not the dinners at fancy restaurants he had promised Lille Mae. It made Lillie Mae want to scream. The big escape she had planned for so long had turned out to be a trap. Worst still, she soon realized that she was pregnant.

As a single girl, there was always the prospect of finding a rich man and moving somewhere far away, where her future still held possibilities. Now things were different. Lillie Mae quickly grew to loathe her husband. She disliked being pregnant, and the anticipation of a child brought her no joy. Instead, she resented the fact that teenage motherhood would keep her from bettering her social status. She even contemplated an abortion, but she never pursued it. Rather, she and Arch moved to New Orleans, where on September 30, 1924, she gave birth to Truman Streckfus Persons, an adorable, perfectly blond and chubby-cheeked little boy.

There was no abrupt ending to Lillie Mae and Arch's marriage, just a disintegration, a slow burning out of their relationship. Lillie Mae soothed herself by allowing other lovers to help her heal. Eventually Lillie Mae and Arch went their separate ways, Lillie Mae moving to New York City in search of the society life she had always craved, while Arch began working on another steamship traveling the Mississippi River.

In the summer of 1930, Lillie Mae and Arch agreed that Truman would remain with Lillie Mae's cousins in Monroeville. Although the couple saw the arrangement as a temporary solution, every member of the family was aware that it was going to be permanent.

It was a dysfunctional family for a boy to grow up in. Arch Persons still traveled around the South trying to figure out a way to make a living, often in ways that were not altogether legal and scheming his way toward earning a buck or two. Up north, Lillie Mae bounced her way from lover to lover, hardly paying any attention to her son's needs, even if she infrequently made it a point to visit Alabama.

☙

Monroeville, Alabama, population 1,355 in 1930, stood between Montgomery and Mobile. At the time of Truman's arrival, the inhabitants' day-to-day activities hadn't changed at all since the previous year, or the year before that, or even the decade that had passed. It was simply one of those small towns populating the Deep South, similar to so many other small towns. Its buildings and homes had originally been painted white but were now sun-bleached and peeling from the scorching summer heat, and from the heavy storms that pummeled them in the winter—at least in those years when there was rain. The classically styled courthouse that dominated so many other southern small-town squares was here too, and those who walked by could catch a glimpse of the time on its clock tower. While the municipality had finally bothered to pave the sidewalks in and around the town's center, the streets that snaked out from the square toward the rest of Monroeville remained as rough as they had always been, all of them built out of clay, which in the summer dried up and enveloped its inhabitants in a shower of dust, while during the winter rains they became a viscous goo.

Truman entered a unique household that he never completely abandoned, regardless of where he'd find himself later in life. The Monroeville home he lived in housed three sisters, all heading toward the later part of middle age: Jeannie, Callie, and Sook Faulk. The big, rambling house on Alabama Avenue had been built years before so that all might live together. Their older brother, Bud, was considered by relatives and acquaintances mostly a recluse, preferring his own company rather than enduring his sisters' squabbles. Truman, while enjoying the bond that formed with Bud, also sought out the company of the women cousins, who provided not only distraction, but also inspiration. Regardless, all the members in the family were gossipy and argumentative, resentful toward others and often toward one another, unforgiving of slights that had occurred decades before or were only imagined.

Jeannie Faulk owned a millinery store in town. She was the matriarch of the family and, from a young age, had taken it upon herself to save her family and extended relations from destitution. She built a business from which all could benefit and erected the sizable house. She ran the household with the same diligence and rigorousness that she did her store, which did not surprise anyone—it was just her way of doing things. Occasionally, one of her sisters, most often Callie, who longed for a life apart from her siblings, tried to rebel against Jeannie and her regulations. But the Faulks were stuck with each other. They were all of a certain age, and their constitutions and attitudes were so well forged that they fought out of habit rather than honest anger, just to have something to do and break the monotony of everyday living.

When Jeannie Faulk shut and locked the store, she walked down the main street toward her house and took with her a fabric pouch containing all the money she had earned that day. When she arrived home, Jeannie opened the little sack and dropped the contents onto the kitchen table. Sook often grabbed a handful of change, to buy a few extras for herself. Before going to bed, Sook called on Truman to join her in her bedroom, where she divided the small loot with her cousin. Sook spent the little stash on chewing tobacco, sending Truman to buy it for her: Brown's Mule was her favorite. She chewed and chewed, and Truman loved to watch her, either when she was walking in the woods searching for herbs, in the fields flying kites, relaxing on the porch staring at the sunset, or in the parlor or the attic, sharing with him fantastic stories she had made up.

Each of the cousins had his or her own peculiar reputation. Aside from Bud the hermit, Jeannie had become infamous for her violent tempers, while Callie, the youngest and prettiest of the three sisters, had been a schoolteacher in her youth and still enjoyed reading and writing, though she now worked as a bookkeeper for the store. Sook, the middle sister, was so shy and reticent that many believed her mentally disabled, although nothing could have been further from the truth. Rather, Sook seemed to have willed herself into a constant state of childhood, which prevented her from getting hurt by anything or anyone. Much like her brother, Bud, Sook avoided the real world as much as possible, and she took on the household duties so that she could remain home. While all the Faulks turned out to be powerful influences on Truman, Sook exerted the strongest creative strength. He would use Sook as inspiration for several of his stories.

Truman appreciated the tall oak trees growing outside the house and lining Alabama Avenue, as he had often climbed them on previous visits, scraping a knee or two. He knew the dog that lived down the street, and he recognized the horse-drawn carriages that passed by their house in the morning on the way to the square. He was also cognizant of the fact that at the end of the road, Alabama Avenue turned into farmland. He grew up as most southern small-town children did: climbing ropes, doing cartwheels, eating good old-fashioned apple pies. During the summer he swam at Hatter's Mill, a popular spot where everybody in town gathered to share a meal and a good wade in the pond. He watched the older children perform cannonballs inside the farthest section of the water, where he was not allowed to go yet. Some neighbors hated the fact that he would not get into fights with other children. No one ever saw Truman physically tangling with

other kids or trying to push another child off his back. Instead, he
ran after the chickens that lived in the backyards, as well as the few
turkeys that kept them company. Sometimes he sat on the porch as
the women of the house entertained the neighbors, chitchatting about
the day's doings. At night, Truman's bedroom was the one right next to
Sook's, and there he enjoyed reading well into the night the stories he
would act out in the daytime, dreaming—like his mother—of places
other than Monroeville.

Because of his size, affect, and attitudes—he was smaller than
those of his age, effeminate, enrapt in his fantasy world—it was difficult for Truman to be accepted by the rest of the community. Most
people eyed him with suspicion, this child with no mother or father
around, a transgressive child whose very origins challenged the norms
of his town. Aside from being harassed for being too small and too
nelly, he was also abused for being too smart. When he started attending school in Monroeville, he could already read and write, a fact that
he was very proud of. He supposed the achievement would at least
endear him to his teacher, if not to the rest of the pupils. Instead, it
had the opposite effect. All of them, the teacher included, disliked
him for it.

Only Nelle Harper Lee, a little girl who lived across a low stone
wall from the Faulks' house, seemed accepting of this peculiar little
boy. Maybe it was because she was an outsider herself. Two years
younger than Truman, she was several inches taller by age eight than
he was. She also already appeared world weary and was considered a
tomboy who did not mind standing up to bullies. Nelle Harper Lee
and Truman Streckfus Persons had bright minds and flourishing
imaginations, and from a young age depended on the fantasy world
they created to pass their time. The two of them often retreated into
vivid storytelling. It was immensely sustaining for Truman to find a

friend with similar likes, and habits, and sensitivities, someone who was living right next door. Their friendship matured and grew, lasting even after Truman moved to New York City to join his mother and her new husband, well into their adult lives. Monroeville, an ordinary, even grim town, would be the childhood home, the going-away place, for two of America's greatest writers, who would remain profoundly essential friends to each other.

SIX

While Truman lived with the Faulks in Monroeville, his parents, Lillie Mae and Arch, still legally married, continued to lead separate lives. New Orleans had been Lillie Mae's original objective, but for her ultimate destination she had always dreamed of New York City. In that regard, Lillie Mae was not unlike many other dreamers, including her son, who were enamored of its wealth, sophistication, glamour, and culture. Ann Woodward would have the same dream, just a few years later. Once Lillie Mae arrived in New York, she found herself enthralled, in no real hurry to go back to Monroeville, even though she had a son there.

In New York, Lillie Mae tried her best to find ways to become part of café society. The term itself had been coined by the gossip writer Maury Paul (known as Cholly Knickerbocker) in 1919, when he noticed six people of different upbringings sitting together around a table dining and chatting amicably. "Society isn't staying home and entertaining anymore," Paul declared. "Society is going out to dinner, out to nightlife and letting down the barriers—that I should see a

Widener, a Goelet, a Carrigan and a Warren all together. It's like a seafood cocktail, with everything from eels to striped bass." According to Paul, New York had become "cafés mad." Everybody who was anybody lived to be seen, gathering for the mere purpose of seeing and being seen. The society doyenne Caroline Astor wouldn't be amused, Maury Paul wrote, if she could "see the manner in which celebrated, and supposedly exclusive ladies of fashion fell over each other in their frantic efforts to obtain advantageous tables in the various restaurants and cafés."

Lucius Beebe, a vocal observer of the times, also attributed the rise of café society to "four or five hundred professional celebrities ranking from grand duchesses to couturiers, stage and screen characters, tavern keepers, debutants, artists, commercial photographers, wine salesmen, literary lights, practitioners of love and professional night club lusters." Across the country, readers gobbled up the stories that were printed on the pages of the tabloids, describing the exploits occurring at such celebrity nightspots as the Stork Club, El Morocco, and Fefe's Monte Carlo.

Maury Paul was there to catch it all. Paul had arrived in New York in 1914 and immediately made it his business to learn all he could about the city's glamorous social leaders. For several years he worked as a society writer for the *Evening Post* and *The Daily Mail*, sharpening his writing skills and keen eye. He was known to the larger public by his byline, Cholly Knickerbocker. During his free time and on most evenings, he spent many hours researching the lives and genealogical histories of his subjects, so as to tie their current exploits and proclivities to those of their ancestors, making his stories richer and seemingly more in-depth than mere tabloid fare. He also had a habit of walking long hours along the city's streets, especially throughout the neighborhoods where the social elite lived, memorizing not only their addresses, but also the ways in which their brownstones had been built and by whom, how the ambient lights changed with the passing of the seasons, what type of trees and bushes they had chosen to plant near their front doors, and, of course, who else lived in the vicinity. He also had a host of insiders he relied on to find out items about upcoming weddings and funerals, engagements that hadn't been disclosed to the public, infidelities, illegitimate children, business dealings, who had earned money illegally, and who had lost their livelihoods. A master of his trade, he became the leading writer about society, both loved and feared. Paul did not exude a frightening air. He was short and relatively rotund and lived in a penthouse apartment with his mother as his roommate. He was fastidious about fashion, and had all of his clothes, including his underwear, shipped from London. And he was particularly fussy about his shoes, some days having them shined at least three times. His assistant, Eve Brown, who was nearly as good as he was about unearthing scoops, was amused at his meticulousness. She also appreciated the "fragile, slim youths with high complexum and curly hair, boys with an airy manner," trailing clouds of perfume into his private office located on 11 West Forty-Second Street, which he used as his place not only to write but also to entertain his friends.

Eve Brown grew well acquainted with Paul's routine. When a story was ready to be written, Paul entered his office, located in his files any information he already possessed on the subject, took off his jacket and flung it onto his chair, removed all his jewelry, including a gold wristwatch and a ring with a red ruby embedded in it, unlatched his belt, sat at his desk, unbuckled his pants, and was ready to work on his story about café society's members and their exploits.

While his writing style was somewhat ornate when compared with the prose by other society writers at the time, beneath the elaboration was a layer of mockery that, to the attuned eye, was not all that well hidden. In fact, he managed to earn the nickname of "Mr. Bitch" while still remaining on speaking terms with those he profiled, even receiving generous and luxurious gifts from them. Society reporting with an edge was an art form in his skilled hands.

◈

This was the society Lillie Mae dreamed of joining. Her start was inauspicious: she found work as a waitress in a restaurant near Wall Street. It was not the glamorous life she had hoped for. But while employed as a waitress, Lillie Mae was also busy in another line of work: husband-hunting. All this while she was still married to Arch, although that marriage existed only on paper. She had come to New York because she was seeking a man who could provide her with all the trappings of wealth. Any day now, she would find that man, whereupon he would propel her into the next level of society she had always desired and believed she deserved.

Arch had his own aspirations, which were not consistently legal. He was forever concocting plans that promised a big payday, which would entice Lillie Mae to reconcile with him. Those plans never worked out. Some landed him a night's sojourn in jail. Some days Arch would arrive at the Faulks' house with a gift or two for Truman, and in moments of enthusiasm would announce his latest endeavor, sure that this was going to be the one with the large payday and bring his family back together once again. Despite his young age, Truman could see that Arch's words were hollow. None of his schemes, Truman understood early on, were ever destined to come to fruition.

Occasionally, Lillie Mae traveled back to Alabama, descending on Monroeville like a dust cloud swathed in perfume, wearing what appeared like well-tailored clothes and hair styled professionally, to the dismay of the townspeople, who wondered what she had done and with whom in order to afford all those fineries. But she never stayed long enough in Monroeville to answer their questions—or to see her son in any meaningful way.

∾

Much like Arch Persons had done years before, Joseph Garcia Capote fell in love with Lillie Mae as soon as he stepped into the restaurant where she worked and saw her. She was fun, vivacious, carefree, unafraid to try new things—uninhibited in a way he had seldom encountered among women. For her part, Lillie Mae was fascinated by what she considered his exotic, Cuban American background. For her, Joe Capote was the stereotypical Latin lover; she was always seeking out men who in some way fulfilled that fantasy profile. Arch was the only one who did not fit the bill.

Joe Capote was exciting, but even more than that, Lillie Mae immediately realized that he made good money and enjoyed spending it rather than saving it, especially on the women he was currently dating. His job on Wall Street paid handsomely, which showed in how well he dressed and how indulgently he lived and ate. While he was not as rich as Lillie Mae had wanted, he was wealthy enough; and he admitted that in his position on Wall Street there were always opportunities for advancement and ways of earning more.

Most people who met Joe Capote did not consider him handsome and were surprised that Lillie Mae had fallen for him. He was squat and round, wore thick glasses, and had a habit of smearing pomade throughout his hair. He opened the collars of his casual shirts to display a few strands of graying hairs. Joe and Lillie Mae thoroughly enjoyed gambling on horses, often attending the races at Belmont. Elenor Friede, who eventually befriended the Capotes while attending a horse race, was not particularly impressed by him. "Joe was a little round man, just a little bigger than Nina. I didn't think he was a very attractive man, although he liked women," she said. And women reciprocated his feelings. "Nina was very jealous," Friede continued. "He couldn't look sideways at a woman, but she'd say, 'I'll get the carving knife.'"

When she met Joe Capote, Lillie Mae felt that she had achieved what she had set out to do when she moved to New York. Eventually she would have the ability to leave her job in the restaurant, occupy an apartment in the city and ultimately a swanky house in the country, and wear clothes from Bonwit Teller. Lillie Mae's relatives should have been happy that she had done so well. But her blooming liaison appeared to irk them, as if she were undeserving of all that Joe Capote was providing.

Lillie Mae had never been in a hurry to legally separate from Arch Persons. However, once she got together with Joe, divorcing Arch became of the utmost importance to her. In order to boost her case, she went so far as to say that Arch had hit her sometimes. For his part, Arch agreed that indeed he had smacked her a few times, but only when she had truly deserved it. No one asked him what that meant, and the admission hurt him in the proceedings.

On November 9, 1931, their divorce became final, and Lillie Mae and Arch were legally bound to one another only through their battle over their son. The custody of Truman became a major source of contention between the two, not because each was eager to begin their parental duties, but because it appeared that in gaining custody of their child each could, in some way, hurt the other at a much deeper level. The judge eventually stipulated that Lillie Mae was to have custody of Truman nine months out of the year, mostly during the school year, and that Arch would have him visit during the summer months. It seemed like a fair and workable custody agreement, if not for the fact that both parents weren't ready or willing to take care of Truman or truly wanted the child with them. The custody battle had been fought only in court, and for the sake of a public judgment. It was obvious Lillie Mae had no real desire to mother Truman; she had argued for sole custody simply to spite Arch. Thus, Truman remained with the Faulks in Monroeville, while Arch and Lillie Mae dropped in and out of his life when their schedule allowed, or when they were reminded that they had a child living with cousins in Monroeville.

SEVEN

During the 1920s, New York City became, for many, the capital of the world. Young people from across the country arrived in large numbers. By the end of World War I, the metropolis was becoming larger than London and well on its way to being the largest city on the planet. By 1940 its population would rise to nearly eight million people, more than the population of Detroit, Philadelphia, and Chicago combined. Manhattan, the Bronx, and Brooklyn, though boroughs of the city itself, were three of the eight most crowded cities in the country. It was then, and continues to be today, one of the most diverse cities in the world.

New York City was home to the most famous and powerful people working in the fields of finance, banking, science, rail transportation, academia, art, literature, publishing, and theater. It had created Broadway plays, the Harlem Renaissance, and the most influential newspapers in the country, many of them written in the different languages of its immigrant population. It was also during this particular time that Wall Street came into its own, starting off nearly a decade of speculation during which the wealthy became even wealthier. People looked to New York City to tell them what was fashionable, what to read, how to cut their hair, how to style their suits, how short to wear their skirts, and how to spend their money. For many Americans, it was as if the city waved a magic wand, spreading its culture, society, and spirit of success across the country. Its economy and example helped fuel the country's aspirations at a time when, according to the young reporter Eric Sevareid, America seemed to have found "a magic key to eternal prosperity."

But the decade hadn't fully ended when, in October 1929, Wall Street crashed. That the economic collapse started in New York City somehow seemed fitting. The plentitude the country had been enjoying until then had also started there. Now the opposite would also happen.

෨

Ann Woodward immediately adored New York. She often meandered around the city simply staring at her surroundings, awed at how far she had come from Kansas City. The frantic streets seemed to have a life of their own, even if they appeared a little squalid. She loved to look up at the grand apartment buildings that lined Central Park and wonder who lived in the penthouses. The roar of yellow taxis cheered her, as did the crowds of men and women constantly hurrying to their individual destinations. There was aspiration in those steps, confidence in the eyes of the passersby she encountered. Even the men who whistled at her as she strode down the pavement in high heels made her smile. In those first days in the city, she threw herself into making the life she had imagined back in Kansas City, determined to make it absolutely different from the life her mother had lived. She intended to follow in the footsteps of her idol, Joan Crawford. No more farm life for her; no more taxi service. She attended auditions, met neighbors, went out for drinks with new people, cut several inches from her hair, and used even more peroxide on it than she did before.

The imposing buildings flanking each side of the street impressed her as she walked on spiked heels to the Powers Agency, located at 247 Park Avenue, the modeling agency she believed was awaiting her arrival. The heels were her best shoes brought from Kansas City, and they suited the dress that clung to her figure. To her disappointment, she found several other girls in the agency's waiting room. Ann had believed the owner was expecting to see her and was stunned when the receptionist told her to drop off her pictures and wait for a call.

Undaunted, Ann returned to the Powers Agency several days in a row, encountering a new set of pretty girls replacing the ones she had met the day before, until one day John Powers himself came out to see her. She was plucky, he told her, gutsy to simply show up and persist until he'd talk to her. He agreed to give her a shot. Her body was too curvaceous to model clothes, Powers said, though she was tall, with generous lips always rouged in the latest colors. He could use her in print advertisements, he told her. She was grateful. While it wasn't what Ann had in mind—she'd wanted to act, not to model—she could make this opportunity a stepping stone to her next destination. Powers also suggested that a little tweak to her nose would not only improve her appearance but also aid her chances of making it as an actress. Somewhere, likely in one of the magazines she favored, Ann had read a short article about Joan Crawford undergoing a similar procedure. And look where it had gotten her! Ann didn't think twice about changing her features. The only issue was finding the money. She had to borrow it from a newly made friend, then embarked on the surgery without hesitation.

The modeling jobs allowed her to save enough money to afford a small apartment at 315 East Fiftieth Street, glamorous by any standards, as it was her own and she could decorate it to her own taste, with plush and colorful curtains, a soft sofa, and photos of her favorite movie stars ripped out from magazines. She also had money and time to audition for off-off-Broadway plays she saw advertised in the local papers, usually the kind of play for which she went in for the lead part but ended up reading for a smaller one. Many of the girls she met through modeling were also actresses, so they shared news of auditions coming up, which they all attended. While she didn't get the big roles she dreamed about, she got bit parts in smaller plays that hardly anyone saw, which gave her the opportunity to fine-tune her skills. Her work in the theater helped her meet agents and producers—and she found she wasn't against dating any of them if they could further her career. Having lovers boosted Ann's confidence.

On the modeling side, Powers booked her plenty of jobs posing for magazine ads for Lux and Camay soap, as well as for makeup campaigns. Soon she began to suspect that Powers was holding back money from what she was earning. She knew she couldn't say something to him, because if she did, her jobs would disappear.

❧

Ann kept a good attitude, always believing that the next audition would thrust her toward stardom. Still, she was often assaulted by moments of paralyzing self-doubt that made her cry. She was now almost twenty-five years old and had been living in New York for three years. Even the nose operation, which Powers had promised would make her more marketable, hadn't helped her. She had been working hard: voice and dance lessons; grooming sessions; even special walking instructions. But she couldn't find a way into the worlds she wanted to join—acting, the theater, Hollywood, and society.

In the late 1930s, Ann joined a traveling acting and dance show. Joan Crawford had started her own career with such a show, so this touring production gave a much-needed boost to her self-esteem. In early January 1940, after the show left Cincinnati and settled in Chicago, Ann wrote her mother telling her that she would be in Kansas City on April 5, playing the Music Hall with her troupe, before leaving for Wichita. Ann hadn't visited Ethel in a few years, and she yearned to reconnect.

As Ann stepped off the train in Kansas City, she was shocked by what she saw. In the intervening years, Ethel's struggles had deepened, and those travails marked her face so badly that Ann didn't recognize her mother right away. Ethel had weakened in strength and in spirit, becoming more gaunt. Even her smile of greeting seemed full of effort. Ann hugged her mother and felt her ribs through her shirt. Her skin had taken on a strange yellow hue. Ethel could hardly speak, ravaged for months by a sore throat that had gone untreated—she didn't have the money to see a doctor. Rather than going out to lunch, as they had planned, Ann rushed her mother to a physician. He'd barely laid eyes on Ethel before advising Ann that Ethel needed to see a specialist in Saint Louis right away. Ann understood by his tight, drawn look that something serious was happening to her mother.

She hired an ambulance to drive them to Barnes Hospital. During the long trip, Ann wondered if her mother's deterioration was due to her years of anxiety, smoking, and sleepless nights. At the hospital Ann paced the corridor outside the examination room, while doctors checked Ethel. Following hours of testing, a physician diagnosed Ethel with a rare form of lung disease that was usually found in cattle, *M. bovis*, a type of tuberculosis. There wasn't much they could do.

Ann's only option was to move her mother to New York.

By 1941, her mother's hospital bills had nearly depleted Ann's savings.
She had to give up the little New York apartment she loved in exchange for a studio. Depression overwhelmed her, as it had her mother.
She no longer went to auditions but instead spent her days at Ethel's
side, in the hospital, where Ethel was now staying permanently, and
as Christmas approached, the lights outside seemed dull, the singing
on the street corners out of tune, and even the snow—which she had
always loved—looked dirty on the city streets. Her own life now reflected her mother's frustrations and bitterness.

Ann often watched her mother as she slept. For Ethel, the strain
of all those years of hardship were showing, as her body readied to
give up. Ann felt sorry for her, for the life she had led, the goals she
had held to with all her might but had never achieved, the bundle of
crumpled five-dollar bills that she had kept stashed in her bra, the
fainting spells that she had so often suffered while in the bathroom, so
tired from lack of sleep, the insults that were hurled at her by the men
who worked for her. Ethel had been of such a distinctive personality,
unstoppable, high strung, that to see her reduced to this scrawny creature was appalling. Ann felt so much pity for her mother; she wished
she could have done more than just find her a better doctor who could
help her die with some dignity.

Ann needed to find a job that would allow her to spend her days
with her mother and work at night. The club Fefe's Monte Carlo was
set to reopen, and she found a job there as a dancer. Located on Fifty-
Fourth Street, near the famed El Morocco, Fefe's offered good pay,
and she knew the place was often frequented by Broadway and Hollywood producers who could help her revive her stalled acting career.
Despite the fact that World War II was now in full swing in Europe,

Manhattan's nightclubs and showplaces kept up their rhythms. The war was still remote to those who attended the most exclusive clubs, not to mention the celebrities who poured in.

Along with El Morocco, the Stork Club was the premier club in the city, dubbed by the gossip columnist Walter Winchell as "the New Yorkiest place in town." The club itself seemed to be a mirror reflecting how café society operated. As soon as its doors opened in the evenings, celebrities and socialites were quickly ushered into the swanky mirror-lined Club Room. Those who managed to pay their way in were allowed a seat in the dining room, located next to the Club Room, which was often overflowing with loud crowds. Nonetheless, from the dining room the regular commoners could stare in glee at the VIPs checking themselves out in the room's mirrors or watching the others who had also been allowed in the Club Room. They pretended to play nice with each other or gossiped with friends about who they had seen and with whom, or who might be having an affair, or who had just split up with whom. Ernest Hemingway was a regular when he visited New York. "If you were at The Stork, you would not have to think. You would just watch the people and listen," he once said.

But the evening wouldn't end at the Stork; it would simply start there. The night wasn't finished until the club-goers visited El Mo. While the Stork gave off a more youthful character, it was the El Morocco that had earned the superior reputation and the patronage of New York's more elite clientele. The club's decor enhanced its notoriety. Divided into two rooms, it featured a champagne area decorated in red velvet with subdued lighting. The next room gave the nightclub its name and was decorated like a sizzling night in the desert, with palm trees, blue walls, low pink lights, and the blue-and-white-zebra-striped banquettes.

John Perona, the owner, said that when the club was founded, "It was speakeasy days and those prohibition agents would raid you and they loved to take an ax and break up the place. So, I told my first decorator to do something simple, just paint the place in stripes. No use having a lot of silk and satin for those raiders to destroy."

Celebrities loved the look. They became so attached to the place that when Perona redecorated the club with a more sophisticated decor, patrons stopped coming. He had the stripes back in less than two days. No publicity was more welcome than having your picture taken against the striped banquettes of El Morocco. Cary Grant gleamed in photographers' flashbulbs there, and so did Ann's favorite, Joan Crawford, among countless others.

∾

Ann worked the midnight and three a.m. shows at Fefe's, leaving the daytime hours free to visit her mother at the hospital and to continue with her auditions. Twice a night the club lights were turned down low and Ann and the other two girls sashayed onto the small stage dressed in white bathing suits, black fishnet stockings, and very high heels. They wore pink and white bunny ears and fluffy cottontails, calling themselves the bunny girls. The stage at Fefe's was only a few feet away from the patrons, allowing them ample view of Ann as she gyrated on the black lacquered platform. Ann lacked inhibition while on the stage, which made her a favorite with the crowd, and which pleased her.

Following their musical numbers, the bunny girls mingled among the patrons, indulging in a drink with one of them in one of the coveted banquettes reserved for private conversations. Many of the girls learned that these men had egos that needed to be massaged, and they were ready to oblige, their own talents on show while focusing on the men. Years later Ann would remember the times she sat at a table chatting up Charlie Chaplin.

Several of the girls were not against accepting gifts from these clients: jewelry, perfume, trips, even money. Men had never given such gifts to Ann's mother, only pain and disappointment, so now Ann took what they offered. There were rumors circulating around the club that Ann did more than just dance, that she was sexually available for money. She always denied it.

∽

In March 1941, just days after turning forty-five, Ethel died in her sleep, alone in a New York hospital room. Ann had visited her mother hours earlier, but a doctor had insisted that Ethel was stable and that Ann should go home to get some sleep herself. As she entered her studio, Ann heard the telephone ringing. Her mother had died just minutes before, the caller said.

Ann knew her mother should be buried back in Kansas alongside her children, but before that, she organized a viewing for Ethel at the Frank E. Campbell Funeral Home in Manhattan. Later, the train bearing her body left New York and arrived at Kansas City's Union Station at six thirty a.m. on March 31.

In Pittsburg, Ann was greeted by her aunts, Lydia and Edna, likely with a certain reserve. The coolness of their relationship with Ethel had developed well before she and Ann had left Pittsburg for Kansas City and had continued. Both Lydia and Edna had disapproved of most of Ethel's actions: the two divorces; the babies she had lost through no fault of her own; the repeated moves for education and jobs; the taxicab company in Kansas City—all had coalesced to make Ethel, in their eyes, seem rough and rebellious, a figure for whom compassion did not come easy. Ann suspected that her aunts believed Ethel had brought her death on herself. In fact, neither one of them even asked how she had died.

On March 31, 1941, Ann buried her mother in the Mount Olive Cemetery, within the Crowell family plot, alongside the children who had passed before her. Ann promised herself to never return to the Midwest again. On returning to New York, grief struck her more strongly than she'd ever thought possible. The small studio seemed to choke her. Not surprisingly, she decided to move again. She also returned to her job at Fefe's Monte Carlo—where she stepped into the next chapter of her life.

EIGHT

William Woodward Sr. was searching for a bit more excitement than his marriage could provide. Ann Eden, dancing onstage, was mesmerizing to him—charismatic and unrestrained, whether dancing provocatively on the stage or circulating among the customers in her little bunny suit. She was absolutely unlike the women in his circle. It was impossible to resist her eyes—they were the color of the stormy Atlantic. He often frequented the club, but when Ann started working there, she made a lasting impression.

The 1930s and the start of the 1940s were not a particularly gratifying time in the life of William Woodward Sr. and his wife, Elsie. Their marriage had become frayed. While William was always valued as a member of the powerful and prominent Woodward family, he was now becoming even more esteemed in New York society for his own accomplishments, including those on the racehorse-breeding circuit. Slowly, he was retreating from his family, moving away from his fifty-five-year-old wife, Elsie, his four daughters, his annoying sisters-in-law, and even his son. Everything within the household seemed to nag and needle at him. It was only the horses that gave him pleasure, and the young women who accompanied him to his various events. He tried to keep these assorted companions a secret, but secrets were hard to keep in their social circles, and word sometimes reached Elsie that her husband had been seen with a number of ladies hanging from his arm.

Ann Eden came into William Woodward Sr.'s life soon after her mother died. One night after her dance, he invited her to his table for a drink. The relationship progressed quickly, with Ann aware from the start that he was a married man unlikely to leave his wife for a show-girl. And while William could not offer her marriage, he provided her, almost as recompense, gifts of money, perfume, jewelry, and fancy, glittering dresses that most days she had no occasion to wear.

❧

The Woodwards were old money. William was handsome, smart, and witty. His style was somewhat Continental for a man of the American establishment. He not only dressed in the latest styles but added a top hat to accentuate his position in life. On his nose rested wide-rimmed spectacles, and, taking a cue from other men in his family, he wore a sleek mustache. He carried a white-tipped cane, though this seemed to be an accessory of fashion more than need. Observers remarked at the inflection in his speech, which gave the impression that he was more at ease with the British royalty than the New York financiers with whom he did business. That was not surprising. Years later, opining on his time in England, *New York* magazine would write that William Woodward Sr. had come to "hone a lifelong practice of acting British."

When William wasn't making money or admiring women, he was breeding horses. The family had owned Belair Stud and Farm since

1898, when James Thomas Woodward, William Woodward's uncle, purchased the mansion and 371 surrounding acres. James Thomas was born in Maryland in 1837, the second son of Mary and Henry Williams Woodward. Educated in Baltimore, he worked first as a dry goods merchant before he moved to New York City and transitioned into the financial world, working for the Hanover National Bank. In 1876, James Thomas Woodward was appointed as one of the bank's directors, eventually becoming its president. Because of his financial acumen, Hanover National Bank became one of the most prominent banks in the country. "[A] fascinating combination of business prudence with sound judgment, ability, and trust in himself . . . makes Mr. Woodward so successful a banker," an 1898 *New York Times* article said of James Thomas Woodward. When he could get away from his duties as a banker, he returned to Maryland to renovate the mansion on the grounds of Belair.

James Thomas Woodward died in April 1910 at his home at 9 East Fifty-Sixth Street in New York City, his death attributed to "paralysis of the brain." He had never married, and in his will he named his nephew, William Woodward Sr., as his sole beneficiary. His estate included an extensive library of first editions and original artwork, not to mention the home in Manhattan, a residence in Newport, Rhode Island, known as "the Cloisters," and the Belair Stud and Farm, which would become the most important place in his nephew's life.

William Woodward Sr. was the only son of James Thomas Woodward's elder brother, also named William, who had died before James Thomas Woodward. William had been born in New York on April 7, 1876, and educated at some of the finest schools in the country, including Groton and Harvard, earning a law degree in 1901. Following a stint in England serving as secretary to Ambassador Joseph Hodges

Choate, William had joined his uncle's bank, eventually becoming a member of its board of directors.

From his father and his uncle, he would someday inherit the Hanover National Bank, but it was Belair Stud and Farm that most excited him, because he had developed a fierce affinity for racehorses while in England. He was intent on enlarging the farm as much as possible, believing that through horse racing, not banking, he would achieve an elite position within a special society. But the banking fortune made him a very marriageable bachelor whose family might not be at the center of high society but was still rich and respected.

∽

He met Elsie Cryder while attending a horse race in Saratoga. He watched from behind as the young Elsie clutched a parasol that matched her yellow dress. She was accompanied by her father, Duncan Cryder, a prominent New York businessman who in 1891, along with a group of businessmen, had founded the Long Island Shinnecock Hills Golf Club. Because of a family scandal involving an uncle, Duncan Cryder had moved the family to Paris, where, according to Elsie, they had indulged in a "life of leisure." That had lasted for several years before the whole family returned to New York in 1899.

But even as he admired the young Elise Cryder, William Woodward was still getting over his attachment to Mary Gaulet, a young woman from a prominent Dutch family who owned magnificent real estate in the Netherlands and in the United States, most especially in New York. While the two had not announced formal plans to wed, the unspoken sentiment was that marriage was in the works. Instead, William and Mary broke up. Now he was intrigued by this new woman who had gone to Saratoga to watch the horse races, but he took some time before he began to court her—and then to marry her.

The Woodwards' Long Island home was a stately brick manor on Cedar Swamp Road in Brookville. It reminded William Sr. of an English estate. It featured sixty acres of wooded fields, meadows, stables for horses, and English gardens. William Sr. was pleased to see foxes running through the property, reminding him of the fox runs in his beloved England. For Elsie the foxes weren't much of a charm. Rather, it was the fact that the property sat next to that of Winthrop Aldrich, a relative of the Rockefellers and a member of the board of directors of Chase National Bank. The Woodwards' own wealth was nowhere near that of the Rockefellers, a matter that irked her.

It peeved Elsie Woodward that despite their prosperity they were still not considered part of the McAllister's "Four Hundred," New York society's most inner circle. The author and social aristocrat Ward McAllister had coined the term "Four Hundred" for the number of socially prominent people who would fit, both literally and symbolically, into the ballroom of the home of socialite Caroline Astor. A reporter once asked McAllister to expand on the idea. "If you go outside that number," McAllister elucidated, "you shake people who are either not at ease in a ballroom or else make other people not at ease."

Long Island's Gold Coast, featuring dozens of villages and estates set on hilly, woody terrain, lies along Long Island Sound on the island's north fork. Long Island had begun to change at the turn of the twentieth century. As the automobile became more popular and reliable, those who could began to search for areas of respite outside the city. With their new mobility, not to mention their money, New York's elite crowds began to take second homes in the seaside towns along the coast of Long Island. This new influx of affluence transformed Long Island's rural counties into a new suburbia for the rich.

What they built were not simple homes that blended in with the surrounding landscapes. In an effort to flaunt their money, the New York City social elite constructed hundreds of glamourous estates, laid out with English gardens and staffed by dozens of servants. The Gold Coast families held connections to almost every industry in the world, including shipping, mining, railroads, and, of course, banking. They had money to spend on not only building their large estates, but also furnishing them with great art and imported decorative pieces. Of course, these estates were often only weekend getaways, as for the most part the families were full-time residents of New York City, where they also owned palatial brownstones as abundantly decorated as their weekend cottages.

The Gold Coast began to glimmer in the country's social consciousness, the exploits of its inhabitants becoming fodder for the social papers as well as novels, including F. Scott Fitzgerald's *The Great Gatsby*. The previously rural area was now an enclave for those who brought their boats in for the summer, and the local inhabitants who had grown used to arising early for a day of fishing now had to compete for space to drop a line with some rich boy wanting to tie up his yacht in the same spot.

∽

Elsie Woodward came from one of America's oldest and finest banking families. Elsie's full name was Elizabeth Ogden Cryder, named after her mother, Elizabeth. She was one of the Cryder triplets, along with Edith and Ethel, identical daughters born in 1883 and brought up in Paris until their return to New York, where they became well known in the city, attending parties and events that they had been invited to and somehow finding their way into the ones they had not. At nearly five foot seven and perfectly coiffed and groomed, they walked down the city's streets with their heads held high, never turning to see who was watching them. Just like her sisters, Elsie grew up accustomed to having, and expecting, the best of everything: the best clothing, the best houses, the best people to socialize with, and ultimately the best spouses for her children. She did not suffer insufficiency or imperfection. While eventually all three sisters had gone on to find good husbands, Elsie had found the most perfect one—or so William Woodward Sr. always reminded her.

〜

When Elsie married William Woodward Sr. in October 1904, a newspaper called the marriage the most brilliant wedding of the year. Decades later, Elsie would still recall arriving in front of Grace Church and being greeted by an enthusiastic crowd eager to catch a glimpse and admire her exquisite bridal gown.

But while Elsie always remembered her wedding day with pleasure—the crowds that gathered to watch her entrance into the church, her intricate dress—she tried, not always with success, to forget certain portions of what followed. Her honeymoon in London was not a success. The weather was gloomy and dreary, but beyond that, she was discomfited to discover that her husband's sexual appetites did not match her own, as she seemed to have none. But it was the salacious article that appeared in a newspaper that bothered her the most, the one that named Mary Gaulet, her husband's previous fiancée, as a better and more beautiful match for William Woodward Sr.

Although her husband was by now the vice president of the Central Hanover Bank, he refused to buy or even rent a house for them to live on their own, as a couple. Instead, they returned to New York and decamped to William's mother's house. His father had died, and William Sr. thought the large, lavish Woodward brownstone, located on Fifty-First Street, was ample enough to accommodate all of them. Elsie was dismayed.

Even more appalling was the fact that soon thereafter William Sr. threw himself into the business of banking and the sport of horse racing. Whenever he was home or had a private moment with his wife, he talked of nothing but horses, the new breeds he was going to acquire and then race, the expansion of his farm, and so on and so forth, to Elsie's endless annoyance.

He had taken over the presidency not only of Hanover National Bank, but also of Belair Stud and Farm. And he soon decided to raise Thoroughbreds for the first time. In fact, by the early 1920s, William Woodward Sr. had developed a full-fledged breeding operation on the grounds of the Belair Stud and Farm, hiring a manager of the Thoroughbred operations to live on the premises with his young family. In 1923, he also hired trainer James "Sunny Jim" Fitzsimmons, who also went by the nickname of "Mr. Fitz," to take over the training of the horses and ready them for competition. It was also during this time that William Woodward Sr. came up with the famous red-and-white spotted silks that would represent the Belair Stud and Farm.

In 1930, all of William Woodward Sr.'s sporting efforts appeared to coalesce: he was voted chairman of the Jockey Club of New York, an accolade he had always desired, and his horse, Gallant Fox, ridden by Earl Sande, won the Triple Crown—the Kentucky Derby, at Louisville's Churchill Downs; the Preakness Stakes at Baltimore's Pimlico; and the Belmont Stakes at New York's Belmont Park. Gallant Fox had been only the second horse in history to do that.

At the end of the 1930 season, Gallant Fox was retired and transferred to Claiborne Stud, located near Paris, Kentucky. Woodward moved his breeding facilities to Kentucky, transferring the colts to Belair for training by the capable hands of Mr. Fitz. Every year, in the spring, William Woodward Sr. and Mr. Fitz traveled to Kentucky to look at the new crop of horses and to figure out which ones could be taken back to Maryland and turned into champions. It was, for William Woodward Sr., one of the most rewarding, if not the most rewarding aspect of his life, giving him the kind of fulfillment and delight that nothing else did, not even his family.

In Kentucky Gallant Fox was bred with the mare Flambino, from which an even more famous horse was born: Omaha. A chestnut colt of a stubborn disposition, Omaha also went on to win the Triple Crown in 1935, along with various other races in the United States and in England. And with success came the money. Not that the Woodward family needed it. But it seemed that as much as they had, the horses provided even more.

When in 1939 William Woodward Sr. appeared on the cover of *Time* magazine, he knew he had made a name for himself that went beyond the one handed down to him by his relatives. He hoped one day to leave Belair to his only son, Billy, to continue his legacy. But his son would not appear to share the same fascination with horses that his father had; actually, his son would not seem to share much with him at all.

∽

As Elsie Woodward began to birth the Woodward children, starting with baby Edith, and as William Woodward's interest seemed more focused on his horses, she concluded that if her husband's interests could lie elsewhere, so could hers. Dozing off in the afternoons became a common hobby, as did complaining about headaches, which also evolved into an excuse to seclude herself in her room away from her mother-in-law.

It was only after Elsie gave birth to their second daughter, Eliza-

beth, whom everybody called Libby, that William Woodward Sr. finally decided to find a house for his family, some five blocks away from
the family manse. Two more daughters, Sarah and Ethel, were born at
9 East Fifty-Sixth Street, and finally a boy, Billy. The arrivals of these
children did not further William Woodward's engagement with his
family. He took frequent trips to England, where he remained longer
and longer to watch the horse races.

Elsie and William's relationship faltered. She knew that during his
frequent trips to England he enjoyed the company of young women,
and that his unfaithfulness continued while in New York. For Elsie,
her company now included the many friends she saw during her salons, which she had started to hold, and which also included people
from the theater world. In fact, by the 1920s Elsie Woodward was
conducting the most well-known social salon in New York, which she
continued to lead until her death.

❧

William Woodward Sr. knew that his wife would not take well to a
scandal, and he had no plans to cause one. Unlike Elsie's uncle, who
had embezzled from his own bank, William Woodward Sr. would not
damage his family's reputation or its ability to thrive in New York.

And so, one night, drinking at a cozy corner table at Fefe's Monte
Carlo, under the cloak of smoky anonymity, William Woodward Sr.
told Ann Eden Crowell that he needed to end their illicit relationship.
But he still wanted to keep her close at hand. He still desired her, and
he'd come up with a perfect scheme: perhaps Ann Eden could use her
seduction skills on his son, Billy Woodward. Even though the society
pages were now crowing about Billy's eligibility as a bachelor, he didn't
seem to want a girlfriend. Woodward Sr. suspected that his son was
still a virgin, and he had also begun hearing rumors that Billy was in

fact a homosexual. Woodward Sr. couldn't have any of that nefarious-
ness around his family. Maybe Ann Eden could teach his offspring
a thing or two about women and turn him around. Ann immediately
said yes. If she couldn't have the father, she would gladly accept the
son.

NINE

Billy Woodward and his friend Bean Baker walked into Fefe's at two forty-five in the morning for a drink. Bean Baker was the more extroverted of the two, and perhaps that's why they had gotten along so well since childhood. Growing up surrounded by four sisters, a mother who ignored him or was preoccupied with hosting teas for her friends or retired to her bedroom with headaches, and a father engrossed with horse breeding, Billy enjoyed having a reckless friend like Bean. Even as an older child, Bean Baker was always eager to try anything dangerous. He kept a collection of guns in his room, with several handguns stashed under his mattress. In time, Billy Woodward would also acquire pistols. Their favorite pastime as teenagers was playing at being hunters while in Billy's large bedroom or aiming loaded shotguns at each other.

Ann was preparing for her three a.m. show when Billy and Bean entered the club. Looking out at the audience from behind the curtained stage, she recognized Billy from a picture William Woodward Sr. had shown her. After the show, Bean invited Ann and a friend to sit at their table. Billy ogled her without saying much of anything. She knew very well the power she had over men, and she knew how to use it.

Billy Woodward was obviously younger than she was, and he did seem virginal. There was indeed something bashful about him, and as the night progressed, he never seemed to become any more comfortable.

Ann lit a cigarette and put it to her lips. He looked at her, at her breasts spilling out from a bra that was too small, and at her legs in those black stockings that drove men wild. Ann could tell right away that the young Billy Woodward had already succumbed to her charms. Years later, when he spoke to friends about the meeting, he would describe that moment at Fefe's as a classic seduction scene plotted by her, something concocted by an experienced harlot in order to get her man. According to Billy, he was a powerless puppet controlled by an older woman.

Shortly after the introduction, Billy and Ann began an affair. And soon after that, they decided to marry. Elsie Woodward was aghast. William Woodward Sr. immediately tried to dissuade Billy, taking him on a father-son trip to their Sag Harbor home. His initial plan had been to initiate his son into sex and to keep in some proximity a woman he enjoyed, and now he was finding himself with an inappropriate potential daughter-in-law. But Billy was smitten. Nothing his parents said would change his mind.

❧

Billy and Ann had their first date at a public and fashionable place, the famous 21 Club on West Fifty-Second Street. He treated Ann to the restaurant's twenty-dollar dinner, considered the best in town. While she was flattered, Ann was always on a diet and didn't touch her meal. Nervous, Billy had only picked at his food too. Trying to show off, Billy had ordered an expensive bottle of champagne and felt relieved when Ann shared it with him. She was amused by this boy of twenty-two, who seemed nervous in her presence. It made her feel so much older than twenty-seven, and wise too. She admitted to him that her mother had recently died and watched for his reaction. He had started to fidget, unsure of what to say. She also revealed that she had often fought with her mother when she was a youngster, a fact that seemed to charm him, because in his family children never argued with their parents; they simply obeyed.

They had also talked about horses, and Billy had been further impressed when Ann revealed herself a fan of the races. She did not tell him she had seen those horses race while she was in the company of his father. She had been able to deduce that he desired her—after these many years in New York, she had come to understand very well what men wanted—but that he didn't know how to go about getting what he lusted for. For once, she had the upper hand. Doubtlessly, she could imagine a life with him that was very different from the one she was currently leading.

Billy, for his part, thought Ann was different, defiant, unwilling to compromise her principles in order to make herself liked. She contrasted dramatically with anyone else his mother had in mind for him, with anyone else she had so far brought to his attention. His parents wouldn't appreciate the idea of her; he already knew that, and that knowledge further bonded him to Ann.

Certainly, she asked about his family, but that was out of politeness, Billy had come to believe. How could a woman like her care where he had gone to school, or what he had studied while in college, or where he now made his home? Where he vacationed or how he made his living? She was beyond those matters, he concluded on their first date.

∾

On Saturday, August 15, 1942, Billy Woodward drove his black Stu-dillac to pick up Ann Eden Crowell at her studio apartment. For the occasion, he donned a red-and-white bow tie, representing the Belair Stud and Farm colors. When he saw Ann, his face blushed nearly the same color as the tie. She wore a green dress, the cloth so flimsy it clung to her body. Her large hat covered her long blond hair, and she held it in place as they sped along the New York highway toward Saratoga.

The ride was different from the one she had taken some years back from Kansas City to New York. Back then, she had driven for miles in a used car she had bought for a few dollars with the meager savings she had accumulated working at a department store, all of her belongings in the trunk, her stockinged feet on the pedal, as it made driving more comfortable. She had slept in the cramped back seat in the parking lots of seedy motels, because she couldn't afford a room. Now she was in the company of a very rich man—a boy, really—who was driving her in an expensive car to watch famous horses run along a track. She felt satisfied.

When they arrived at Saratoga's track, a valet took their car and Billy directed her toward the clubhouse, where members of the elite crowd, including his family, were gathering for the occasion. He nor-mally despised these elaborate social gatherings, as he did his required appearances at charity balls and galas, with his family and his family's friends. He performed all these social functions with dread, consider-ing them nothing more than unwelcome duties imposed on him by his station in life. But this day was different. He suspected that he was going to relish this outing. He already knew that he did not want to be complacent about the way his life was unfolding, allowing everybody else to make choices and decisions for him, including job prospects and whom to marry. By bringing Ann Eden here, he was, in essence, thumbing his nose against the establishment among which he had been born and raised.

Ann arrived at the races enveloped in a cloud of perfume and smoke from a cigarette. Elsie Woodward was dismayed. Why had Billy chosen to introduce his fiancée in a public place, during one of the few outings his mother had recently ventured out to attend? As of late Elsie Woodward had been retreating from public life more and more, and most society people were stunned to finally see her attending an outdoor event, especially a horse race. She had aged, many agreed. It seemed she no longer paid attention to fashion; her garments were a very dark shade of black or blue, resembling mourning clothes.

Who was the curious girl with Billy? Normally, when meeting the young people surrounding her children, Elsie quickly assessed their social standing. Elsie immediately disliked Ann and all that she represented and was fearful of what this pairing might mean for the family. The young woman was bold, brazen, loud. She smoked and drank liquor freely. To Elsie's immense dismay, Ann even reached out and removed a red rose from the flower arrangement on the nearby table and inserted it in Billy's lapel. Ann thought it would be an endearing gesture, but judging from everyone's appalled looks, she realized that she had done something improper. As the races started, she squealed in delight, and while Billy's sisters tried to shush her, he let Ann be, enjoying everyone else's sense of discomfort.

In Elsie Woodward's eyes, Ann was nothing more than the classic gold digger. Certainly, as a young woman she had had her own social transgressions—Elsie once had the audacity to enter a formal affair smoking a cigarette, and Grace Vanderbilt had admonished her loudly for all to hear—but this woman was a walking, talking, social transgression. The girl continuing to inhale cigarettes despite the many disapproving glances directed her way. She was either oblivious to the stares or simply didn't care about them. Both possibilities bothered Elsie. She understood right away that Ann had a defiant will, the kind that wouldn't easily be broken by a few sharp rebukes from the likes of Grace Vanderbilt or Elsie Woodward.

William Woodward Sr. seemed uncomfortable in Ann's presence. Ann smiled widely at him, but of course she wasn't going to reveal anything about their relationship. Ann wouldn't tell Elsie that her husband had invited her to the tracks once before, or that they had once spent a lovely weekend together in Maryland while Elsie and the rest of the family were on vacation elsewhere. And she certainly wasn't going to tell Elsie, or Billy for that matter, that it had been William Woodward Sr.'s idea that she rid Billy of his virginity.

Even without these revelations, Elsie Woodward was completely appalled. Perhaps it was Ann's clothes, the way they clung to her figure; or her ample breasts, rising from a dress a size or two too small; or the colors, too bright, too tropical, just too something. Elsie believed the girl was nothing more than a money-hungry woman only after Billy's $10 million trust, which was often publicized in the newspapers. "One look and I knew the whole story," Elsie told her friends later. "I wish Billy had just married one of the attractive housemaids. At least we would have known where she came from."

From the moment Billy was born, Elsie had been plotting his future, particularly his marriage, which she wanted to be to a debutante who would usher him and, by extension, the whole family, into an even higher tier of social standing. Starting in Billy's childhood, Elsie had cast about for the right young girl to become the daughter-in-law who would meet her high standards. She had lately become intrigued by Sarah Churchill, the child who was endowed not on one, but on two fronts: a royal on the English side, and a fortunate heir from the Vanderbilts on the other. Sarah's mother was Consuelo Vanderbilt Churchill, the Duchess of Marlborough. What a pair they would make, Billy and Sarah. But that dream was dashed when Ann entered the picture. An affair, a youthful crush on someone out of his class that would eventually blow over—much like a bad bout of influenza—that was one thing. But to marry such a person was a profound error.

Ann understood right away that she was not welcome. She had not expected to be greeted enthusiastically by Elsie Woodward, or by any of her kin. Still, their behavior seemed out of character even for the likes of them. It was not much different from the resentment Ethel had received from her male competitors when she had opened her taxi company back in Kansas City. It turned out that Ethel had taught Ann quite a lot about standing firm in the face of adversaries. And she became more resolute in her pursuit of Billy Woodward.

❧

While Elsie Woodward was peeved by her son's indiscretion, not to mention by what those indiscretions were doing to the family's reputation, she was used to scandal, as much as she loathed to admit it. In 1891, when she was only eight years old, her uncle W. Wetmore Cryder, then president of the Madison Square Bank, had been indicted for embezzling nearly forty thousand dollars from the institution he headed. Wetmore had been a well-regarded member of the New York society and a financier; a member of several respected private clubs, including the Knickerbocker; and the owner of a mansion in Tuxedo Park, an enclave where some of the wealthiest New Yorkers had their homes. But everything collapsed when he was charged with embezzlement and soon after arrested and sent to prison. Elsie's family had had to escape to Europe. She knew from girlhood how easy it was to be exiled from society. Now the family preferred not to think too much about that time, or about the uncle.

After the trip to the races, when she was back in the city, Elsie hired a private investigator to dig into Ann's background. Elsie had a way of moving swiftly when it came to her family. Days later, Elsie pored over the investigator's report. Ann's mother, she learned, had been married and divorced twice, and she had indulged in several affairs. The people Ethel had associated with while working in the taxi company were, many of them, criminals. And what to say of Ann's father and his failed enterprises? Looking at Ann's birth certificate, Elsie saw that the girl hadn't even been born at home or in a hospital but in a "black box," a shack behind her family's farm where the animals were slaughtered.

Elsie also became quickly acquainted with Ann's work at Fefe's, strutting in her little bunny costume. Elsie was appalled to learn that Ann was showing off to her girlfriends a thick gold bracelet made at the turn of the century. Elsie knew that this was the bracelet Billy's grand-uncle James had given Billy's grandmother decades earlier. How could her son be giving away the family's heirlooms to a harlot?

Elsie confronted Billy about Ann and told him what she had learned about the woman he planned to bring into the Woodward family. She went so far as to disclose that during her earlier years as a traveling actress, Ann Eden had even enjoyed an illicit affair with the actor Franchot Tone, while he was still married to Joan Crawford. Ann would prove to be a stain on the family, not to mention what she would do to Billy himself—it wouldn't end well, she warned him. She was a hazard, Elsie believed, and her husband, Billy's father, agreed. Elsie would not have put it this directly to her son, but she knew what young men were like, and she would have intimated to Billy that Ann was the kind of woman an otherwise respectable gentleman would have a little fun with for a while, but one he never truly and openly became involved with, much less introduced to his family and friends. But Billy wouldn't entertain any of his mother's arguments. Hearing them seemed to have the opposite effect on Billy. He found it titillating that this girl, a woman who had seduced a man to commit adultery on a movie star wife, now wanted him. He was impressed with Ann, and a little bit with himself too.

No one who knew Billy thought him the rebellious type. Going out with Ann was the first act of true disobedience Elsie or anyone else could remember. He spent most of his nights at her small studio, returning home in the early-morning hours. It gave him so much pleasure to know that his actions were thought of as illicit and scandalous, almost dirty. He found himself enjoying Ann all the more.

Despite Elsie's warnings, Billy Woodward and Ann Eden became engaged. But each had different reasons for being ecstatic. For Billy, dating someone like Ann meant a clear break from convention, a sign that he was an individual, a man who could make his own decisions and was not bound by familial duties. And for Ann Eden, Billy Woodward came from the world she had always dreamed of. If she played her cards right and found a place in not only his bed but also his heart, the relationship could write the next chapter in her life.

❦

Billy Woodward enlisted in the navy in December 1942 as World War II summoned young American men into combat. The notion that he might die in the war seemed to make his affair with Ann feel even more urgent, and incredibly tragic; it was possible their time together would be grievously short. Ann found herself crying often about such a possibility. However, the war had now given him the opportunity to prove himself in the eyes of his father, and donning his navy uniform made him feel like an adult, somehow no longer under his mother's thumb.

When he was called away to the gunnery school in Tacoma, Washington, it was Ann who initiated talks of imminent marriage. She felt the need to belong to him, she told him, and the idea that something might happen to him while abroad made her feel abandoned. Billy didn't immediately assent but promised her that he would think about it during their separation, which might be long. And despite the great terror of war, there seemed to be something romantic about it as well: he, a dashing young man going off to help his country, while back in New York City Ann was waiting for him.

Left behind back east, Ann was certain that he would forget about her, even though he'd promised to marry her. She had seen how young, marriageable women looked at him when they were out together. But when his letter arrived, asking her if there was someone whose permission he needed to ask before marrying her, she was elated and said no, there was nobody. She did not tell him that she was not an orphan, as she had said to him earlier, that her father was still alive, even though she had not seen him or spoken to him in many years. If one day he were to find out, she was certain that he would understand why she had lied to him.

Because Billy was still in Tacoma, waiting to be shipped out, it seemed obvious that they should marry there, and that Ann should join him out west. Ann packed for the cross-country train trip to Washington State quickly. She mentioned to her girlfriends how excited she was to finally begin this next stage of her life. But before she went, Elsie Woodward invited her to tea at her house in Manhattan.

There, seated among her daughters, Elsie announced that they would not be attending the wedding, being so far away, and besides, being a wartime wedding, no one would expect them to go. Elsie also mentioned that now, with Ann becoming part of the family, it would be important for her that she'd learn to socialize with a new kind of people, implying that her former acquaintances should remain just that, former. Ann understood right away what she meant. Elsie Woodward had learned of her job at Fefe's. She would need to give up her work in that establishment. Ann didn't mind that at all. She had some money saved up, and she assumed her husband would take care of her afterward. But what would happen if Elsie and her daughters knew that both William Woodward Sr. and William Woodward Jr. had been patrons at Fefe's? What would the women say to that? What would they think of the father and son drinking and flirting in the nightclub late at night?

In a clear signal of his mother's disapproval, Billy's marriage announcement did not appear in the pages of the *New York Times*, as had those of his siblings—Elsie shoved it deep in the *Newport Mercury and Weekly News*, hoping that no one would see it.

TEN

Immediately following the wedding ceremony, the Woodward family and friends agreed that this would be an ill-fated marriage. Of course, many knew of the rumors circulating that Billy was a homosexual, and those still persisted. In that case, marriage was not such a terrible scheme. But despite general displeasure, or because of it, Billy and Ann Woodward seemed happy at the start of their marriage, attending parties, going on short vacations, dining intimately in dimly-lit and well-known restaurants while in Tacoma and later in New York. The Woodward family awaited the moment when the novelty wore off and the marriage imploded.

While Billy was away in the navy, Ann awaited the arrival of her first child in an apartment on the top floor of the Woodwards' house. Strangely enough, this mirrored Elsie's early experience in her own marriage, when she and William Woodward Sr. had lived in her mother-in-law's home. Elsie Woodward did not seem to recall her own unhappiness at the situation. Instead, Elsie watched as Ann tried her hand at various projects she had read about, such as table setting, going about the house rearranging the flowers and plants, her belly growing. As Ann's pregnancy progressed, so did Elsie's anger, and rather than having anything to do with her daughter-in-law, Elsie preferred to spend more time in her room, keeping as far from Ann as she could.

Billy's time in the war was harrowing. He had been aboard the USS *Liscome Bay* on November 24, 1943, when the carrier was attacked by a Japanese submarine. The ship went down, taking with it an admiral, its captain, 53 officers, and another 591 enlisted men. Billy was one of just 272 crew members to survive.

When he returned from the war, he was determined to live with a vengeance the life he had nearly lost, shedding more of the repression he'd felt as bearer of the Woodward name, amplifying the defiance he had demonstrated in marrying Ann. The disciplined life of a family man didn't fit his new plans; being a playboy and enjoying his freedom and his status suited him better. He was ambivalent toward his wife, and even more so toward the job at the bank his father had provided for him. Ann herself seemed like a new person to him, swollen and ready to give birth; she was not part of his new plans either. Nor was there a proposal to move out of his parents' house. In July 1944, much as Elsie had done decades before, Ann gave birth to her first child, William III, known as Woody, in the third-floor bedroom of her in-laws' house in Manhattan.

By the late 1940s, Billy, Ann, Woody, and their second son, James Woodward, who had been born on January 14, 1948, were still living at the Woodwards', and it did not appear that they were going to move out any time soon. Billy was in no hurry to settle into happy domesticity. As long as they were under his parents' roof, he could dodge the responsibility of being an adult and continue with his old ways.

Ann became tired of the situation and put her foot down. If her husband wasn't going to think about their family, then she would. And a five-story brownstone on East Seventy-Third Street would serve as the perfect family home for them. Billy was unsure about the move; having a home and a family of his own made him feel squeamish. However, after listening to Ann and getting an earful from his mother, he bought the house in the summer of 1948, just before running away on a sailing trip with friends, as if fleeing the act he had just committed was a rebuke to adulthood.

For Ann the house was the fulfillment of a dream. She had a lovely brownstone in Manhattan, two new sons, a cook, a maid, and several butlers. While her husband appeared to be growing bored with her and their domestic situation, she had decided to dedicate herself even more to finding ways to attract his attention again.

❧

In photographs, they appeared to be the perfect couple, mingling with New York's upper crust, meeting and entertaining aristocrats, savoring fine dining, and traveling across the United States and Europe. Ann adored her new life: a rich husband, a town house on the Upper East Side, and a large estate on Long Island's North Shore, in the rarified town of Oyster Bay Cove. From the start, her job appeared to be devoting herself to becoming Mrs. Woodward, bent on pleasing her husband, and working hard to remaking herself into the kind of lady she had fantasized about becoming.

While during her previous life she had been accustomed to gulping down tepid coffee from chipped enamel cups in the back room of the taxi company, she now drank champagne from crystal glasses polished by servants. Instead of grooming her eyebrows with tweezers she'd stolen from a drugstore, as she had back in Kansas City, she had them tended to by Manhattan's best aestheticians. She was far from

Kansas and her mother's taxi company, where she had nodded off on the dirty cot behind the counter, smelling the odor of the men's room in the movie theater.

Ann knew she was the subject of much gossip. William Woodward Sr. had tried his best to keep his previous relationship with her a secret, but some of his closest friends somehow knew. It was convenient, they said, that the Woodwards had kept it all in the family. Ann found it all slightly amusing—hypocritical, really—for many of the women who spread the rumors had done much worse than she had, marrying old English lords for money and titles, or oil tycoons with scores of girlfriends on the side. However, the rumors and disdain caused most in their circle to keep her at arm's length. She had no one close to show her how to navigate her new environment, and someone always seemed to be ready to pounce on her with a snide comment if she made a mistake.

Behind the happy photographs, there was tension. Ann's past of dancing in nightclubs was behind her, but Billy didn't want to forget those days. It was precisely those unbridled moments that had appealed to him. And now—with her etiquette and speech lessons, with trying to learn French, even with her attempts to fold napkins into animal shapes that he could not wait to unfold—she was transforming herself into the kind of woman he liked the least: one who resembled his mother and his sisters and every other debutante he had known for years who had thumbed their noses at those they considered commoners. Ann was learning to emulate everything about them, from their clothing, to their perfumes, to their postures. All those qualities that had first entranced Billy—her free spirit, her lack of finesse, her ability to say precisely what she thought, the freedom she displayed with her body, the allure she held over men—now seemed overexaggerated, but in a way, also fake.

Billy now understood that everything she had done had just been a way to con him into falling for her. Ann had indeed been a very good actress, he often mused, better than most people had ever given her credit for. She had been interested only in achieving status, and nothing else. And he had provided that for her. His mother had been right all along. The disappointment Billy felt was deep and long lasting, augmented with a hefty dose of anger. While attending parties, he often watched as his wife chatted with his friends and made what he considered to be a fool of herself, trying to speak of things she had no knowledge of, like banking or international travel, or trying out her French. He humiliated her at every possible opportunity, much as his mother did, even berating her for things that his friends knew had initially seemed endearing to him. And despite her cultivated confidence, her husband's words and rebukes often made her feel inadequate, and she responded with promises to try harder and do better.

She hired a speech therapist, who worked to get rid of her Kansas accent and to imbue her speech with a tone she believed gave her a hint of class and foreign allure. She found a tutor to brief her on the topics she needed to know about so that her husband's family and his old friends would become new friends of hers. She read books on English and American antiques, trying to figure out the difference between the two, and which were more prized by collectors; she took language lessons and found an affinity for French; and she began to read cookbooks, even collecting recipes from magazines she liked and organizing them in notebooks alongside etiquette advice; and she learned the many ways to fold a napkin and when to use which fork and spoon.

However, she never quite gave up her distinctive style in clothing. She enjoyed wearing attractive dresses she knew caught men's attention, something that Billy began to deplore as his friends stared at her bosom. Soon he began to insult her, telling her not to flirt like a hooker. These outbursts occurred in front of many of their friends, and she was hurt by his words. She promised to find a new style that was flattering to her figure—and one that was more subdued.

∽

Fissures in the marriage soon became more obvious to others. Billy was in no mood to work the steady banking job his father had held for him. And while Ann gave birth to their sons, Billy seemed to take little interest in the milestones of fatherhood. He preferred to go out drinking, carousing with women, and staying in bed until noon, then repeating the same cycle all over again the next day. When Ann complained, he began to quiet her with expensive jewelry and property, but still their arguments intensified.

Ann had initially been able to keep a hold on her husband through her sexual expertise. He had been inexperienced with women, eager to engage and practice new things. When she came into his life, she had proved to be a satisfying teacher, one with an excellent repertoire of skills. But as time went by, and as Billy and Bean explored more and more of Manhattan's nightlife, Ann's tricks began to seem dated, as he met and became involved with younger people who were even more interesting to him than a former chorus girl from Kansas. Maybe their relationship was indeed what his mother had warned him against— a youthful, lustful affair, a rebellious act on his part that he had taken too far—and now he was living with the consequences.

Through the 1940s and early 1950s, Billy Woodward was known as a playboy in New York society. In 1946 he became reacquainted with Princess Marina Torlonia. At the time Marina was married to Francis "Frank" Shields, an amateur tennis player who had reached his professional apex mostly in the 1920s and 1930s. Marina and her husband shared two children. She would go on to have four husbands. Marina was a woman Billy had been somewhat acquainted and friendly with since childhood, but with whom he had lost touch in recent years. She was the type of woman his mother told him he should have always gone after, a woman with a background not unlike his own. She did not hunger for status, as Ann did.

Despite their both being married, neither had any qualms about pursuing an affair, and many of Marina's friends hoped that Billy would be able to convince Ann to grant him a divorce. Even with the scandal that would surely erupt if the match was made official, Elsie and William Woodward approved of the relationship.

The liaison devastated Ann, who was pregnant again. The birth of their second son meant nothing to Billy. He was still intent on divorcing Ann and pursuing his new lover. While she stayed home with a new child, the affair between Billy and Marina continued. That fall, Marina, who was living on the West Coast, left her husband and moved to New York City to be nearer to Billy. Ann and Billy fought often about it, and he began to hit her more severely, the bruises she received showing through the makeup she so carefully applied. It was Dr. John Prutting, Ann's physician, who helped Ann through these times, becoming not only a confidant but also agreeing to provide her with the medications she needed for migraines, insomnia, and depression. Her new divorce attorney, Sol Rosenblatt, offered the legal advice that she sought.

In September 1948, Billy and Ann officially separated. Rosenblatt, as her attorney, recommended she not allow Billy or the Woodwards to see the children. Rosenblatt was known for using heavy-handed tactics to get his clients, mostly society women, all that they deserved, and likely even more than they expected, from their soon-to-be ex-husbands. One of the few Jewish lawyers in their Long Island group, Rosenblatt had acquired the nickname "the Fixer," as he was known to have a large group of acquaintances on retainer who owed him favors. He was born in Oklahoma and studied at Harvard. Like many who were not born into wealth, he loved society people. Their problems were common and unique all at once. He still had the scar on his leg from the day a hit man had shot him while J. P. Morgan's will was being contested.

Rosenblatt thought the Woodwards were simply another high-profile couple going their separate ways. Sometimes he met Ann for lunch at La Côte Basque, a restaurant in New York, and they'd chat for hours about travels, families, children, celebrity women, and horses, while gulping down some especially good wine. Eventually Ann would broach the subject of her husband, and Sol Rosenblatt offered his handkerchief as the tears flowed.

It was at this point in their relationship that, unbeknownst to Ann, Billy changed his will, determined to leave Ann with as little as possible. In December 1948 Billy asked Ann to officially divorce. On the sidelines, Marina and her supporters kept watch, quietly waiting for Billy and Ann to reach an agreement. Elsie and William Woodward even agreed to pay Ann $2 million as long as she signed the paperwork.

Each Woodward hired a detective to spy on the other. Ann's detective showed her photographs of her husband and Marina taking romantic walks in Central Park.

Billy employed his own detective not only to follow Ann but even to tap her telephone. He discovered that during their separation she had an affair. By New York law, Billy could have used that information during the divorce proceedings and refused to pay the $2 million settlement his parents had promised. However, the fact that she had landed a high-profile lover seemed to excite him. Another man had yearned for his wife. While he now spent most of his time with Marina, a princess herself, he still visited Ann from time to time, and when he saw her the two of them inevitably landed in bed.

He was still attracted to her, he quickly realized. She had always possessed an allure that would never leave her, a hold on him hard to break. And with that awareness he began to distance himself from Marina, and to the displeasure of his parents, he halted the divorce proceedings. To those who inquired he lied and said that Ann had asked for too much money, that it was more convenient to remain married to her and have his affairs on the side. It was a story that would follow their marriage for years afterward, of Ann bribing him into staying married by asking for an obscene amount of money in return for her leaving.

Billy had agreed not to divorce Ann. But there was a humiliating caveat that went along with the proposal to remain together: Billy wanted to continue having his affairs. Ann would need great fortitude to abide by his request. Nonetheless, she eventually accepted her husband's terms, with no small amount of regret. In the earliest days of their courtship and marriage, she had always been able to sway him to see her point of view. But now that was difficult, if not impossible to do. She would have to redouble her efforts.

∽

In December 1948 or January 1949, Mannie Page, a man in his thirties, became the Woodwards' chauffeur. Like the other employees, he lived in their brownstone, where all the staff were housed in rooms on the fifth floor. The rest of the personnel had warned him about the drama of the Woodwards' squabbles, but he didn't think much of it. He was just happy to have found work for such a well-to-do family; the pay they offered was more than what he could have made elsewhere.

In December 1949, Ann and Billy Woodward gave a cocktail party to celebrate Ann's thirty-fourth birthday. They invited some sixty guests to the glitzy affair. Following the party, the festivities continued, moving from their brownstone to the El Morocco night-club.

The staff all retired after the party but were awakened about two thirty a.m. by loud screams and a police siren. Mannie Page opened the door to his room and noticed the rest of the staff in their night-clothes spying from slivers of opened doors. The screams were coming from the third floor, where Ann and Billy Woodward had their bed-room.

Mannie Page tiptoed to the stairwell, debating the possibility of walking downstairs to assist, when he heard Ann accusing Billy of being a good-for-nothing husband, urging him to go back to his "Ital-ian whores." When Mannie made it to the bottom of the stairs, he saw Ann scratch Billy's face with her nails, at which point he hit her, giving her a black eye and tearing at her dress.

Billy then rushed out of the house, while Ann locked herself in the bedroom and did not come out for three days. Billy returned the next day and asked Mannie Page to pack him a bag so that he could go away for a few days. When Ann reemerged from her room, she gave orders to the staff not to let the elder Woodwards see their grandsons.

A week or so later Billy and Ann made up, going away to the Carib-bean islands on a short vacation together, returning rejuvenated and reconciled, it seemed—until they hosted another social gathering at the house. The last departing guest was barely on the sidewalk when they began to argue again.

On that night, Mannie Page hadn't even made it up the staircase to his room when he heard Billy accuse his wife of leaning too much into the male guests and Ann accuse her husband of being too friendly with the women guests. When Billy told Ann that he wanted a divorce, Ann became physically and verbally abusive, at which point Billy left the house, taking rooms at the Brook Club.

When he was asked about it later, Mannie Page admitted that he never saw any firearms in the house, but he felt that Ann and Billy Woodward didn't need them. Their hands were usually enough to make their point. Ann flung bottles, shoes, ashtrays at Billy, and Billy retaliated by slapping her face.

❧

With the death of William Woodward Sr. on September 25, 1953, when he was seventy-seven years old, Billy became the sole inheritor of Belair Stud and Farm, with William Sr. declaring in his bequest his hope that the "farm may mean as much to my son as it has to my uncle and myself and that he may spend many happy days there maintaining the place in a modest and simple way as has been our habit."

Although in his youth Billy hadn't seemed interested in horse breeding and racing, when Belair Stud and Farm passed to him, he discovered a newfound appreciation for the sport, as well as for the colt Nashua, which his father had wished to see race in England. Now Nashua remained on the grounds in Maryland, and Billy Woodward decided that instead of sending the horse across the Atlantic, he would have him trained in the United States and race him only on American tracks. No one knew what prompted that choice. Perhaps it was because his father had owned Nashua and now that the horse belonged to him, he wanted to assert his own authority over it. Either way, it would turn out to be one of the best decisions Billy made. Thanks to the discipline of Mr. Fitz, the trainer, by 1954 Nashua had won six out of the eight races he entered in, and had arrived in second place in the other two.

In the spring of 1955, due to an apparent touch of flu, Nashua lost the Kentucky Derby. Nevertheless, he won the other two races in the Triple Crown, the Preakness and the Belmont Stakes. Watching the races from their private box in the stands, Billy and Ann enjoyed all the pageantry—the music, the outfits, the drinking, and the mingling with other social elites—and then, when the races ended, they walked into the winner's circle to meet up with the jockeys.

∽

By now, forty-year-old Ann had also become more involved in the operations of the stud farm and in Nashua's progress, something Elsie Woodward could not accept and insisted that Billy put a stop to. This had been her husband's domain, Elsie insisted, and she did not want Ann to assert herself there. Regardless, because of Nashua, Billy's and Ann's fame had increased. Ann landed on the lists of the best-dressed women, and they met like-minded couples. Ann was there to reap all the rewards, including trips to Paris and London, newspaper and magazine covers, and adventures all over the world, including a hunting trip to India.

The couple's arguments took on a whole new dimension after, feeling vulnerable one night in bed, Ann told Billy how she had first met his father at Fefe's Monte Carlo before she'd met him. Ann immediately saw that she had made a mistake. It didn't take Billy long to assume that his father and Ann had had an affair, and Ann had to spend all night trying to soothe him, assuring him that her relationship with his father had been an innocent friendship. Billy eventually claimed to believe her, but nonetheless he felt humiliated by the revelation that his father had known his lover before he did.

The mounting tension within their relationship was evident even to outsiders. Both Billy and Ann drank heavily and, emboldened by the liquor, sparred dramatically in public. They seemed to spite each other with amorous encounters, which in turn would lead to a fight, followed by a sexual reconciliation. For Billy, it was with women who worked at his father's bank or women whom his closest friends introduced him to when he went out. Ann was never at a loss for lovers either. A beautiful woman with plenty of men in her circle, she enjoyed having her husband's high-profile married friends visit their house on Long Island when she was there on weekends, the children off at their friends' frequent birthday parties or horseback riding lessons. Often Ann could see her husband's roving eyes sweeping the room when they were attending an event together; she would become hostile if a woman even neared him. Ann particularly hated the rumors that Billy recruited men as lovers. Despite his having been married for years now, these stories about Billy persisted. In fact, during a spat witnessed by dozens of partygoers, Ann screamed at Billy, "Why don't you just bring a man into our bed! That's what you want anyway!"

∾

It was, everybody knew, a volatile relationship, yet Ann never gave up on Billy—she seethed every time another woman got anywhere near him, and the force of her jealousy eventually achieved the same notoriety she herself did in the society pages. Finally, the emotional storms battering her appeared overwhelming. At one point she even refused to eat, her previously porcelainlike skin taking on a deathlike pallor, not unlike the face of her mother all those years before.

Since Billy would continue to have his affairs, Ann packed her suitcases, much as she and her mother had done years before, and in an effort to find a measure of contentment elsewhere, she decamped to England, where her position as Mrs. Woodward was properly honored, much more so than it was in Manhattan. There, she began a liaison with forty-four-year-old Lord William Astor, a wealthy married man whose family owned large swaths of real estate in England and the United States.

When she returned to New York, she brought with her a newfound happiness and self-confidence that she seemed to wrap around her like a silk shawl. Weeks had passed since her leaving, weeks during which she had had an affair with an aristocrat, while learning to ride horses and shoot pistols. Billy wanted to be disgusted by her sexual exploits, but he was nonetheless impressed that she had commanded the interest of such a man.

Elsie found out about Ann's affair and made Ann aware of what she thought of it, and of her; how appalled she was, and how horrifying she believed Ann to be. While Elsie didn't like or approve of husbands straying from their wives, the fact remained that she understood their proclivities. Wives, on the other hand, had their duties to fulfill, certain rules to obey, which did not include having lovers. Ann was embarrassing not only herself, but also her husband, not to mention the entire Woodward clan and the name they had given her.

Nonetheless Ann knew that by then she had become just the front of the Woodward marriage. Her husband wanted to keep up a certain facade in the papers while having his fun. Ann was mortified by this turn of events and wasn't sure how much longer she could stand it.

ELEVEN

⌒※⌒

Joseph Garcia Capote received his divorce on March 18, 1932. Less than two weeks later, he and Lillie Mae got married. In September, Lillie Mae decided that she wanted to be a mother to her child and asked her cousins to send Truman to live with her in New York. Before he left for his new home, young Truman decided he wanted to leave his mark on the small town: he announced that he was going to throw a party. Despite being only eight years old, he took weeks to plan his farewell celebration, showing the same type of attention to detail he displayed decades later while planning his famous Black and White masquerade ball at the Plaza Hotel.

In sending out his invitations, young Truman instructed his guests to show up at the bash dressed in costume, although this was a rarity for the children of Monroeville. And the attendees were not only the town's children. Of course, his cousins were to be there, as well as Nelle Harper Lee and some school friends. He also invited Sonny Bouler, who would be immortalized in Harper Lee's *To Kill a Mockingbird* as Boo Radley, and John White, a Black field-worker he knew very well.

The children played games Truman had devised himself and enjoyed refreshments Sook had prepared. They listened to music from Jeannie's phonograph. Everything was progressing well until the Ku Klux Klan showed up, having heard that John White was an attendee. Members of the Klan despised the idea of a Black man associating with white people—children, no less—and unceremoniously grabbed one of the masked guests they believed was White, dragging him outside for what they said was their way of teaching him a lesson. Ripping off the mask, they found they had taken the wrong person: under the disguise was Sonny Bouler, shaking violently from fear. John White had been hidden away when the Ku Klux Klan showed up.

∾

It seemed that finally Truman's dream was about to come true. He had often yearned to be a part of his mother's life, to live with her in New York. However, once he got there he soon began to look back at his days in Monroeville with nostalgia.

On February 14, 1935, Truman Streckfus Persons was adopted by Joseph Garcia Capote, thus becoming Truman Capote. Truman Capote quickly got accustomed to his new name, and even suggested to his own father that he be referred to by his new appellation. In the fall of 1936, he wrote a letter to Arch Persons while boarding at the Saint John's Military Academy in Ossining, New York. "As you probably know my name was changed from Person's [sic] to Capote," Truman explained to Arch, "and I would appreciate it if in the future you would address me as Truman Capote, as everyone knows me by that name." Arch was not pleased.

In gaining a stepfather, Truman Capote also secured a considerate parent who worked to make life more settled for him. Lillie Mae, who now went by the name of Nina, was delighted by her husband's attention to her son, and by her New York life in general. She finally felt a part of the world she had always craved to join. She was no longer the little southern girl from Monroeville but a worldly New York matron with a husband who made a good living, a son in private school, and enough money to afford anything she desired.

Truman's mother was eerily similar to Ann Woodward. Just like Ann Woodward, who had changed her name from Angeline Crowell to Ann Eden Crowell and eventually to Ann Woodward, Nina had changed her name from what she thought was the lowly, small-town-sounding Lillie Mae to Nina, which seemed more high class to her, with a touch of sophistication and European chic. Just like Ann, Nina had also moved from a small town to New York City in search of a better life. And just like Ann, Nina had been lured in by the wealth of café society members, by the glamour and security that the rarified class had to offer.

They lived in an apartment Joe Capote rented in Brooklyn. While Nina enjoyed the demands and bustle of the city, for Truman Capote, who had spent his childhood in a small southern town, the transition to urban life initially proved difficult. In New York, his mother was absorbed with her new husband, who required total devotion from her. Much as she had done while back in Monroeville, she assumed that her son was fine on his own. Truman missed Alabama, where he had received some measure of attention from his relatives. He started to mythologize his days in Monroeville and the people he had known— even his parents—glossing over their flaws and allowing them to become the parents he had always wanted and not those they had really been.

The family was not truly happy with life in New York and in June 1939 moved to Greenwich, Connecticut. Joe Capote located a house on Orchard Drive in the semiaffluent section of the city called Mill-brook. Nina relished life in Connecticut, and for a while she felt at home. Her days were now filled with shopping, long lunches, even longer dinners, and fun cocktail parties. And everywhere, there was alcohol. After shopping, she visited the country club with her new girlfriends, gossiping, playing cards, and drinking. The banter they traded started off lightly, but later became pointed and often vicious, even downright mean. It was a new way of living for Joe and Nina, one they easily fell into.

For Truman Capote, this move was not as difficult as the earlier ones. Arriving at Greenwich High School already a sophomore, he was the target of a few snide remarks, but he was accustomed to those. He was also becoming such an interesting and amusing young man that it was easier to attract attention and friendships.

While Greenwich didn't offer the excitement of New York City, Truman Capote did find two things he had lacked in the city: a new friend, Phoebe Pierce, and the support of a new teacher, Catherine Wood. Phoebe Pierce became his best friend in the North, fulfilling the same role Nelle Harper Lee had fulfilled in the South. Phoebe was beautiful, and just like Truman and Harper Lee herself, she also had literary ambitions. Truman and Phoebe took to sneaking off to Manhattan, where they visited museums and listened to music in cafés. And while in Monroeville he had never found a teacher who had supported his creative and literary ambitions, much less known what to do with his obvious writing talent, in Connecticut Truman found an English teacher who recognized his unusual gifts. Catherine Wood (whom Truman Capote took to calling "Woody") viewed his inattention to school subjects not as uninterest in education or signs of a poor intellect, but hints that he was not being challenged enough. His was a temperament that needed to be recognized, pushed, and encouraged, and she meant to do just that. She even predicted that his future as a writer would be a bright one.

In June 1942, the Capotes left the Connecticut suburbs and returned to New York City.

~

To those who had watched Nina grow up, and to those who came to
know her later, it appeared that the life she had built with Joe Capote
and Truman was an accomplishment. They had a beautiful place to
live. Joe left the house every morning for a steady job on Wall Street,
and their lifestyle hinted they had plenty of money. Nina had shed
her southern skin to become one of those Manhattan women she had
always admired and wanted to be: polished, sophisticated, glamorous.

However, Truman's loneliness became more pronounced. He was
lonely at home and away from it. His mother's attitude toward him
grew more volatile as he grew older, so that now, when she was drunk,
she showed him either more ambivalence or anger. And the drinking
itself increased each day; in fact, she was never too far from a glass of
liquor. Looking at her son, she often realized that she did not precisely
love him, nor did she truly hate him. And for his part, this netherworld
state in which he lived also did not allow him to love her thoroughly,
or to hate her completely.

~

By the time Truman finished high school at the Franklin School,
the relationship between his mother and stepfather had deteriorated.
After discovering that Joe Capote had cheated on her several times,
Nina drank more. In years past, she had indulged in liquor while in
the company of friends or during lunches and dinners, and at parties;
now she drank a lot at home, and alone. When she was drunk, she
took her anger out on Truman, particularly in the presence of those
few close friends he brought home. Joe Capote, still infatuated with

his wife despite his affairs, blamed Truman for all her problems. Joe mentioned to friends that Nina feared her boy was displaying homosexual tendencies, leaving her frightened and ashamed and numbing herself with alcohol.

Joe's affairs and indiscretions contributed to Nina's depression and humiliation. Nina knew about them because she employed the help of private investigators. The more Nina learned about his affairs, the more she drank. And the more she drank, the more she verbally abused Truman. She never missed an opportunity to remind him of the disappointment she felt in him—he was not the child she had wanted, and he certainly wasn't becoming the man she had hoped for.

By now Truman Capote knew who he was and was not hiding it. In an era when homosexuality was generally condemned, he was not afraid to let the world know that he was homosexual. Even at the start of his career, when many young gay writers of his era might have feared that being open about their sexual orientation would hurt them, Truman Capote was who he was. Nor did he make any efforts to hide his likes and dislikes in order to please others, most especially his mother.

TWELVE

Unlike Ann Woodward, Truman Capote was granted entry into New York's society because of his brilliance. The author Anaïs Nin met Capote at a party she hosted at her apartment. Nin recalled him as a "small, slender young man, with hair over his eyes, extending the slightest and most boneless hand. He seemed fragile and easily wounded." As was the case for Anaïs Nin, there was something about Truman Capote that beguiled most people. With his small stature, blond hair, baby face, and blue eyes, he still had the look of a very young boy. He often spoke theatrically, exaggerating his southern drawl. But his intelligence and talent were obviously those of someone much more mature. While Anaïs Nin had never met him before, she had heard of him, as well as read his much-talked-about short story "Miriam." The party was a gathering of poets, writers, critics, and publishers, and there Truman Capote met the writer Gore Vidal for the first time.

"Almost from the beginning," Nin said, "Gore and Truman sized each other up as future rivals. After all, there could be only one *enfant terrible*. Gore was almost a historian, dealing in facts, whereas

Truman came from the Southern school of recounters, meaning he never wanted a fact to get in the way of a good story. Gore camouflaged his homosexuality, whereas Truman used it to draw attention to himself. The more outrageous he was, the more onlookers he attracted."

In late 1942 or the early months of 1943, Truman Capote began his part-time job as a copyboy at *The New Yorker*. Copyboys hardly ever moved up to writing positions, but Truman had expectations.

In 1944 he left *The New Yorker*, returning home to Alabama and taking with him the unfinished manuscript of a novel he was working on called *Summer Crossing*. He believed he knew the story well and was planning to finish it while living in more familiar territory. *Summer Crossing* took place within the world of Manhattan's socialites, with Grady McNeil as its protagonist, the seventeen-year-old daughter of rich and prominent parents who leave her alone for a summer in the city while the family travels to Europe. Truman sensed that he was familiar not only with the character but also the society she inhabited, after having taken notes and observed as much as he could from his early years living adjacent to New York high society. But the reality was that despite all the work he had done, the text lacked something—authenticity. It did not sparkle with an insider's knowledge of this world but read as if someone was observing it from the outside rather than completely embroiled in it. Nonetheless, Capote planned on finishing the book while surrounded by the familiar people and places he had grown up with.

Monroeville was as sleepy as ever, especially in the hot and drowsy days of summer. Most of its residents spent their time sitting on front porches, whether their own or their neighbors', visiting, telling stories, sharing lemonade and iced tea. Whether these stories were true or not didn't matter. They were embellished with each retelling, so that soon they lost their original kernel of truth, a virtue and an all-too-common characteristic of southern storytelling that Truman Capote absorbed from the very start. The home where Truman's relatives lived had such a porch, a big wooden one that framed the entire house and made it a particularly enticing place to share these talks.

In Monroeville *Summer Crossing* was proving difficult to write. Lately, it had started to feel "thin, clever, unfelt." Capote had returned to Alabama in the hopes of being able to fix it, but the opposite was happening. His eyes were opening up to the manuscript's flaws. As he walked near a stream one day, thinking through the book's plot and prose, childhood memories came to him, along with the story and themes for an entirely different book. This new story arrived to him virtually completed, he later claimed. He continued his walk by an abandoned mill he knew from his childhood, until he reached his relatives' home when night was already falling. He skipped dinner and went straight to his room. "I said goodnight, locked myself in my room, tossed the manuscript of *Summer Crossing* into the bottom drawer, collected several sharp pencils and a fresh pad of yellow lined papers, got into bed fully clothed, and with pathetic optimism wrote: 'Other Voices, Other Rooms—a novel by Truman Capote,'" he would say later. This time he knew he would have no trouble finishing this novel.

No one knows for sure if Truman's story of the genesis of *Other Voices, Other Rooms* is entirely true. With Truman's tendency for enriching his narratives, there could have been a touch of fabrication to the sequence of events. But there was something much more romantic and special to him about the idea of this book coming to him fully formed, given the torments he was enduring with *Summer Crossing*. Plus, it made a good tale.

Days later Truman bought a bus ticket for his birth city of New Orleans, and rented a room on noisy Royal Street, in the French Quarter. There, he continued to write throughout the night and to sleep during the day, his plan being to finish part of his new novel, as well as a handful of short stories he had brought with him. Truman would need the next two years to bring the manuscript to completion. What materialized was a rich and poetic work unlike anything *Summer Crossing* had ever been.

The book's setting was the rural South, a place Truman knew well, rather than New York City, a place he was still discovering. The gothic atmosphere of *Other Voices, Other Rooms* was one Truman had been steeped in since childhood. The pages dripped with the languor of a summer afternoon sitting on those familiar front porches.

Joel Harrison Knox, the thirteen-year-old protagonist of *Other Voices, Other Rooms*, was reminiscent of Truman himself. Raised in New Orleans, after the passing of his mother he was sent to live in a backwater town in the South with a father he had never met, and who had abandoned the family during the boy's youth. While Truman denied the idea that his book was in any way autobiographical, for readers it was not difficult to compare what they knew about Truman's life with the fictional life of Joel Knox. Just like Joel, Truman had been born in New Orleans; he had hardly seen his father and had spent most of his childhood in rural Alabama while being raised by a cast of eccentric relatives, many of whom eventually made their way into his work.

❧

Truman Capote was not shy, nor was he against pestering editors. One morning in the spring of 1945, following his return to New York City from New Orleans, he showed up at the offices of *Mademoi-*

selle magazine wanting to speak to its fiction editor, George Davis. It was not customary to simply show up to see the editor of a magazine, but then Truman was not a customary writer. George Davis couldn't see him right away, so Truman simply sat in the reception room and waited. There was an eagerness and capriciousness in young Truman that endeared him to many, if not all, he came across. George Davis had cultivated a reputation for being crusty; he was not necessarily up for a stunt.

Much like Ann Woodward when she showed up at the modeling agency to speak to its president during her early years in New York City, Truman Capote was just as plucky. And something about Capote, about his self-confidence and his offer to simply sit in the waiting room while Davis read his work, made Davis like the young writer. George Davis immediately rejected the first two submissions, "The Walls Are Cold," and a portion of *Summer Crossing*, which Truman Capote had continued to work on despite moving on to other writings. Nonetheless, Davis asked Capote if he had more work to show him. Of course he did. Davis was immediately captivated by the strange tale of a lonely woman's meeting with a naughty little girl. This supernatural story, "Miriam," was intriguing, pulpy, and gave a hint of Truman's talent with the southern gothic genre. Davis accepted it right away. During that same year, Truman Capote also sold stories to *Story* and *Harper's Bazaar*. By the end of 1946, Herschel Brickell, who edited the annual anthology of the O. Henry Prize stories, called Truman "the most remarkable talent of the year" and included "Miriam" in the annual anthology.

Throughout 1945 and 1946 Truman continued working on *Other Voices, Other Rooms*. He had pressed on with his schedule of working at night propped up while on his bed, a set of yellow notebooks on bent knees. As was now his habit, he did not go to sleep until the early-morning hours, then woke up around noon, whereupon he joined friends for lunch and a drink. It was a routine that he was to keep for most of the rest of his life, changing it only as he grew older, when in the last decade of his life his actual writing process almost disappeared.

The book eventually found a publisher with Random House, and upon the book's publication in 1947, many of the reviews were glowing. The writer Somerset Maugham called Truman Capote "the hope of modern literature," while others compared him to Eudora Welty, William Faulkner, Carson McCullers, Oscar Wilde, and, of course, Edgar Allan Poe. However, there were those who were less than impressed, or even outright dismissive, including the critic from the *New York Times*. Regardless of the reviews, Truman Capote later went on to call the book "a satisfying conclusion to the first cycle of my development." And without even seeing the final manuscript to *Other Voices, Other Rooms*, the movie production company Twentieth Century Fox optioned it for fifteen hundred dollars.

Following the publication of *Other Voices, Other Rooms*, and after receiving so many positive reviews, Truman Capote returned to the offices of *Mademoiselle* to speak to George Davis again and to seek his opinion about the book. "Well," Davis replied, blunt as always. "I suppose someone had to write the fairy *Huckleberry Finn*."

❧

Nineteen forty-eight proved to be a spectacular year for Truman Capote. *Other Voices, Other Rooms* landed in reviewers' hands and finally critics were able to read for themselves the book they had heard so much about. "The darling of the Gods," his editors at Random House called him. Capote, at the time of its writing, said he hadn't noticed the autobiographical overtones to the book. Some twenty-five years later, in an interview, he admitted, *"Other Voices, Other Rooms* was an attempt to exorcise demons, an unconscious, altogether in-tuitive attempt, for I was not aware, except for a few incidents and descriptions, of its being in any serious degree autobiographical. Re-reading now, I find such self-deception unpardonable."

Few readers thought this remark honest, as the protagonist not only resembled him, but several of the characters had clearly been plucked right out of Monroeville, their habits and proclivities obvi-ously found in people he had known there. And this was a habit that would continue for the rest of his days.

Suddenly, New York City became manageable for Truman, shrunk to a relatively small circle of privileged and successful people. He was busy meeting editors, magazine and book publishers, and writers who sought to befriend him. "New York is like a city made out of modeling clay," Truman once said. "You can make it whatever you want. It's the only city in the world in which you can have totally separate lives, groups of friends that didn't know one another or anything about one another."

Also in 1948, Truman Capote met the man with whom he was to have the longest and deepest relationship of his life, Jack Dunphy. Jack Dunphy was as quiet as Truman Capote was loud, as antisocial as Truman Capote was social. Maybe it was because of that incongruity that Truman felt a need to get close to him.

At thirty-four, Dunphy was nearly a decade older than Capote, and a member of a large Irish family, one of six children raised in Phila-delphia. Dunphy had also dreamed of becoming a writer but was from a poor family always strapped for money, and he worked in a factory in order to support himself. As a youngster, Jack Dunphy had also enjoyed dancing, and he had enrolled in dance lessons to develop his skills. As it turned out, he had a natural ability for it, and that revelation shocked but delighted him. While dancing had not been a part of his original life plan, he thought that maybe this new skill could take him away from the drudgery of his factory job and open up some opportunities.

Following several auditions in New York, he found a steady role as a member of a chorus line. He met professionals in the dance field, including the actress Joan McCracken, with whom he was cast in the musical *Oklahoma!* McCracken ended up the star of the musical, and she and Dunphy became romantically involved. They later married, only to separate and divorce when rumors of her infidelities proved to be true.

When World War II erupted, Dunphy enlisted in the army and was sent to Europe. By the time he returned to the United States his marriage was over, and he decided to close himself off against any relationship with women. "Women were very distasteful to me, and I decided I wanted to go to bed with men," Dunphy said later in life. "I had been denying crushes on men before, but I had never thought of doing anything about them. I knew the jars of honey were there, but I didn't know they could be opened."

While Jack Dunphy enjoyed dancing, he still fantasized about writing. It was his first and deepest ambition, and he continued to believe he could somehow fulfill it. He took advantage of those nights while working to complete a manuscript titled *John Fury*, which depicted a world not unlike the one he had grown up in, populated by poor Irish characters resembling his own family. Shortly after his book was published, he encountered Truman Capote at the home of their mutual friend, the writer and editor Leo Lerman. With his tall dancer's body, red hair, and blue eyes, Jack Dunphy immediately caught

Truman Capote's attention. Capote also made an impression on Dunphy. He may not have been as physically attractive as Jack Dunphy was, but at the time Truman Capote was still alluring and beautiful. If there was someone Truman wanted to impress, he was certain to show off his many other gifts too: his intellect, his wittiness, his conversational skill, and his southern charm. When he wanted to be, he could also be extremely kind. And he was already familiar with Jack Dunphy, saying to friends, "I had a terrific crush on him without ever having seen him." Truman made certain Dunphy knew about that too.

∾

In 1954, still riding on the success of his novel and living abroad, Truman received word that his stepfather had been discovered embezzling money from his job. Maybe he needed to maintain Nina's style of living and fund their habits, which included gambling. As a result, he was fired from his job on Wall Street. The ensuing scandal embarrassed Nina, who was also alarmed at what the loss of his income meant for their lifestyle. Nina found herself in an unusual position: How would she explain this to her privileged girlfriends? It seemed as if the past was catching up to her. Nina's face, tight and withdrawn, exposed her depression and worries; she no longer exuded beauty and vitality. Not surprisingly, she didn't want to see any of her friends.

Nina had attempted suicide once before. But the next time she tried her hand at it, she swallowed a heavier dose of Seconal. Joe found her the next morning sprawled on the floor, unconscious. As with her first attempt, there were signs that she had likely regretted her actions at the last moment: the telephone was off the hook, probably having been knocked off its cradle when she reached out to try to call for help. And one of the windows in her room was ajar, the assumption being that she might have thought a whiff of fresh air would have reinvigorated her. Joe called for an ambulance, and she was rushed to the Knickerbocker Hospital, where she died on Monday, January 4. She was only weeks shy of her forty-ninth birthday.

Although it was true that Truman Capote had a complicated relationship with his mother, Nina's death hit him profoundly. "She didn't have to do it," he told a friend. "She didn't have to die. I've got money." In the midst of his grief, he didn't realize that her misery wasn't entirely about needing money—after all, he had already been supporting Nina and Joe for months. For Nina, it was the public scandal her husband's crime had inspired that she couldn't tolerate. She had lost her place in a world that she had spent her entire life securing.

On January 7, her funeral was held at the Frank E. Campbell funeral parlor in Manhattan. Her relatives from Monroeville refused to travel north for the service. They insisted that she be buried back in Alabama, but it was not what she had wanted. In fact, there was not going to be a burial at all. Nina had made it very clear that, when she died, she was to be cremated, which went against her relatives' beliefs. Following the cremation, her remains were placed into a crypt at the Westchester County Crematorium.

While for Truman Capote the world had been upended, there were those who never liked Nina, such as Truman's lover, Jack Dunphy. "She was forever trying to make him over, make a man of him. . . . It was the commencement of her life-long determination to dominate a spirit she no more understood than she did the turnings of the moon," he said once. "She would have liked to sit on him and smother him . . . she did not really want him, and never had. . . . I disliked her immensely. . . . He did not love her, but he wanted her to love him."

Arch Persons did not attend his ex-wife's funeral. However, he arrived in New York only days afterward. His reasons became obvious right away: he was there to learn whether or not Nina had left behind anything he could lay claim to, most especially money. But Nina and Joe had been in dire financial straits. "There's nothing here for you," Truman Capote told Arch. "You're not my father. Joe's my father. He's taken care of me."

∾

It is possible that Truman Capote loathed the socialite Ann Woodward because she reminded him so much of his mother. But he may also have been so cruel to her because Ann Woodward seemed too much like him as well. Both had undertaken a series of moves to shake off their earliest lives. Like Capote, Ann Woodward had also worked hard to infiltrate a society into which she didn't belong, and where she'd come to learn she had always been ridiculed, no matter how carefully she had been mimicking those around her.

The same had happened to Capote. He had accessed a literary establishment where he clearly did not belong, and those around him were aware of it. His writing might have been admired, some of the time, but he was a peculiarity, an outsider. Oliver Smith, the Broadway set designer Truman had counted as his friend, once told a reporter that Truman was like a cat he knew: "He was just an alley cat that wandered around the neighborhood eating whenever he could. He was thin—very, very thin—and he would stand on the porch looking wistfully into the kitchen. He was determined to get into the house, but I didn't want him. I had four other cats, which was a big enough feline population. Well, we eventually fed him on the porch, but still didn't allow him in. Finally, he got himself into the kitchen, and of course now he just rules the house. He's just huge! He can't get enough to eat. Truman's craving for a luxurious environment was something like that cat's." He might as well have been describing Ann Woodward herself.

THIRTEEN

※

On the evening of October 29, 1955, Billy and Ann Woodward attended a party at the house of George and Edith Baker to honor the Duke and Duchess of Windsor. The Woodwards and the Windsors had known each other for over a dozen years. Ann in particular had an affinity for the duchess, the former Wallis Simpson, a woman not unlike herself who was often maligned in the press and never liked by her husband's family. The couples saw each other at least two or three times a year, often when the Woodwards traveled to England, but also when the Windsors visited the United States to watch the horse races and to make the rounds of high society. However, at the Bakers', the seating arrangements were spread out over two rooms, and the Woodwards and Windsors found themselves sitting at different tables. Nonetheless, they did manage to converge and chat, especially about Billy's horse Nashua.

During the day, the rich autumn colors painted a lush landscape around the Oyster Bay Cove area, but at night they were hardly visible. Thunder and lightning crashed in the distance and came closer and closer as Ann and Billy drove to the Bakers' home. The roads were shrouded in fog, and during the drive over Ann and Billy got into another argument, this one about Billy's recent trip to Kansas to buy a plane. He wanted the plane so he could fly back and forth between Long Island and Belair Stud and Farm, in Maryland. By air, he could make the trip between the two locations in about an hour and forty-five minutes. It was a trip he wanted to do every weekend, and whenever else he could find the time.

This plane was a Helio Courier, a small four-seater invented and patented by a professor at the Massachusetts Institute of Technology and built in Kansas. Ann had begged him to look elsewhere, partly because the state of Kansas was a sore spot for her. She hadn't returned there since burying her mother. But Billy had not reconsidered. A friend from Groton, Steward Clement, had informed him that the best place to buy such a plane was in none other than Pittsburg, Kansas, the very town that Ann's mother had sought to escape. When Billy heard that, he laughed through the telephone, as Stewart later recalled. "My wife was manufactured there, too," Billy told Clement. The plane manufacturing company was on West Fourth Street, only two miles away from the farm Ann had grown up on.

∞

As they left for the party, the maid Annie Schroeder saw them out of the house and locked one of the main front doors behind her. She then went into Billy's and Ann's bedrooms to straighten up, making up the beds and cleaning the bathrooms. Annie had been advised that a prowler was roaming the area, and she was tense and listening for any unusual sounds, her vivid imagination hurrying her on. She tidied up the rooms, placing pillows and bedding where they belonged, picking up the gowns that Ann Woodward had tried on and discarded, folding up expensive brassieres and underwear and returning them to their drawers.

She then walked back to the kitchen to throw half-emptied bottles in the garbage, wash glasses left in the sink and on the table, and fold dish towels. Then, because it was part of her job, she waited until the Woodward children were due home. The boys were out with friends, and she had been instructed to wait up for them before she herself retired to her room for the night.

When the children came back home, they rushed upstairs to their bedrooms, and Annie finally went to her own bedroom, where she pinned her hair up and prepared for her eleven p.m. bedtime. In those moments hovering between awareness and slumber, she heard the telephone ringing and wondered who would be calling at that hour. She did not get up to find out, because she decided that it was not her job to do so.

Hours later, she woke up when she heard the telephone ringing again—or what she thought was the telephone. "I don't want to swear to the time," she would later tell Assistant District Attorney Edward Robinson. "I didn't know what it was, but it was after I heard those rings that I heard bangs. One bang was louder."

She did not get up to check on the noise. But those bangs—there were two—were far apart. "It wasn't bang, bang," she said by way of an explanation. "It was bang—bang."

It was then that she realized that she had not heard a telephone ringing, or the alarm, but blasts that sounded like gunshots. She did not hear any shrieking or other human sounds. She did not hear Mrs. Woodward screaming for help. And while logically she knew that a shooting had occurred, somewhere, at least, she did not get up to check on what had happened, or where. It was only when someone knocked on her bedroom door and told her to get up that she did so, finally leaving her room.

~

Billy and Ann Woodward arrived at the Bakers' party at eight thirty. They were some of the first guests there to make an appearance. The first person they bumped into was Sid Freeman, a well-known pianist hired to provide entertainment for the evening. They greeted each other, but quickly Ann excused herself to visit the powder room and check her makeup.

Billy Woodward and Sid Freeman picked up a drink and started to chat. Immediately Billy brought up the subject of the prowler menacing so many North Shore houses. Sid Freeman could sense from Billy not only apprehension but anticipation, as Billy Woodward confessed that they might be expecting "some excitement around their place," given the unrest the prowler was creating. But they were prepared, Billy said, should the prowler show up again.

Sid Freeman listened attentively, then said, "I hope you're well-armed," at which point Billy Woodward replied, "Yes, I have a pistol." He told Freeman that as they were preparing to leave the house for the party, Billy had taken one of his guns and stashed it in the car. He'd decided that if they should come upon the intruder as they returned from the party, he'd take care of the man himself. Before Billy could elaborate on his plan, Harry Evans, another attendee who'd just arrived, interrupted their conversation.

Ann Woodward looked wonderful in an evening gown of a soft blue-gray reminiscent of a dove's feathers. Billy had picked out the dress himself, accustomed as he was by then to buying clothes for her that were not too brazen, too look-at-me revealing, even as Ann had put on a few pounds. His mother had introduced that idea into his mind, and he had followed through. Never mind that Ann was routinely photographed as one of the best-dressed women in New York.

While she often left her long blond tresses loose around her shoulders, tonight she had decided on something different. She had twined her hair in a tight bun at the back of her neck, leaving only a tendril to curl at the side. Her necklace glittered against her neck and down her bosom, which she had dusted with a slightly shiny powder. Her beauty was not entirely waning, at least not this evening.

By now, Ann Woodward's metamorphosis into a respectable society matron was complete. While to Elsie Woodward, Ann would always remain the hick from the Midwest who stole her son, by 1955 very little endured of the young woman who'd driven to New York from Kansas City in a used car. Speech classes had done away with Ann's accent, and numerous etiquette lessons had gotten rid of her brash laughter and awkward, forward manners. Even her clothes, once loud and clingy, were now mostly understated and classy. Ann felt that she had washed herself clean of the past. Most people didn't know of her early days in Pittsburg, Kansas, or of her mother's taxi cab company in Kansas City. Unless they took the time to research her background, no one would find out either.

Attendees at the party later recalled both Ann and Billy Woodward looking lovely but being extremely agitated. Guests would tell police about Ann going around the Bakers' house asking anyone who would listen to her, "Have you heard about the prowler?" The recent rush of robberies in their neighborhood seemed to have been her main concern that night. She feared that she was being watched, Ann told a guest, and revealed that Billy had armed himself with a gun, intending to shoot the intruder if he made his way into their house. Someone told Ann that she had become obsessed, to which Ann gave an uneasy smile and confessed that her dread was so great, that night she was also going to sleep with a shotgun next to her bed. There was a sense of foreboding in the air, the feeling that something was about to happen soon, if the prowler wasn't caught.

❧

During her typical week at her Manhattan brownstone, Ann missed the house in Oyster Bay Cove. While she loved the city, she truly felt at ease in the wooded enclave on Long Island. Their home, on Berry Hill Road, was considered one of the smaller ones in the area, though Ann was pleased by it. She had nicknamed the twelve-room wood-and-stucco structure the Playhouse, which she thought sounded whimsical. On its north side the house was attached to a rather large building that previously had housed an indoor tennis court, but which was now leased by Cinerama as a movie theater. The Woodwards had also agreed to let Cinerama use a swath of space in the rear of the east side of the property, which had once accommodated a music room but that now the Woodwards no longer had any use for.

Ann liked sleeping in her downstairs bedroom. There were two large rectangular windows looking out to the front of the house and a smaller circular window in the bathroom. Her husband was a little further down the hall, in his own smaller bedroom, with only one window.

The house was situated within bramble, bushes, and trees. To the right front of the house was a tall old tree whose limbs extended all the way to the roof, and with the slightest of breezes the branches brushed against Ann's window, sounding as if long nails were scraping against the glass.

Ann's night table was crowded: a lamp; a radio for when she couldn't sleep or for when she needed to hear the latest news; a water bottle to keep herself hydrated—water was so important for the skin, she had learned as a youngster; her cigarettes, which she couldn't do without; a flashlight, in case she needed to see in the middle of the night. She also kept another night table in her room, this one slightly larger and burdened with a telephone, another water bottle and glass, another radio, and a large metal pillbox.

She often liked to walk to her closet and browse through her garments. When in Oyster Bay, Billy and Ann attended many social events, so her closet, accessed by wide double doors, held many a boutique's worth of clothes, from country wear to daytime dressy clothes to evening gowns. Her dressing table sat between the two windows, and there she kept her cosmetics, her perfumes, and her extra bottles of medications that Dr. Prutting prescribed for her migraines, cramps, anxiety, and generalized pain. She suffered from so many ailments, as she often complained to her family and friends. She was glad Dr. Prutting was liberal with his prescription pad. One of her dearest purchases, a phonograph, was on a small console not far from her bed. She kept a few books on the small table by her bed, along with a warm blanket that she reached out for more frequently than the books. It was a comfortable room, and she savored being in it when not in their primary home in the city.

The children also enjoyed being in Oyster Bay, and they had many friends there. During the 1951–1952 school year, they had attended the Greenvale School, staying on their property on Berry Hill Road with their caregiver, Annie Schroeder, before they were transferred to the Buckley School in New York City. By 1955 Schroeder had been employed as the children's nanny for nearly five years, though she increasingly yearned to spend more time at her Brooklyn apartment, finding excuses to escape there whenever she could.

Mrs. Woodward was a difficult person to work for, as Annie Schroeder had come to realize; she was inflexible and fiercely impatient with the help, and quick to discharge those who did not obey her orders. A woman named Ingeborg Sorenson had been hired as a cook, and she was even more difficult than Mrs. Woodward, jealous and irritable, changing things around the house at her whims and without consulting anyone. Mrs. Woodward got rid of her. Annie Schroeder tried her best to stay on Mrs. Woodward's good side. She did not want to become Mrs. Woodward's next victim.

∽

The boys were excited to be in Oyster Bay this Halloween weekend of 1955, even if they were aware of the hostility between their parents, and between their mother and the staff. They looked forward to the weekend; they were scheduled for riding lessons and to attend an evening picnic with other local children organized by their riding instructor. Both Woody, eleven, and Jimmy, who was seven, went to bed willingly that Friday night because their father had promised them that on the following morning, he was going to take them to the local airport to show them the new plane he had just bought. And if they acted like little gentlemen, Billy Woodward had told his children, he would even treat them to a short flight.

Until their arrival that weekend, the Woodwards hadn't been aware of the presence in the neighborhood of a prowler, although the local police had been busy searching for an intruder who had been breaking into other residents' homes and stealing smaller goods, such as radios, articles of clothing to sell, and even food. The Woodwards' neighbor Harriet Aldrich Bering and her husband had told Billy that the previous night the prowler had been around their own property. They should be careful, the Berings warned Billy and Ann when they arrived that Friday evening, and make sure to take precautions. As Billy and Ann discussed the situation, Ann was suddenly seized by an overwhelming feeling of anxiety.

And, as it happened, early in the morning of Saturday the twenty-ninth, Lee Principe, who took care of their property, informed Billy that it appeared as if the prowler had spent the night in their garage; he'd found a window broken. Principe had also discovered cans of open food in a nearby cabana and noticed footprints along the grounds near the main entrance. Principe called the police and was told that they were looking for a young German man whom they believed was responsible for the recent string of break-ins. Minutes after Lee Principe told Billy this, Billy telephoned the Oyster Bay Cove chief of police, Russell Haff, to report the incident. Furthermore, Ann's poodle had woken her up in the middle of the night with ferocious barking, though the dog never barked unprovoked, she'd insisted.

Despite her apprehension, Ann Woodward decided to keep up with her day of errands. Looking through her vanity set, she realized that she had made a mistake in not bringing any cosmetics with her from the city. Those she had left behind the last time they were in Oyster Bay Cove had gone rancid, and she decided to drive into town and buy what she needed.

She took the keys to her husband's black Ford Thunderbird and drove to Snouder's Corner Drug Store in Oyster Bay. It was a cool day, a touch breezy, low-level clouds that promised rain quietly traversing a sky sunless and gray. At the store, Ann browsed for some time, selecting what she needed and a lot she just wanted, until she had filled several bags with cosmetics, and then engaged in short spurts of conversation with John T. Saunders, its clerk, a horse racing fanatic and fan of Nashua. Ann told him the horse would be withdrawn from any races for the next three months in order to rest.

Ann asked John Saunders to help her bring the bags to her car, and he did, depositing them into the back seat of the Thunderbird. Then Ann Woodward returned home, trying to distract herself from the prowler and focus on the party later that evening.

~

While at the party, with the Duke and Duchess of Windsor working the next room, Ann told a guest that while their home itself hadn't been burglarized yet, there had been signs that someone had been snooping on their property. As partygoers listened to Ann, Mr. and Mrs. Gimmell could not really tell if she was serious about the threat she felt, as Ann seemed sober one moment then appeared flippant the next. During the conversation, Mrs. Mary Gimmell suggested that if both were truly so frightened by the prowler, instead of shooting him and staining their expensive floors and furniture, they should think of dissolving a good handful of sleeping pills into a tall glass of milk, or maybe take out some cheese and leave it on the kitchen table for him to feast on. The woman then laughed at her own wit. That way, Mrs. Gimmel advised the Woodwards, Billy could then simply call the police to come and arrest him without dirtying up his hands. Smiling indulgently, Billy Woodward said he would consider that plan.

Sitting down for dinner, Billy found himself next to Mrs. Margarita Phipps, a genial woman always intrigued by a good story. Admitting that his wife was all wired up about the prowler, Billy told Mrs. Phipps that both he and Ann feared that the prowler might return to their property that night. Just in case, he went on, he had brought a gun with him for protection, though he had left it in the car. Billy had not elaborated on what he planned to do if he came across the intruder. But Mrs. Phipps could imagine it, and she had looked around the table to see if anyone else had heard them chat—there was, after all, Mrs. Guest, Mrs. Schiff, John Rutherford, and several others. But it appeared that no one else had been privy to their conversation.

One person with whom Billy Woodward spoke privately about his misgivings was Spitwood White. The two had known each other for decades and had spent time in the navy together. White was aware of Billy and Ann's marital issues, but this evening Billy didn't confide in White about them. Billy was more interested in talking about the prowler. He had a plan to catch him, Billy told White, and he mentioned again he had brought a gun with him for protection, and that he kept it stashed in the car.

❧

When Billy and Ann left the party, at about one o'clock in the morning, now Sunday, October 30, many of the attendees wondered if they would quarrel on the way home. The Woodwards, activated by alcohol, were known not just to quarrel in public but to have their arguments erupt in private, after a social event. They did indeed argue—continuing their earlier fight about the plane Billy had just bought in Kansas—the Helio Courier. He was meant to buy that plane, he had told his mother. Ann did not agree; not only was she not in favor of his buying the plane, but she was upset that he had gone to Pittsburg, Kansas, to do it.

Ann had not been back to Pittsburg, Kansas, or the farm she'd lived on as a child, in several years, despite having relatives there. She still recalled it as a bleak, gray, and somber place, and wondered what Billy would think of it. Nonetheless, she had asked Billy if he wanted her to go with him; but he'd refused, saying he preferred to travel there alone. Ann hadn't insisted. Traveling by himself, Billy would find out more than Ann ever wanted him to know.

When Billy landed in Pittsburg, Vernon Marsh, the owner of the manufacturing company, picked him up at the airport and drove him to the plant. Billy stared wide-eyed as they passed by abandoned and run-down farms surrounded by ramshackle fences. It was mid-October, the steely gray colors of the sky unwelcoming and threatening a storm. The grayness of the weather made the area look even more painfully distressed, and the barren branches and parched fields only reinforced that impression. He took in the once painted houses now bleached raw and peeling thanks to the harsh weather and hot sun. There were rusty cars and old bicycles on front lawns. The few people he glimpsed looked depressed and resigned. A sense of hopelessness dominated the landscape, and it made Billy think of Ann.

Chatting with Vernon, Billy had mentioned that Ann was originally from the area. Vernon quickly recognized the Crowell surname and told Billy that she still had a few relatives in the vicinity; what's more, the old farm where she and her family had lived was still standing, albeit in shambles. Billy declined the invitation to see it.

After Billy decided on which plane to buy, Marsh dropped him off at the drugstore, where Billy found a stool and asked for a drink. He struck up a conversation with the man behind the counter and revealed that he was married to Ann Woodward, previously known as Angeline or Ann Eden Crowell. The man's ears had immediately perked up. He was initially hesitant to talk, but with a little urging from Billy, he spoke up. Billy quickly learned more than he had ever known about Ann's mother, Ethel Crowell, and her two failed marriages, and of her various adventures with other men. And the man had revealed to Billy the history of Jesse-Claude, Ann's father, who had not died in the war, as Ann had always claimed, but was a retired streetcar conductor alive and living in Detroit in near poverty. Billy had nearly choked on his drink. He'd recalled his mother's words about Ann and wondered what Elsie would have to say now. And then Billy came to realize that if everything he had learned about his wife was actually true, he now had good ammunition for a quick divorce by blackmailing her. While he had wanted to reconcile and work on their marriage after they had each engaged in an affair, Billy had come to conclude that he was

William Woodward Sr. was a well-known banker and owner of horses. He met Ann Eden before his son, Billy Woodward, did. Here he is attending the races with his wife, Elsie, and one of their daughters.

Soon after arriving in New York, Ann Eden—later to become Ann Woodward—began working as a model. Here she is working for the CBS Corporation.

Because Ann and Billy Woodward came from different sides of the track, family and friends believed their marriage would never last. They always put up a good front, despite their differences.

After she married Billy, Ann became known for her sense of style.

Initially, Billy had no interest in horses. After William Woodward Sr. died and Billy inherited the stables and horses, he became more interested in the sport of kings. In this photograph Ann and Billy are standing next to their greatest horse, Nashua.

Although Billy never particularly enjoyed social events, he made an effort when they featured his horses. Here, he and Ann pose after Nashua won a race.

Over the years, Ann took a particular liking to hunting. Here she holds a photograph that captures one of her proudest moments— shooting one of the biggest tigers in India.

Jimmy and William Woodward were Ann and Billy's two sons. They were asleep the night of the shooting and always said they didn't hear anything. Just like their mother, they both died by suicide.

Paul Wirths had been robbing houses around the Woodwards' home on Halloween weekend of 1955. He ran out of the house when he heard gunshots.

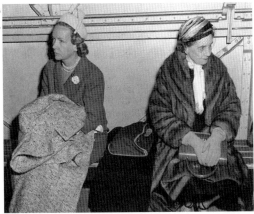

Elsie Woodward was never fond of her daughter-in-law, Ann. The two fought over everything—from the treatment of Billy and the children, to the clothes Ann chose to wear. Here they are after the death of Billy, on one of the very few occasions they had the chance to be together.

Although Billy's family thought Ann should be charged with murder, a grand jury did not agree. Here, Ann is seen leaving the police department following a lengthy interrogation by Assistant District Attorney Edward Robinson.

Truman Capote was a handsome and mischievous little boy who resembled his mother, Lillie Mae, in height and coloring. His relatives enjoyed taking his picture, and this is one of the most famous that exists of him as a child.

Truman Capote and Harper Lee struck up a friendship while living next door to each other in Monroeville, Alabama. Here they are standing in the kitchen of the Deweys' home while researching *In Cold Blood.*

Truman's masterpiece, *In Cold Blood,* put the true crime genre on the map. In this portrait he is standing in front of the small post office located in Holcomb, Kansas, where the murders took place.

One of the most well-known and eccentric writers of his generation, Truman achieved the apex of his career with the publication of *In Cold Blood*.

Katherine Graham was the guest of honor at Truman's famous Black and White Ball, a party he gave for himself, to celebrate his book *In Cold Blood*.

C. Z. Guest was one of Truman's friends and one of his so-called swans. She was also one of the few people who did not abandon him after the debacle following *Esquire's* publication of "La Côte Basque."

First Lady Jackie Kennedy's younger sister, Lee Radziwill, was also Truman's friend and one of his swans. She came to rely on him for personal and professional advice when she desired a career in entertainment.

Barbara "Babe" Paley and William Paley became Truman's friends, with Babe herself becoming his best friend and his favorite swan. He ended up betraying that friendship with the publication of "La Côte Basque."

tired of Ann. Now, suddenly, he understood that he could get rid of Ann permanently without having to give her a penny. Furthermore, he knew that he could also keep the children. He had abruptly left the drugstore and gone to his hotel to place a telephone call.

Ann had picked up the receiver right away. She asked about his plane and, hesitantly, about his time in Kansas. He told her that most people he met were very friendly, and that they remembered her and Ethel quite well. Maybe before returning to New York, he would also visit her father; after all, he was alive, not dead, as she had always told him. Did she know that he lived in Detroit?

Ann acknowledged her father was alive and that she had not told Billy the truth. People always embellished their backgrounds to fit in society, she had insisted. These were just little white lies. Besides, she had been an actress during her younger years, he knew that. She had changed her name just like she had changed her past, including the fact that her father was alive, to adjust to her new life.

And then, to frighten her a little more, Billy told his wife that he had found out so much dirt on her that his lawyers would be very pleased with his visit to Kansas. After the divorce, she would never see the children again, nor would she be able to reside in any of their homes in New York. It was high time that she returned to Kansas, Billy continued.

Billy's words must have filled Ann with despair and horror. What exactly did he plan to do with what he had learned? She had never believed him capable of stooping to such low actions, but apparently she had been mistaken.

Later, after the shooting, people who knew the couple personally would talk about this particular incident as the inciting factor in the murder. Everything that followed, they said, could be traced back to Billy Woodward's trip to Kansas.

FOURTEEN

❧

When Billy and Ann returned home from the party that October night, Billy took the pistol from the glove compartment of their car and, together with Ann, searched the house to make certain no one had broken in. They checked the refrigerator to see if any of their food had been consumed, or if anything they'd left on the counter had been eaten or taken. Everything seemed in order. Their maid had straightened the kitchen, thus almost everything was put back in the cabinets. Sloppy, their miniature poodle, rushed toward them, happy to have them home—especially Ann, who doted on her like a daughter.

From the gun cabinet, Billy removed a shotgun and handed it to Ann, advising her to keep it by the side of the bed. He chose one for himself as well. Billy knew that if they found the prowler lurking on their property, he could shoot him. So could Ann. The act would be considered self-defense, he had explained to her earlier. While Ann was obviously afraid of the intruder, she might have enjoyed feeling closer to her husband, the two of them searching all the rooms in the house to make sure they were secure. They even inspected the clubhouse again. In the aftermath of Billy's call from Kansas, Ann might still have been hopeful that her marriage could be saved, but she could have suspected that this closeness she was sensing now was only a temporary reprieve.

When they finished, they whispered their goodnights to each other and retired to their separate bedrooms. By now Ann was tired and reeked of alcohol and cigarettes, and she yearned to remove her makeup and swallow a handful of pills that would render her numb and sleepy.

In her room, Ann placed the shotgun on a chair next to her bed. She was more than familiar with this gun. Ann had purchased the twelve-bore double-barrel Churchill "Imperial" model sidelock ejector shotgun the previous September in London. She had paid a little over two thousand dollars, a price she didn't think too exorbitant for such a piece. But more than the price, she had liked one feature about the shotgun: its weight. Coming in at a bit over five pounds, it was a relatively light shotgun, perfectly fine for her to handle. Most women she knew did not appreciate the craftmanship of guns. In fact, when a few of her acquaintances had learned of her purchase, she had had to explain that the shotgun had been a gift from her husband.

She now unfurled her hair from the bun and began her nightly routine of changing into a nightgown. Always unable to stand the cold, she donned a quilted and fancifully trimmed bed jacket. She also wore her bra to bed, confident that wearing a bra while sleeping would prevent her breasts from drooping. She splashed water on her face, then wiped away her cosmetics. She had educated herself on the different ways to apply and remove makeup during her theatrical days, and she had never lost her touch. Even better than the professionals, she often mused. But beautiful as she was, her naked face was beginning to show her age. She had also started to worry about gaining weight, thus had resumed some of the exercises she had performed during her days as a model, realizing that they had been easier when she was younger. She brushed her teeth, then smeared cold cream over her skin and swallowed some sleeping pills before sliding into bed. By now Ann had made it a habit to ingest several Seconals and Thorazines with a glass or two—or three—of beer just before going to bed. The mix sometimes worked, and sometimes worked only to make her toss and turn fitfully in bed until dawn, listening to the wind and the rain and her own thoughts. Then she pulled on a sleeping mask and hoped for rest.

Ann no longer slept like she used to. Uncertainty plagued her. She had grown accustomed to waking up with a start in the middle of the night, baffled by new waves of anxiety, while her heart pounded in fear, before she reached for a new bottle of pills Dr. Prutting had prescribed her. Elsie Woodward had recommended that she see Dr. Ben Keane, who was the family doctor and who for years had taken care of everything that ailed the Woodwards. However, Ann suspected Dr. Keane would report everything they talked about to Elsie. Long ago Ann had come to realize that nothing was sacred with Elsie, or with the rest of the Woodwards, or anybody who worked for them. She preferred to remain with Dr. Prutting and his generous prescription pad.

In the next bedroom, Billy was about to take a shower. While he owned plenty of pajamas, even some fancy ones Ann had purchased for him, he preferred to sleep in the nude, and this night was no different.

As Ann would tell it later, not long after she had gone to bed, she heard a crash. She also heard Sloppy growling. Ann knew the dog hardly ever barked, let alone growled, unless she came across strangers. In her mentally hazy state, she thought of the prowler. Ann tore off her sleeping mask and got up, grabbing her shotgun on the way to the door. The butt of the gun fit snuggly into her armpit, and she felt a rush of adrenaline just thinking that she might come face-to-face with the prowler she had been worrying so much about for a few days now.

She slowly opened her bedroom door and peered into the corridor. There was a large window at the end of the hallway dressed in gauzy curtains, a thin sliver of moon somewhat visible through the glass, its feeble light entering through the pale fabric and highlighting a shadow next to Billy's room. In the near darkness, as she would tell investigators later, Ann heard the rustling of feet and spotted the outline of a shadow. She aimed toward the end of the corridor, and with the skill of a trained marksman she unloaded her shotgun. Birdshot slammed across the hall and toward the staircase, the smell of gunpowder filled the air and stung her nose. She ran across the corridor in her bare feet toward the intruder on the floor, and saw the naked body fully splayed out. She suddenly realized her mistake and screamed. The man at her feet in a pool of blood was her husband.

Almost immediately Ann Woodward ran down to the basement, where the gun cabinet was located, and threw several shotgun shells back inside. She was afraid, she said later, that if she kept the shells by her side, she would be tempted to shoot herself. She then ran back upstairs, kicked her shotgun by Billy's side, and moved away from the body to go to the telephone at the other end of the hallway. Ann picked up the receiver, but somehow, she would say, she could not dial the number for the police department.

On that Sunday morning, two telephone operators, Gladys Francis and Gertrude Gallagher, were working the Oyster Bay 6 Exchange, part of the New York Telephone Company. At exactly 2:07 a.m., Gladys Francis picked up a call from a hysterical woman who was screaming for help. It was difficult for Gladys Francis to distinguish the woman's words, and in fact the only thing she could understand was that the woman was screaming "playhouse." Both she and Gertrude Gallagher, who was listening in, had an inkling that this call might be coming from the vicinity of the Cinerama Corporation.

Gertrude Gallagher then connected what she now believed was an emergency call to the Second Precinct of the local police department, while still keeping the line open and listening to the conversation. The sergeant at the Second Precinct asked the operators to try to get the woman's name and address, as well as to figure out from where the call was originating. But the caller was too frantic and unable to speak coherently.

At the same time another call was coming in from a man named Steve Smith, who said he worked on the Cinerama grounds. He stated that while making his rounds he had heard a woman screaming and believed that it was coming from the Woodwards' main house. While Gladys Francis spoke to this person, Gertrude Gallagher, whose line was still open with the woman who had called a few minutes earlier, passed along this information to the Second Precinct, who in turn called out for help to the Oyster Bay Cove Police.

By now, several minutes had passed since the initial call, so that by the time it was determined that the call was from the Woodward estate, precious time had been wasted.

After finally telling the police her location and then hanging up, Ann Woodward had the presence of mind to call her lawyer, Sol Rosenblatt.

∽

Ann Woodward's earsplitting shrieks had reached the ears of the man on duty at the estate, but strangely enough, her children slept undisturbed. Steve Smith heard two sharp noises spaced just seconds apart. He believed them to be the clatter of someone trying to break into the building. He was walking back from the kitchen across the tennis court when he heard a woman calling for help. "Something terrible has happened!" the woman screamed, without giving details of the shooting. She then told Smith she could not let him in, because she didn't have the key on hand to open the main door, which opened from the inside. Smith rushed back to his office and placed the call to the police department at about ten minutes after two. And waited for them to arrive. Later, he would tell investigators that when he first reached the front door, he saw a light on in the hallway, which was how he realized right away that it was Ann Woodward screaming for help.

"It is very, very important" for the investigation to know what he saw, Assistant District Attorney Edward Robinson would tell Smith.

"Yes, I could see the light on in the hallway and I could hear her screaming."

"Are you sure it was the overhead light, the one that is on now in the hallway?" Robinson pressed, when he again spoke to Smith a day later. But Smith's memories had not changed.

"Yes, there was a light. I didn't pay any attention. I couldn't tell you."

"Is it possible it was a light shining coming from one of the bedrooms?"

"That I couldn't tell you," Steve Smith admitted. "I know there was a light lit when I got to the door. Whether it was the hall light or what, I don't know. But it was lit up and I tried the door."

"But they say this hall light was out when they arrived," Robinson said of the police. "Are you positive it was on when you got here?"

"I am positive it was on. The two lights were on, this one in the middle here and the one inside," he said, pointing to a photograph of the house and indicating the hall light and the one in Billy Wood-ward's bedroom.

How was that possible? Robinson asked himself. Did Ann Wood-ward turn off the light in the few seconds it took for Steve Smith to go and call the police?

∽

Thirty-two-year-old Thomas Costello worked for the police depart-ment of the County of Nassau. On Sunday, October 30, 1955, he was working the one-to-eight a.m. shift. Minutes after two o'clock, after he had completed surveying the grounds of the Pine Hollow Country Club, he met Detectives Moylan and Boyd, who had been assigned to do the same thing, because a prowler might be in the area. They found no one and left in separate cars to resume their respective patrols.

Moments later, at 2:14, Costello, along with car 695, received a call from the Oyster Bay Cove Police Department about a disturbance at the Woodward estate. Picking up the call, Costello answered that he would be proceeding to the scene. When he arrived there, at 2:24, he found not only Detectives Moylan and Boyd, but also Oyster Bay Cove patrolman Henri Cormier. They were met by Steve Smith. As he led them to the main door, they could clearly hear a woman screaming. It was dark, and Moylan shined a flashlight through the glass front door.

Moylan rushed to kick in the door, but it would not budge. Costello went to the first window to the right of the door, which turned out to be Ann Woodward's bedroom, and found it to be slightly open. He pushed it open all the way in and climbed through, finding the room entirely in darkness. He then rushed out of the room and into the hallway, where he found Ann Woodward lying atop Billy Woodward, who was sprawled in a pool of blood, while she cried out, "My darling, my darling." At first glance, Costello believed the victim to be only seriously wounded. He rushed to the front door, which was only a short distance from this bedroom, but Costello found he couldn't get it open; there must have been some sort of locking mechanism he couldn't figure out. By then Moylan had come in, having also entered the house through Ann Woodward's bedroom window. Costello explained what he had found and told Moylan to stay with the victim while he went to find the back door in order to open it and allow the rest of the officers to enter the house. Throughout, he never took notice of anyone else in the house, not even a dog.

Costello found the telephone and called for more police, a doctor, and an ambulance. When Dr. Francis Moore, who worked for the coroner's office, arrived only a short while later, he pronounced Billy Woodward dead.

By the time Lieutenant E. Barry arrived on the scene and told Costello to resume his post, it was close to three o'clock. And as he stepped out of the now-open front door, Costello noticed something he had missed before, when he was busy trying to reach the screaming woman inside: the black Thunderbird parked in front of the house.

Earlier in the evening, around one a.m., when Costello was starting his rounds, at the Murphy Fuel Oil Company on Pine Hollow Road, he noticed a black Ford Thunderbird driving at a steady rate southbound on Pine Hollow Road, a man at the wheel and a woman in the passenger seat. When he was done checking the doors Costello drove toward a police call box and passed the Thunderbird again.

At the time, he did not know who the car belonged to, but seeing the car parked in the driveway, he realized that he had bumped into the Woodwards just minutes before the shooting occurred.

❧

At 2:15 a.m. Russ Haff, Oyster Bay's chief of police, had received a radio call to hurry to the Woodwards' house. When he made it to the house, lights were flooding the driveway. He inhaled the smell of wet grass and damp earth as he stepped out of the car and walked into the house. He and the other officers entering the building could still hear Ann screaming. Oddly enough, the children and the staff were nowhere to be seen. When the officers reached the site of the shooting, they noticed a naked man on the floor, the side and back of his head blown apart by a gunshot, and a blond woman hovering over him with blood smeared all over her face, hands, and nightclothes. Fearing an intruder was still roaming the house, they drew their weapons, and several of them began searching the nearby woods while others remained with Ann. Haff instructed the men to fan out throughout the house and along the estate to search for the intruder.

Haff bent down and asked Ann if she had seen the man who had shot Billy. Ann shook her head and screamed, "No, no." Haff placed his hand on her shoulder and asked her if she had seen anything at all, or perhaps heard anything prior to the shots. Ann inhaled deeply and, looking up at him, whispered, "I fired the shot, we both had guns, I thought it was the man that has been around here."

Haff later said that in order to remember her words correctly, he removed a paper napkin from his jacket and jotted them down. He quickly instructed the men to stop searching, as there was no intruder, and explained to the others as best he could what had just happened. Walking into Ann's bedroom, Haff stared at the luxurious furniture, at the bluish-gray evening gown hanging behind an open closet door, and at the night table. He took an inventory of all the prescription bottles on it. He then opened Ann's night table drawer, where he found additional pill bottles.

Ann could not be comforted. At almost three o'clock in the

morning, Dr. Francis Moore asked the detective watching over Ann to leave them alone while he examined her. He took her pulse and chatted for a few minutes. But when Dr. Moore asked her to remove her bloody nightclothes in order to examine her further, Ann refused, afraid that he would notice the bruises on her body and deduce that they'd been inflicted by Billy during one of their fights. She continued to scream and moan, until Dr. Moore gave her a sedative, ten milligrams of Thorazine, which calmed her almost right away. Dr. Moore would be criticized for his actions, because giving a murder suspect a sedative was not normal practice, and now Ann wouldn't be able to clearly remember all that had happened. His action would be viewed by the press as extending special treatment to a wealthy subject.

By four o'clock, Claire Moore, a registered nurse and not a relative of Dr. Francis Moore, arrived on the premises and entered Ann's bedroom, where Ann was now lying in bed. She grasped Ann's hand in hers and assured her that she was there to help her. Afraid that Ann would try to commit suicide, Claire Moore filled three paper bags with the pill bottles scattered around the room, as Ann watched and meekly begged Claire not to take her medications away.

❧

Soon the house was crowded with various law officials walking inside and outside: Assistant Chief of Police Jim Farrell, District Attorney Frank Gullotta, Chief Assistant District Attorney Edward Robinson, and Chief of Detectives Stuyvesant Pinnell.

Jim Farrell was nicknamed by many in the community "Gentleman Jim." He liked to mingle with the area's well-to-do, even enjoying a round or two of golf with them, often including members of the Pratt family, into which Libby Woodward, Billy's sister, had married.

Frank Gullotta and Edward Robinson wanted to question Ann immediately, but the sedative Dr. Moore had administered had done its job, and instead of crying hysterically, Ann sat stone cold and expressionless on a couch in her bedroom. She was in no position to talk to them or anyone else, and the men eventually agreed they'd have to wait. At least, Gullotta told Robinson, they had the confession that Russ Haff had written on a napkin when he'd first arrived on the scene.

Frank Gullotta had heard many unpleasant words from his own golf friends about Ann Woodward. With them, he made no effort to hide his aversion for her, describing Ann in the same terms that Elsie Woodward most often reserved for her daughter-in-law: a social climber and gold digger who had scammed her way into the family. Gullotta was forty-seven years old and originally from Brooklyn, educated at Columbia and Saint John's School of Law. He had become district attorney when the position became suddenly vacant, later winning election in his own right. He was, for the most part, a reserved man with a grim view of human nature. Now, looking at the scene before him and going over the details he'd learned from the detectives, Gullotta immediately made up his mind that Ann was guilty of murder. He just needed more concrete evidence to back it up. He instructed the officers on the scene to search the house for "physical evidence, anything that might indicate there was bad blood between the Woodwards, or any other reason for her to kill him," as he would testify later. They had to collect all the evidence before they could tie the threads together, he told them. He intended to prove her guilt. He wanted her in prison, where he thought she belonged. The persona that she tried to adopt that night, and continued to maintain, of the meek, terrified widow, belied her true nature, Gullotta surmised. He would stand by his beliefs for the rest of his days.

⁊

The police concentrated on the murder weapon, lying on the floor and slightly to the right of Ann Woodward's bedroom door, the muzzle pointing northeast. Near the shotgun were round pieces of paper, wads from the cartridges themselves. Billy Woodward's bedroom door had been damaged by the blasts, most especially around the handle. The position of the body appeared odd to several of the officers, for Billy was neither inside his bedroom nor was he outside it; rather, he was located somewhere in between. Behind his body, the investigators could see into his room, sparsely furnished. Near the foot of the single bed was a bureau with a lamp and some magazines, and near that bureau was situated another single bed, this one stripped of its bedding. There was also a small table with another lamp, a water bottle, an ashtray, cigarettes, and eyeglasses. Close by, an electric heater and an extension cord were noticed. Near the window was a chair, and next to that chair was a door leading into the bathroom. Near the bathroom, on a desk against a wall, the investigators found a shotgun—a .410 double barrel. On the desk was a lamp, writing paper and pens, a flashlight, and a semiautomatic pistol inside a black leather holster. On a chair far from the desk, a tuxedo was laid out, along with a cream-colored shirt, a black tie, and a pair of moccasin-type shoes on the floor. Those were the clothes, they determined, that Billy Woodward had worn earlier that evening at the Bakers' party.

Right away the police were puzzled by several things regarding the Woodward shooting: Had Billy also heard the crash, as Ann claimed she'd heard, and come to his bedroom door to see what was happening? If so, why wasn't he armed? Why wasn't his gun anywhere near his person? And why was he naked? Had he simply just come out of the shower when he heard the noise, if there had been a noise at all, or was he going to see his wife for an amorous encounter? They eventually also found out that there was a twenty-minute lapse between the time of the shooting and the timing of Ann's screams, at least as given by Smith. What had she done during those twenty minutes? Was it possible that she had been screaming all along and Smith had heard her screaming only twenty minutes later? Or had she done something more sinister during that lapse, such as set up the crime scene and her alibi, then started hollering in order to attract attention? And why hadn't the children heard anything?

Billy Bancroft, Billy's nephew, arrived at the home at almost four thirty in the morning to identify his uncle's body. He shuddered at seeing Billy in such condition and the house trampled on by strangers. His uncle was very protective of his things; he would have hated seeing what these people were doing to his belongings. After talking to the police, Bancroft entered Ann's bedroom. He found her sitting at the edge of the bed, looking disheveled and numbed by the shock. He pitied her then, as he always had, this person who had come into their family only to find herself mocked by everyone and highly disliked. It had always been obvious to him that his uncle had physically abused his wife, even though she had tried hard to hide the fact and to deny it. Ann had become adept at it, managing to conceal her bruises beneath thick layers of makeup.

While he was still at the Playhouse, Billy Bancroft called Billy Woodward's older sister, Libby, now Mrs. John T. Pratt, to inform her about what had occurred, and to ask her to come to the house on Oyster Bay Cove. She arrived from the city a few hours later, her intentions being to remove her nephews from the scene and to take them to the home of their grandmother Woodward in the city.

Investigators wanted to interview Libby Woodward Pratt, but she was so impatient to take the children from the estate that they could barely get her response to the killing or to determine how she felt about the whole affair between her brother and sister-in-law. She truly didn't know very much about the private lives of her brother and his wife, she told the detectives; she was older than her brother by almost fifteen years, thus they tended to travel in very different social circles. She then led the children from the house and into a chauffeured car, and quickly sped toward the city.

FIFTEEN

⌒✦⌒

In the morning, rumors spread quickly through Oyster Bay Cove. The wealth and status of the Woodward couple, the circumstances surrounding the shooting, and the way Ann was treated immediately afterward—unlike any regular suspect—naturally fueled speculation. Everyone had an opinion. It was true that most of the Woodwards' friends had long predicted the marriage was not going to last. Most had visualized a divorce. Murder had never entered anyone's mind.

Along with everyone else, the Duke and Duchess of Windsor were surprised to hear about the shooting. The duchess had always believed them "an ideal couple," so the suggestions that immediately started to circulate about them, most especially about Ann, were troubling to her. Mrs. Lynn Slater, who had also attended the party at the Bakers' the previous night, invited many of the available guests who had been there to a luncheon she threw together the following day. The purpose of this lunch was to chronicle all that had occurred at the party and to gossip about the strange sequence of events.

Detectives got wind of this luncheon and showed up, later questioning those party attendees who had decided against attending Mrs. Slater's get-together. When asked by the detectives, the Duchess of Windsor admitted that she was surprised by the Woodwards' developing saga. She and Ann had spent the previous night chatting about Billy's pride and joy—his horse Nashua—and she hadn't noticed anything untoward about Ann. But when the detectives interviewed Elsa Maxwell, they heard an entirely different story. Maxwell was shocked to hear that the Duchess of Windsor had told them she found the Woodwards an ideal couple, because everybody at the party was aware theirs was a tumultuous relationship, and that each had hired an investigator to spy on the other, a process that had been going on for months.

While Ann Woodward had several investigators working for her, the one she preferred and relied on was Walter C. Keir, who operated the Keir Investigating Bureau Inc., at 225 West Fifty-Seventh Street. Ann had employed him dozens of times between December 1948 and June 1955, mostly during the period Billy had asked her for a divorce and later when she suspected him of having some little affair.

She always felt secure in having a man like Walter C. Keir to call on when she felt the chill of suspicion blowing. Once, she had asked Keir to check on a Canadian woman named Fernanda Mantel. Another time she had sought details on a New Yorker who went by the name of Sally Parson. Keir was especially useful when Ann took extended trips abroad. On those occasions, she knew Billy needed a leash. During one of those journeys she had come to suspect that her husband had even bought himself an apartment at the Blackstone Hotel in New York, although Keir had found nothing concrete that said he had.

Not many people were aware of it, but Billy and Ann Woodward had once again separated during May 1955, and Billy had moved out of the house and gone to live at the Brook Club. Despite leading separate lives for a while, Ann still wanted to keep track of him, hiring Keir to see if indeed Billy was spending his time alone or in the company of other women. Keir hadn't turned up anything worthwhile, but he had mentioned to Ann that he suspected Billy Woodward had become aware of his following him and was making certain not to be caught. Ann agreed that Billy was on to her. Ann was also certain that Billy was cheating on her, and for a second, she had wondered if Billy was paying Walter C. Keir double the money she was in order to stop his investigations and thwart her suspicions.

After interviewing Keir, the detectives also spoke with Alfred G. Vanderbilt Jr., who had been a very close friend of William Woodward Sr. He was shown a list of those who had been guests at the Bakers' party, and he nodded, agreeing that they were, more or less, the usual couples Billy and Ann socialized with in the city and while in the country. When detectives probed a bit further about what he thought of the Woodward marriage, Vanderbilt paused, then replied rather diplomatically that he believed they had a marriage not unlike other marriages, where arguments often sneaked up during conversations. Ann was not the easiest person to get along with, Vanderbilt admitted, nor was she excessively popular in their "social set." Then he waited for the detectives to leave, saying no more.

❧

The night of the party, Billy had spent his time sitting next to Brenda Frazier, the young woman who was currently the glamour queen of the gossip papers and the most photographed personality of the era. She had become famous for being one of the hottest debutantes and granted the cover of *Life*. Many readers of those papers were mystified as to why she was so notorious. Mostly, she attended parties, debutante balls, and spent her evenings in various nightclubs on the arms of different men. Regardless, that evening at the Bakers' party she was a hit, coyly bantering with the men, laughing audaciously and loudly for many to hear even from across a room, and Billy Woodward had made time to flirt with her too. Those in the know speculated that he and Ann must have fought about his behavior toward Frazier.

That Ann had mistaken Billy for a burglar seemed far-fetched, many surmised, as Billy had stood just feet from her, stark naked from a shower. No matter how dark it was and how scared she was, how could Ann not recognize her husband, his height, weight, shape, standing only a few feet from her? While she insisted that her vision had been obscured, Billy's friends argued that no room was ever completely dark; that there had to have been ambient light coming from somewhere, enough to tell that there was someone there, otherwise she would not have fired. Did she know that it was her husband, and were her motives malevolent? And she was obviously very good with a rifle and had the reflexes of a markswoman. Most of them recalled the photograph taken of Ann on safari some years earlier, a picture now framed on her mantelpiece, Ann posing with a rifle in hand, next to a dead tiger.

People knew that Billy wanted to divorce her. Better to be a widow than a divorcée, they opined. They buzzed about the possibility that Ann had murdered Billy to get to the money. They had no idea that his millions were tied up in a trust, mostly for the children, and that she could not get her hands on it. In fact, Ann herself wasn't even aware of that fact, and she would not learn of it until a few days after the murder. The reality was that, financially, she would have been better off being the ex–Mrs. Woodward, rather than the widow of the late Mr. Billy Woodward.

Two detectives, Don Stark and Henry Koel, spoke to as many people who attended the party as they could, as well as to friends like the Bakers, and Bean's sisters, who thought the idea of Ann being a murderer ludicrous. Titi Baker Schiff said, "Ann is a shrewd woman, he [Billy] was worth much more to her alive than dead."

When asked, most people were of two minds. "There was no prowler," said Liz Fondows. "Ann made him up. She tried to protect herself because she murdered Billy Woodward in cold blood." But Mrs. I. Townsend Burden told the police investigators, "Everybody was scared about the prowler starting a few days before the shooting. We lived in Mill Neck, twenty minutes away, and went to the same club. . . . I was particularly nervous about him. I started locking the front door."

Others had a hard time believing Ann had murdered Billy simply because she was a woman. "Ann was not tough or strong enough to have murdered Billy," said Ned Patterson.

Was there even a real threat from a prowler, or had Ann connived the risk to abet her murder scheme? "He was my best friend," said Charles Walker of Billy Woodward. "I talked to these people at the party. . . . She [Ann] had them going about the prowler. There wasn't any prowler. She was plotting the murder. I'm convinced it just gave her an excuse to go get the shotgun and have it by her bed. He didn't care about the prowler. She mentioned the prowler and talked it up. It was all part of her premeditated plan to murder Billy. She was a strong lady and she could carry off something like that once she decided on it."

But Charles Schwartz, another party guest, said, "Everybody knew that a prowler was in the neighborhood. I had one conversation afterward with Elsie about standing by her. The police just called and asked if we had anything special to say. We didn't. We had just been at the Bakers' and said that we and everybody else were taking about the prowler."

Reporters covering the case learned that Billy Woodward had placed a telephone call to the police department just days before his own murder. "Mr. Woodward was concerned," Haff told reporters, "that the man lurking around his property might be a crackpot from the track who'd lost a bet and was nursing a vengeance against the Woodwards because of Nashua's success."

The detectives also spoke to several of the staff members, particularly those who no longer worked for the Woodwards. They had much to say.

They found forty-eight-year-old Ingeborg Sorenson working at a new address as a housekeeper, and while she had a lot of work to finish, she did not mind sitting down for a few minutes to talk about her previous employers. She told the detectives she had noticed right away how Mr. Woodward treated his wife "as a person who was sick." While they often argued, Sorenson went on, Billy Woodward sometimes enjoyed ignoring Ann altogether, which angered Ann even more. It was a game he played, Sorenson said, as he knew how to tick her off. Sorenson had never noticed guns in their bedroom, she said, but she was aware that they stored them in a locked metal cabinet down in their basement. And as far as she knew, only Ann Woodward had the keys to that cabinet.

Then Sorenson reported something that struck the detectives as interesting. As far as she was aware, Sorenson said, Ann Woodward almost always used earplugs when she went to bed. When asked how she knew this, and how she could be certain this was a common occurrence, Sorenson responded that she used to serve Ann coffee in bed in the morning, and when she entered her bedroom, she would notice Ann pluck out the earplugs from her ears. In addition, Sorenson was cognizant of the fact that Mrs. Ann Woodward often ingested sleeping pills. Sorenson had once overheard a telephone call in which

Ann ordered her personal secretary to get refills on her pills. Furthermore, it was common knowledge within the staff, not to mention the family, that Ann Woodward had two or three bottles of beer each evening prior to going to bed.

The detectives asked Sorenson what her overall feelings were about Ann Woodward, although it was easy to suspect them. "During the time I was employed by the Woodwards I became of the opinion that Mrs. Woodward was sick, mentally, in that when she became upset, she would lose her temper and control," she replied. "I was not actually surprised when I heard that Mr. Woodward had been shot by Mrs. Woodward."

❧

Elsie Woodward was not told about her son's death right away. At seventy-two, she was grieving the loss of one of her sisters. Her family had decided to let her sleep until morning, but by nine o'clock they knew they couldn't delay the news any longer. Billy Bancroft arrived at Elsie's house on Eighty-Sixth Street and presented himself to her along with other relatives, a few friends, and Elsie's butler.

Confusion and grief contorted Elsie's face when she learned of Billy's death. People in the room would remember the hard lines that formed when she was told that Ann had been the one who pulled the trigger. Elsie believed that the malicious girl from Kansas who had conned her son into marrying her had now shot and killed him on purpose. Elsie, and most of the Woodward clan, would always believe that Ann had murdered Billy, although to the outside world they would claim otherwise. They were a family who did not appreciate interferences, and Elsie feared that if Ann were investigated for murder, people would begin to question the family's other ghosts and indiscretions, something that she intended to avoid at all costs. Elsie had always guarded the family's privacy. She certainly did not intend to have a murderous profiteer ruin it now.

Elsie Woodward immediately called Walter Gray Dunnington, the family lawyer, and told him that Ann had murdered Billy. Dunnington was stunned and, after expressing his condolences, asked Elsie what she wanted him to do. She instructed him to make sure her grandsons were protected. Dunnington immediately understood her meaning and promised Elsie that Billy's children would no longer be in Ann's custody, and that he would make certain that they would continue to live with their grandmother. They were already safely in her house.

Back at the Playhouse, Ann could hear people rambling all over her house, though she did not have the strength to get up and check to see what they were doing. She remained sequestered in her bedroom. In the morning, Assistant District Attorney Edward Robinson, along with a stenographer and Claire Moore, the nurse, returned to her bedroom. They needed to question her, Robinson said, about what had happened the night before. But he saw that she was still under the protective haze of the medicines, and that she would not be of any help. She did inquire about the welfare of her children, and as far as her husband was concerned, she kept on repeating "My darling, my darling." Following a few more attempts to speak to her, they finally left her alone, as she appeared to wish they would.

But as the hours passed, the Thorazine began to wear off. Ann began to resent the people walking all over her house. The Woodwards had been so careful with this residence, Ann herself choosing each piece of furniture and decorative object, each item hanging from the walls, each little knickknack on the expensive tables and bureaus.

Now strangers were dusting for fingerprints, taking measurements, walking on her imported rugs with muddied boots.

She was becoming distressed, an officer reported after he went to check on her. Robinson assigned Detective Albright to stay with her. His job was not to question her—though, if she spoke about the ordeal, he was not to stop her—but to simply watch over her as the police continued with tasks around the house.

And for some reason, perhaps simply out of the desire to chat with someone, Ann Woodward suddenly felt the need to unburden herself. Albright appeared to be friendly and warm. She quietly told him of the events that had occurred the previous evening, at the Bakers' party at Peacock Point. Billy had decided to take a pistol with him, stashing it in the glove compartment, though she had not wanted him to do so, she said. They had spoken of the prowler on their way there, and Billy felt more secure by having the pistol with him. She could not remember what time they had left the party or the exact time they had made it home, but regardless of that, Billy had feared that the prowler might try to enter the house that night, which was why he had convinced her to take a loaded shotgun into her bedroom and advised her to place it next to her bed.

Detective Albright listened, allowed Ann to talk, occasionally lit a cigarette. Ann continued. At one point, she said, not long after having gone to bed, she heard her poodle barking, and also a noise that to her had seemed unfamiliar. She got up, reached for her shotgun, and, holding it in her hands, walked to the door and peeked at the hall. Then she shot. She could not see anything at that point, as none of the lights were on.

During the conversation, Ann's doctor, John Prutting, arrived from New York. Immediately, he requested that she be moved from her home to Doctors Hospital, on the Upper East Side in New York City, where she could receive the proper treatment from him. She was in a fragile state, obviously not well, he said. He could arrange to have her moved in a private ambulance, and if Detective Albright wished, he could follow them in a departmental car and stay at the hospital until his presence was no longer needed, as long as he did not interfere with Mrs. Woodward's recovery. Albright was not keen on this directive, but after speaking to his superiors, it was decided that Ann Woodward could be moved to New York City as soon as the arrangements were made.

〜

The headlines of the local and national newspapers were lurid and did nothing to tamp down suspicions about Ann: "Showgirl Wife Kills Heir With Shotgun Blast!" screamed *Life* magazine, while in the *New York Times* the news article began, "Not in this century have circumstances combined to produce so sensational a shooting—a tragedy involving people of great wealth, the meteoric career of a poor girl carried to the heights of fame, and elements of mystery." The press was on the hunt, and Ann Woodward was their prey.

When Sol Rosenblatt arrived at the Playhouse at midmorning, he had had a difficult time entering the premises, because reporters were now camped outside the home and the police would not allow anyone inside. It was only when he threatened the police department with a lawsuit that he was allowed passage.

Rosenblatt put his hands on Ann's shoulders to still her, and immediately she calmed down. She began to cry; then, in a quiet voice, barely above a whisper, she explained what had happened. He patted her hand and didn't push for details beyond the ones she recited. He simply interpreted to her the common-law rule that she was legally allowed to defend herself if someone entered her house with the intent to do harm; in other words, she could shoot and kill an intruder. Ann had been the homeowner who had clearly feared for her safety and that of her family; she had shot the person she had believed was the prowler. She shouldn't worry, Rosenblatt told her; it had all been a terrible accident. Ann nodded, but she wasn't entirely convinced. He also advised her to say as little as possible. While she could not take back what she had already admitted to, she should not volunteer any more information. He would do the talking for her, he told her, unless he instructed her otherwise. Then he went on to explain in very fine detail the story she should stick to when questioned by the police and the lawyers. And he suspected that Billy's family was not going to make it easy for her, he informed her.

By the time Sol Rosenblatt left the Playhouse, some two hours later, he had devised a plan. He immediately called J. Russell Sprague, a local politician who also owned a law firm, well connected in the community and known to trade favors. Rosenblatt asked Sprague to make sure the district attorney did not charge Ann Woodward with murder or put her in jail immediately. Also, because Rosenblatt was a divorce lawyer, he wanted Sprague to help him find a good criminal attorney to represent Ann. And they would have to work fast. He suspected that with the Woodwards' influence, the case would move relatively quickly through the justice system.

❧

On October 31, while still in the hospital, Ann Woodward was visited by Assistant District Attorney Edward Robinson, District Attorney Frank Gullotta, as well as a stenographer, Nathan Birchall. Present also was Dr. John Prutting. Following several basic questions they'd already asked before, Robinson asked Ann if there were any lights on in Billy Woodward's room.

"I don't know," Ann replied. "I don't remember any lights."

"Did you see your husband at all as you fired?" Robinson asked.

"I didn't see anything," Ann told them. "I just heard the noise and fired in the direction of the noise. I really didn't intend to even hit anybody. I just intended that they would know that, you know, we were protected. And whatever it was would go away."

❧

Billy and Ann shared at least one passion, the detectives and Robinson learned: they liked to hunt. Both had developed a love for big game hunting, which they indulged with several trips to India, where Ann, who had become a keen markswoman, shot the biggest tiger ever killed by a woman. Ann Woodward was proud of a photograph that memorialized the hunting event, and she kept it in a frame on her mantelpiece. The oil magnate Russell Havenstrite later wrote to Robinson that Ann was "the most dangerous woman with a gun I ever saw. She shot without looking."

Havenstrite had been friendly with William Woodward Sr. through the horse racing circuit, but he hadn't met the younger Billy Woodward until later, after his marriage to Ann, when both couples were invited to travel to India in the fall of 1952 as guests of the maharaja of Jaipur.

The plan had been to go tiger shooting, and at first Ann Woodward had shown little interest in hunting. The couples flew to visit the maharaja of Penna, a brother-in-law of the maharaja of Jaipur, all of them traveling in Havenstrite's private DC-3. While the holiday continued for a few more days, the Havenstrites eventually returned home to the West Coast, while Ann and Billy remained for a while longer.

Russell Havenstrite was not sorry to depart. In fact, he was eager to have nothing to do with Ann Woodward anymore. "She was very demanding of everyone," he eventually said. "Couldn't pick up a glass of water two feet away." He recalled a particular evening in Delhi when the whole group agreed to go out for dinner. Ann chose not to join them and remained behind in her room. But upon the group's return she somehow had expected Billy to have brought her dinner, and when he didn't, she flew into a rage and made a scene that embarrassed her husband and everyone around him. The group discreetly dispersed out of respect for Billy Woodward. Even as they left for the privacy of their own rooms, they could still hear Ann screaming at Billy about his thoughtlessness.

When the Havenstrites and Woodwards next saw each other in New York that fall, Billy Woodward was clearly ill. He admitted that he had caught infectious hepatitis while in India, shortly after the Havenstrites had left. They had had to return to New York early, Billy said, to Ann's chagrin, because they had been scheduled to remain not for just one extra month but two. He was still to recover completely, though he felt a lot better, even if he didn't look like it. The couples had dinner in the city a few times, and at the Woodwards' home, where the Havenstrites met the children.

The two couples corresponded frequently after that, keeping the conversation and friendship light, as the Havenstrites didn't particularly care for Ann Woodward. Then Ann wrote to let them know that she had received an invitation from the maharaja of Jaipur for the couples to travel to his country to shoot tigers in the spring of 1953. Ann's excitement was apparent, as she described the maharaja's evocation of man-eating tigers roaming his neighborhood and his desire to hunt them. Aside from her enthusiasm, another thing also appeared clearly obvious in Ann's letter: she had taken up shooting. The Havenstrites agreed to the trip and planned to meet the Woodwards in New York.

When the Havenstrites arrived in New York, they discovered that

Billy Woodward could not join them, because he had to travel to Florida for business related to his horses, which he was more excited about than a trip to India. Ann was displeased and wondered for a time if she should go tiger hunting on her own, but after some debate she decided to go forward with her preparations. By the time she arrived in Jaipur, weeks later, Russell Havenstrite stated, "she was excited to shoot tigers."

The trip started off badly. Ann Woodward and Russell Havenstrite did not quite see eye to eye, mostly, he would later say, because she had "such a miserable disposition and she and I didn't get along at any time." It became obvious right away that she and Billy had not been getting along. Russell Havenstrite speculated that Billy's trip to Florida had been an excuse to get away from his wife.

At the time, Ann was not a very good shot. She once aimed at Russell's head instead of a bird, almost killing him. "She would just get very excited and rattled when she shot," he said. The guides were frightened of her. "The men would practically hold her gun to keep her from shooting; she was stubborn and didn't want to take advice from anyone."

Ann rattled on about her anxieties. She was afraid that Billy was going to divorce her, that he was growing tired of her, of their marriage, of their life together. She had doubts about his fidelity. She even admitted that she had hired a private detective to keep track of him, although she suspected that Billy had become aware of him, because she had been hiring the same man for years. Ann kept wondering if she should be returning home, and Russell Havenstrite and his wife tried their best to push her to do so, but Ann stayed on.

Ann's erratic behavior with guns persisted. At each stopover, the new guides were warned against her—the maharaja of Jaipur would write a letter to them alerting them that "Mrs. Woodward was dangerous with guns and inexperienced and that they should watch her at all times and should have someone with her at all times." During that period, she could not be allowed to shoot at birds, or any large animals that she had in her gunsight.

One day, tired and fearful for his life, Russell Havenstrite decided to give her a lesson in the middle of a hunt. He told her that when she saw her prey "to line up the sight on her gun and point it at the tiger first and pull the trigger." To hold it steady and use her imagination, he told her. Moments later, a tiger came out in the clearing and she shot at it, killing it. Ann Woodward was giddy. "I remember what you told me and did it," Ann Woodward told Russell Havenstrite, expressing gratitude for his lessons. It was the first time she had a clue about what she was doing with a rifle, and for the rest of the hunting trip, she continued to refine her skills, shooting and killing on every occasion that she could.

"I don't know what to say about her, she is just so irrational, highstrung, and nervous," Russell Havenstrite said. "I don't think she is a very stable person around firearms. You couldn't tell Anne [sic] anything, she resented any advice, except that one particular time when I tried to show her what to shoot, and she went out and shot the biggest tiger in the party."

SIXTEEN

By October 1955 a young German named Paul Wirths had not reported to his parole officer for a few months. Frank Steiner, a detective from the Second Precinct in Nassau County who had arrested Wirths for burglarizing homes and stealing food, money, and on one occasion a gun, sent out a bulletin to find him.

Paul Wirths was tall and thin, with a fair complexion, blond hair, and green eyes. He was twenty-three and called himself a bricklayer, although he had not been employed in that job since traveling to the United States from Germany just the year before. His last official address was in a rooming house in Hempstead, New York, on Long Island; however, he could now no longer afford the rent and slept anywhere he could—in garages he broke into, in parks and on benches, in cars he stole, and on city streets.

For money, he had been breaking into houses and robbing them of small items, which he later pawned. Within those houses he also helped himself to food he found in the refrigerators, his preference leaning to cold-meat sandwiches, milk, beer, and sweets, especially strawberry and lemon meringue pie, which Long Islanders seemed to be fond of. He burglarized homes in Hempstead, Garden City, Kings Park, Old Westbury, and several other towns east of New York City, then moved on into the wealthier neighborhoods of Oyster Bay Cove.

Although he usually went to these places on foot, he sometimes left by car. One night he stole a 1950 Oldsmobile from a garage and then abandoned it in Huntington. In East Hills he got away with a Ford station wagon, which he discarded in Kings Park. In Kings Park he stole a 1953 Lincoln sedan, which he drove to Old Westbury. He then helped himself to a Chevrolet station wagon, which he exchanged for a gray 1955 Buick. Wirths also stole guns. A .22-caliber Remington rifle; a shotgun somewhere else; two sixteen-gauge shotgun shells elsewhere.

It didn't take long for police to find Wirths after the bulletin went out. A day later, two Huntington patrolmen out on their rounds saw Wirths inside the Suffolk Grill in Huntington, eating a hamburger and drinking a milkshake. Concerned that Wirths might be armed, the patrolmen waited until he finished his lunch and left the restaurant. Wirths immediately ran and they gave quick chase as they yelled after him to stop. When he didn't, one of the officers fired a warning shot into the air. Wirths, trying to jump into a 1952 Ford convertible he had stolen from a garage in Westbury on the night of October 31, stopped and let himself be apprehended. While searching inside the car, the officers found a twenty-gauge J. C. Higgins shotgun, two pocketknives, one black table knife, a traveling bag containing two pairs of golf shoes, a Hungarian pearl choker, a yellow gold pinky ring with a large purple stone, a handful of silk shirts, several boxes of matches, a jacket too big for him, size nine gloves, and other assorted items that obviously did not belong to him.

At the police station, Wirths was greeted by Detective Frank Steiner, who told him that his crimes had made a woman shoot her husband.

Wirths understood right away that he was being "accused of murder," his confession later read, and soon admitted that he had been at the Woodwards' house—but on Friday night, not Saturday, twenty-four hours before Billy Woodward was shot. Paul Wirths conceded that he had spied on Billy until he had fallen asleep, and then, at dawn on Saturday morning, he'd broken into the pool house and helped himself to canned food. It was precisely the story Ann and Billy had told the guests at the Bakers' party, of waking up on Saturday and finding that someone had been on their grounds.

But there was something about Paul Wirths's story that didn't ring true, or perhaps didn't fit the narrative some of the detectives had already formed in their minds. This was especially true for Detective Steiner. Prior to returning Wirths to his cell, Steiner told him that he should really think hard about telling the truth about what had happened at the Woodward estate. If he had done nothing wrong, Steiner asked him, then he had nothing to fear. Correct? In fact, he had nothing to lose either, Steiner went on. His words could actually help people. Wirths nodded, whispering that he would think about it.

The following day Wirths asked to speak to Detective Steiner. When the two men met again, Wirths admitted he'd been doing a lot of pondering. He had decided to tell the truth regarding what had happened at the Woodward estate, chiefly about the time of the shooting. He spoke quickly, somberly, stating that he had been anxious about telling the truth, fearing that admitting his presence on the grounds of the house on Saturday night, October 29, would get him involved in a situation he wanted to stay away from. But the whole ordeal bothered him, he said, especially the situation with "the kids." Their father had died, and now there was a risk that their mother could go to jail too. He had grown up without a mother himself, and he didn't want that to happen to the Woodward children, especially if he were to be the cause of it. Paul Wirths thus agreed to give the details of what happened the night and early morning of October 29 and October 30.

∽

Paul Wirths spent the early part of the evening of Saturday, October 29, 1955, roaming the woods surrounding the Pine Hollow Country Club. Around eight p.m. he broke a windowpane and crept into the clubhouse's snack area, opening a refrigerator and retrieving sandwiches and milk, which he ate on a bench outside. When he noticed a police car with the lights on driving up the driveway, he took off from the bench, running toward the neighboring house, which he now knew belonged to the Woodwards. He hid within tall shrubs and bushes, fearing he might be discovered. Moments later, while still hiding behind the bushes, he noticed two men, likely two employees of the club, leaving the Cinerama building. He also saw that the Woodward house was all lit up. Curious, he left his hiding spot and quietly looked through a kitchen window.

A short time later, he observed a small woman walking to the rear of the house, likely the maid, although he was not precisely sure about the time. He continued to loiter around the property for hours, all the while carrying with him the twenty-gauge shotgun he had stolen from a previous break-in in Kings Park. By now it was past midnight on October 30. The weather had become cold and damp, and he was growing tired and somewhat sleepy. He was hungry too, a constant in his life. Sometime later, he heard a car come up the driveway and was barely quick enough to jump and hide behind a cement pillar located just to the right of the main front door. He heard the car stop and saw a man and a woman step out into the courtyard in front of the house. He could not help but admire their fancy clothes and in particular the woman's face, which he found beautiful. They were quiet until they reached the main door, then he heard a few muffled words and could understand only something about a "key." They entered, and, according to Wirths, the house, which had been dark until then, became lit by a faint light somewhere at the far end of a corridor.

Paul Wirths waited what he determined must have been some ten minutes, and then he saw several lights go on almost at the same time in rooms located parallel to the main entrance. Having taken a survey of the property earlier in the evening, and on the day before as well, he knew those rooms to be the bedrooms. He walked to the bedroom located to the right of the door, but he could not see inside, as the dark-colored shades were drawn. As he snooped around, walking back and forth between the two bedroom windows, he also noticed that the bathroom lights had gone on. Slowly, each light in the house began to dim. It was at that moment that he made the decision to break into the Woodwards' house, because, as he told the detectives, "It looked like the people had money," which he was after, as he wanted to go to Florida for a "new start."

He waited a few moments longer, wanting to give the people inside time to fall asleep. When nearly an hour had passed, he started to climb up a tree to the right of the front of the house. It was not an easy feat, because he was holding the shotgun in one hand. As he climbed, one of the tree branches noisily snapped and fell off, nearly bringing him down as well, but he managed to hold on. He wondered if anyone inside had heard the commotion, but when no lights came on, he continued scaling upward. He climbed across another thick branch and onto a flat portion of the roof located near the front of the house. Once on the roof, he slowly walked to a glass door that led into the house's second story—all the while holding his shotgun.

Wirths tried the handle of this glass door. It was unlocked, but some drapes blew into his face and his foot caught in them as he walked inside. As he tried to untangle, the butt of his shotgun hit the glass, breaking a portion of it. Despite the noise, no one came, no light went on. When he freed himself from the drapes, he took a moment and looked around, realizing that he was inside a bedroom, as there was enough natural light to distinguish a double bed with only a mattress on it, its actual bedding folded on a chair. The next thing he knew, he heard a shot so loud, "to him [it] sounded like a cannon going off." He could not tell which way the shot came from, but he knew enough about shotguns to understand that it was coming from inside the house—there were echoes all around him.

Paul Wirths didn't wait to see if anyone was coming after him. He ran out of the room as fast as he could and rushed across the flat roof with his own shotgun still clutched in his hand. Rather than climb back down the tree, he took a chance and jumped off, landing on the ground by the kitchen. He then ran toward the woods, crossing Route 25A. Making the decision to head west, he continued to traverse the woods until he saw a farm. He searched the barn located on the property and found it empty. Given that it was now dawn and it was also raining, he decided to stay there to sleep. At nearly noon the next day he left the barn to see if there was any activity outside. As he walked the perimeter of the barn, he stumbled, and his own shotgun went off. Fearing that someone might have heard the blast, he ran back into the barn.

Paul Wirths lingered in the barn until nightfall, at which point he left and from a nearby garage stole a 1955 Ford station wagon. For the next few days he continued to break into garages in the neighborhood, stealing several cars and whatever else he could find, including money, food, and clothing, until he swiped the 1952 Ford convertible in which he was found.

When asked why he had initially told detectives a different story of his movements and actions, especially about the timing, he admitted that he did not want to get more involved in the Woodward murder case than he already was.

After his confession, the detectives drove Paul Wirths to the Woodward house in the hope that he could show them precisely all his movements. Reporters followed the tour as Wirths grinned at them, displaying missing teeth that had been knocked out during a fight with a homeowner.

When they returned to the police station, it was Frank Steiner who walked Paul Wirths back to his cell. He had done well, Steiner told him, very well.

∾

When the news of Paul Wirths's confession appeared in the papers, many were suspicious. Those who never believed Ann Woodward were not inclined to believe Paul Wirths. Obviously, they agreed, someone had paid Wirths to give a false confession. Some wondered if Frank Steiner had bribed him. Perhaps Steiner himself had been bribed. The rumors were so rampant that Steiner had to go on record stating, "I never took a penny from anybody, nor did I give Paul Wirths any money." Not everyone believed him. Had Sol Rosenstein handed Steiner a fee to convince Wirths to say those things in order to bolster Ann's claim of an intruder?

Rumors swirled that maybe Elsie Woodward had somehow enticed Paul Wirths into a confession to support Ann's story. Friends of Elsie's knew that she loathed her daughter-in-law. Even so, Elsie could not permit her family to be torn apart by innuendoes and fabrications, especially on account of Ann. It was easier to dish out money to cover up the dirty deeds, many surmised, and pretend to support Ann while safeguarding the Woodward family. Elsie knew Billy harbored secrets that should never be known—that he had physically and emotionally abused Ann; that he had had lovers, perhaps of both sexes; that he had taken to watching pornography while having sex with his lovers; that he had solicited prostitutes. Private matters had to remain private.

SEVENTEEN

❧

As Paul Wirths told his story, Ann slept in her room at Doctors Hospital. Dr. Prutting had come to believe that she was on the verge of a nervous breakdown, and so he'd injected her with another massive dose of sedatives. During her few moments of lucidity, she spoke of her husband, having convinced herself that Billy was not really dead but off somewhere on one of his affairs. Or, she feared he'd picked up a man who resembled his best friend, Bean Baker, in an effort to really hurt her. But then she'd realize that he was with none of those people, having died in her arms, or rather, by her hands. And then she'd yearn to see her children, though Elsie would not send them to her.

When Dr. Prutting wasn't available to take care of Ann, it was his wife, Dr. Jane Aldenn, who did. Dr. Aldenn believed the shooting had been an accident and not premeditated, and she made her theories known during the many interviews she granted to reporters. "Ann had no center. She only lived to please Billy, she was desperate to keep him and her position as Mrs. William Woodward," Dr. Aldenn said. "Her marriage was her career, and he stabilized her. I don't buy her shooting him as a conscious decision. Once he was gone, she was distraught. Still, subconsciously she had to hate his hold over her."

Billy Woodward's funeral would take place on November 2, at eleven o'clock, at the Saint James' Church in New York City, followed by a burial at the Woodlawn Cemetery in the Bronx. Ann Woodward would not attend, because she was still hospitalized. The Woodwards' servants were given the morning off to attend. The flags at the various clubs to which Billy had belonged—the Union Club, the Jockey Club, and the Brook—were flown at half mast.

Ann sent a blanket of white chrysanthemums interspersed with red carnations, the colors of the Belair Stud and Farm. The flowers were placed over the casket, with an inscription that said, "To Dunk from Monk"—Ann and Billy's pet names when they first married. Elsie Woodward was appalled by the flowers and thought the arrangement in poor taste. However, she allowed it, as it would have seemed unusual for Billy's wife not to have done at least this much.

The legal case against Ann looked weak, Elsie's lawyers explained to her. If she was brought to trial, chances were good that everything Elsie dreaded would come to fruition. Lawyers would dig deep into Ann and Billy's marriage. Details would be unearthed, and, in the end, Billy would be the one to come up looking like an abuser and deserving of his ending—likely Ann would be acquitted.

During a press conference on November 4, 1955, Police Chief Pinnell announced that the district attorney had decided to submit the evidence to a grand jury. "If the grand jury dismisses the shooting as an accident," Pinnel said, "we won't press charges." The grand jury would convene on Friday, November 25, in Nassau County.

Hearing that the evidence was going to a grand jury, Elsie decided to visit Ann. By now ten days had passed since the shooting. Elsie's rage was still burning, and Ann, sitting in her hospital chair, could see it despite her mother-in-law's black mourning veil. Elsie didn't sit down, nor did she lift her veil when she spoke, her voice flat and direct. She informed Ann that the newspapers, many of their friends, and most people in the community suspected Ann of deliberately killing Billy. Ann whimpered and tried to speak, but as soon as she opened her mouth Elsie held up her hand, and for a moment Ann was unsure if her mother-in-law intended to stop her from talking or wanted to strike her. It was a massive scandal, Elsie said, her voice solemn, but she and her family had the power to put an end to it. Ann had only to agree to let the children go.

Ann had never fully realized her mother-in-law's contempt for her until then. Elsie was undoubtedly resentful of Ann's hold over her son, jealous even. Elsie had always wanted control of Billy, and she'd been able to assert that dominance until he had met Ann. Ann had never imagined that she would have to fight her mother-in-law over her sons. She didn't know it yet, but Elsie didn't want to raise the boys herself. She had already contacted a prestigious boarding school in Switzerland, where she intended to send them.

In the hospital room Elsie Woodward revealed Billy's revised will, which had been drawn up during his love affair with Marina Torlonia. Although Ann had known about the affair, and she and Billy had almost separated before reconciling, she had not been aware he had reworked his will. Ann's eyes widened with humiliation on learning the new terms—she would receive only the minimum that was legally owed to her by the state. Elsie, for her part, was very pleased that her son had taken her advice and hadn't changed the terms once again when he had reunited with Ann. She even went so far as to tell Ann that in her opinion, Billy had actually been far too generous to someone like her, because as far as she was concerned, she didn't deserve anything. Ann still owned the house in Oyster Bay Cove, where the

shooting had occurred, and their house in Manhattan, along with furniture, jewelry, a yearly allowance, and a sizable amount of cash. Even
with all of that, Billy would have been more useful to Ann alive than
dead.

Ann was shocked but not entirely surprised that her husband had
turned against her. She knew that Elsie would be pleased to finally get
rid of her, even if it had cost her son. And Ann understood her very
limited options. She was uneasy at having to leave the children in her
mother-in-law's care. And it was during this meeting that Elsie told
Ann she would send the boys to the school in Switzerland. Having
no choice, Ann agreed. The two women's decision would never be
explained fully to her two boys. Weeks after their father was killed on
the very day he had taken them to fly in his new airplane, the two boys
would be exiled from the only family they had left.

EIGHTEEN

⁓⚜⁓

On November 21, 1955, Ann Woodward went to Mineola to be questioned by Edward Robinson. Reporters camped outside the police headquarters trailed after her in the hopes that she'd make a comment, but she refused to indulge them. Her lawyer cut a path through the journalists, as she hid her face beneath a dark shawl. Ever since she had married Billy, she had been the willing subject of these newsmen's stories and photographs, which had once made her feel special. But now she wanted nothing more than to be left alone.

Three weeks had passed since the shooting. Although she was still under her doctor's care, Robinson hoped that she would be capable of answering more questions than she had been on the night of Billy's death. And her lawyers had agreed to this meeting. Robinson immediately asked if there were any issues in their marriage that she wanted to share, at which point she shrugged and said, "I would say we had an average married life."

If that was so, Robinson probed, why had she hired detectives to follow her husband soon after they were married? "Were you suspicious of Mr. Woodward?"

"Well, I was curious," Ann admitted.

"Had you heard rumors of something?" Robinson asked.

"Well, I think I had the feeling that he was—I don't know, maybe stopping to have a drink or seeing a girl, and I just was curious to find out."

"Did you know who the girl was?"

"As I said, I wasn't sure, but I had an idea that it might be . . ." Ann trailed off. "I mean, a certain girl. But I didn't know her."

Edward Robinson asked her about other times she had hired a detective, as well as the times she had had her husband followed during his affair with Marina Torlonia. Ann became evasive, pleading for additional time to recall facts, or simply stating that what she had learned hadn't been all that important.

Robinson asked about an argument they had had while in Miami in February 1955. "Do you remember that?" She did, but again, she was reluctant to talk about it.

"What happened?"

"I remember that it was a Saturday night and we had been out," Ann said softly. "I don't know, we got into some argument and for some reason my husband started to choke me, and that frightened me terribly because he was very big and strong, and when he started to choke me, I was terrified because he was so strong. And so, I screamed and someone else in the building must have heard me and called the police."

"Did an ashtray get mixed up in that some place along the line?"

"I don't remember all the details," Ann said.

"Was it possible that you threw an ashtray at him during the course of that argument?"

"It is possible. Women throw things. That is the female instinct."

"Did the Police arrive at the room?"

"Yes, I remember the Police being there," Ann agreed.

"There was no action taken, though, was there?" Robinson asked.

"Oh, there wasn't any action to take," Ann replied, as if indignant that he should have suggested such a thing.

"Had Mr. Woodward been drinking that night?"

"It was a Saturday night and we had been out. I would think in all probability, yes."

"Had you been drinking?"

"I may have."

"You do drink, do you, Mrs. Woodward?"

"I drink very little."

"Were there any other effects as far as your relations with Mr. Woodward over this thing in Miami?"

"Oh, no," said Ann. "We went out to a big lunch party the next day, and it didn't mean a thing. As a matter of fact, in *Time* magazine there is a picture that was taken the very next day. It was the Duchess of Windsor and the Duke of Windsor and the Sanfords. We all had lunch the very next day. It didn't mean anything. Our arguments didn't ever mean anything." The memory of that day seemed to bring her alive.

Robinson changed the subject. "Had you heard anything about prowlers before you came out on Friday night?"

"I had not heard anything about the prowler," Ann said. "No."

Robinson asked how long they had been sleeping in the bedrooms downstairs. Ann acknowledged that it had been several months, having made the switch just before summer, although she could not recall the exact date. She left the bedrooms upstairs ready for guests, she explained, with the beds already made, although Paul Wirths had told Robinson that when he entered through one of the bedroom's doors, he had noticed that one of the beds was unmade, the bedding folded on one of the chairs nearby. Ann Woodward did not know why that would be. She had given instructions to her maids to fix them. She would have to reprimand them, she told Robinson.

She had woken up very late that Saturday morning of the party, she told Robinson, not until her husband had entered her bedroom, sat on her bed, and told her how glad he was that she was finally awake. Their oldest son was with him. The boy was excited, Ann went on. He had spent the morning with his father and his brother, up in Billy's plane, and enthusiastically told his mother everything about his flying adventure. It was only after the boy had left her room that Billy told Ann that it looked as if someone had broken into his car the night before. Whoever had been in the garage had managed to get only as far as the glove compartment. Billy went on to reveal what Principe had told him about the cabana and the footprints. Principe said a prowler had been breaking into homes around the area in the previous week, and that he suspected that it was the same person who had been in their garage.

When Ann had finally arisen from bed, she and Billy had looked around their property. They found where the cabana had been broken into, the prowler having entered through a window he had shattered. It also appeared that the prowler had dragged a chaise lounge out of the cabana and slept on it. Everything that had been stored in a small refrigerator was also removed and strewn around the floor.

Ann felt that the man who had broken into their home was likely still roaming around there that weekend, she told Edward Robinson. He was probably watching them as they searched the property. She started speaking French with Billy, assuming the prowler did not know the language, and together they continued looking over the property, finding further evidence, including scraps of food, empty beer cans, and half-eaten sweets.

They also found a rock in the garage, realizing the prowler had used it to break into the ammunition box, which in their minds meant that the prowler also possessed a gun.

"What car was that, the Studelac?" Robinson wanted to know.

"The Studebaker," Ann said. "This is the thing that terrified us again . . . was the fact that the car we had come from New York in the very night before, had been broken into just as soon as we had parked it in the garage. So again, the prowler was just right there, right at the place I mean, we said he might have been right in the garage, even, or behind the garage or anywhere when we came into the garage, and it is a long walk from the garage to the house."

Ann dabbed her eyes. "So my husband said—I mean, that the prowler had a gun; he must have had a gun if he tried to steal the shells; and that if he was that close and breaking in the night before, that we had better start to take some real precautions and arm ourselves and be prepared for the prowler."

They talked about getting someone to guard the house, Ann told Robinson, but neither one was thrilled with that solution.

The children were going to a picnic held by their riding instructor that evening, and Ann and Billy were scheduled to attend a party at the Bakers' home. Ann told Edward Robinson that before they left, she and her husband instructed the maid to wait up for the children, who would be home between eight thirty and nine o'clock, and then to make sure to lock all the doors before retiring for the night. Ann showed the woman how to do it. This was a whole new awareness for their safety, as they usually would not have locked the front door too, because it was a thick and heavy double door.

Billy decided to take the Ford Thunderbird to the party, because it was faster and slicker, and he liked driving it on the streets of Long Island. The party was scheduled for eight thirty; however, Ann and Billy found themselves arriving at their destination early. "We drove around a little bit before we went in," Ann Woodward said. They roamed around the area for a while, admiring the homes and the Halloween decorations.

It was at this moment on that Saturday night that Ann Woodward made it a point to put on her jewelry. She had brought these particular pearls and matching earrings from the city with her and had planned on donning them for the party. However, once they arrived in Oyster Bay Cove and learned of the prowler, she was reluctant to wear them immediately upon leaving the house, afraid they would entice the robber if he saw them. She had stashed the pieces in a little soft fabric bag and carried them with her in the car, searching for a moment to put them on before entering the party. Arriving early to the Bakers' house worked out perfectly; she had plenty of time to prepare.

Billy Woodward had brought a gun. Earlier in the day he had gone down to the gun cabinet in the basement and removed a nine-millimeter pistol. It was now safely stowed in the glove compartment of the Thunderbird.

At the party, Edward Robinson wanted to know, whom did Ann talk to about the prowler?

"Oh, we talked to—well, everybody that—I mean, nearly everybody that I talked to, anyway, I discussed the prowler with," Ann told him. "And Billy talked about the prowler, and I think Billy said that he brought a gun and he had put the gun in—and he was going to protect us on the way over and back."

When they returned home, Ann continued, the lights in the driveway on the Berry Hill Road side of the house were lit, just as they had left them. It was a long driveway, so it made sense to have some lights on as they drove up to the main door. The lights on the property's other driveways had been kept dark, as usual. They pulled up in front of the house and left the car there, instead of parking it in the garage.

Billy removed the gun from the glove compartment and asked Ann for the house keys. As she fumbled through her purse, she could not find them. Nor could she locate the small fabric purse holding her jewelry, which she had removed as soon as they left the party. She didn't mention this to her husband, fearing the prowler would overhear their conversation, but she did say she could not find the key. And that's when Billy Woodward walked to her bedroom window and crawled through it, Ann Woodward told Edward Robinson.

"Are you sure of that, Mrs. Woodward?" Robinson asked, looking up at her. "Are you sure that he went in that window, or did he just speak about going in?"

Ann reflected for a moment. "I think he went in through that window because I know I had the feeling then again that it was just so easy for the prowler to get in the house."

Edward Robinson nodded and cleared his throat. "You see," he began, "his clothes don't show anything at all that would indicate that he had gone to the point of climbing in that window, and there is a heavy wisteria vine in front of it. Unless you are positive on that statement—that is why I am asking you about it now. As your counsel will tell you, unless you are positive about it, I wouldn't want you to make the statement."

Ann Woodward thought further about what she had just stated. "It may be possible that we talked about it. That might be possible. I mean, I can't remember exactly . . ."

"Who eventually opened the door?"

"I had a key and opened the door," Ann admitted. She said she had searched deeper into her purse and eventually found the key.

Once inside, Billy then went to check around the house, while Ann walked to the back hall and up the stairs to make sure the children were sleeping. She stood outside their rooms and heard them breathing. Her husband eventually joined her, and they returned downstairs, to the sitting room, at which point Billy suggested going to the basement and retrieving the shotguns from the cabinet for both of them. They should both be armed, he had advised Ann, in case the prowler made his appearance.

Ann opened the gun cabinet and even removed extra shells for good measure, which she hid inside her bra, she told Robinson. Those extra ones she eventually returned to the cabinet right after the shooting, accidentally spilling several of them on the floor.

When they separated for the evening, she rested her shotgun on the little slipper chair on the left side of the room, next to her bed.

And before she knew it, she heard a noise, Ann Woodward said. "Something or someone. I don't know what I thought was in the house. And it all happened so terribly fast. The whole thing. I just did it so quick," she said.

Edward Robinson waited a moment before asking, "Do you know whether there were any lights on down in the hall when you fired?"

"It was dark," Ann said.

"Did you see any shadows or think you saw any shadows?"

"Well, I thought there was somebody on the stairs."

"You thought you saw somebody on the stairs?" Robinson asked. How could she have, if it was as dark as she had previously said?

"I don't know," she replied. "I just thought that I saw somebody or something that was moving on the stairs," she said. "I don't know. I had the feeling of being—I don't know. I may have turned on the light, but I just had . . ."

"Did you have a light in your bedroom?"

"There was no light," she said, shaking her head.

"Did you call out, 'who's there?' or anything like that when you went out in the hall or when you went to the door?" Robinson inquired, scribbling some notes down in his notepad.

"No, I just jumped up and ran over and shot. That's why it was so horrible. That's the whole tragedy, the tragedy of the thing."

Edward Robinson wondered if she had given any thought that perhaps it could have been the maid walking down the hall, and not a stranger at all. Ann shook her head. "I didn't think about anything. It all happened so fast I didn't think. Don't you realize that I didn't even think? That's what is so horrible."

"But you didn't call out when you went out to the door at all? You just went out and fired?"

"I just rushed to the door and fired. It happened so fast."

"You are sure that it was in darkness as far as you know when you went to the door and fired?" Robinson asked. Ann nodded. "Now, as you know, I have told you this before, we found a light on down at the far end of Mr. Woodward's bedroom, down by his bed. Do you know whether that was on or not? Was it lighted?"

Ann thought a moment. "I may have turned it on. I may have."

"Well, you didn't go into his bedroom after it happened, did you?"

"I went to him and held him in my arms."

"I know that," said Robinson. "But you didn't go any further than that, did you?"

"I don't remember," she said.

"Where is the switch for the light in the hall? The one that lights the chandelier that hangs in the hallway?"

"It is in the hall, as you come in the door."

"That's right," Robinson said. "Do you recall turning that switch on or lighting that light after the shot?"

"I don't remember what I did. I may have. I very well may have. I don't remember."

"But you did realize what had happened at that time? I am trying to find out how you could see that in the dark."

Ann finally whispered, "I must have turned the light on. Because I remember seeing somebody that didn't have any clothes on and realizing that that was my husband."

Edward Robinson did not reply. He was done with her.

∽

On Friday, November 25, the grand jury began its inquiry into the death of William Woodward Jr., with Edward Robinson supervising. District Attorney Frank Gullotta was there too, and while he believed a visit to the crime scene was essential for the jury members to get a sense of what had occurred, the grand jury did not agree with him and declined to go to the Woodwards' estate. There was a long list of experts to get through, along with gun authorities, and many photographs to examine, and witnesses who were ready to testify. And, of course, there was Ann Woodward herself, who needed to be heard.

Sitting across from the all-male jury, Ann was on the stand for a total of thirty-one minutes, cross-examined by Edward Robinson, who stopped every so often to allow her a break to dab her eyes with her monogrammed handkerchief. She appeared bereft, all present agreed later, but then, she had been an actress, as the papers pointed out; how difficult was it to pull off that stunt? Many other jury members also agreed that her testimony was impressive, recalling details from the night of the shooting that had escaped her when she was first questioned: the sound of a branch snapping outside her bedroom; the dog barking even more viciously than she had previously recalled; the moonlight, which had not been shining that bright after all.

While in court, Ann broke down several times when she felt particularly overwhelmed. Members of the grand jury later reasoned that she made for a very compelling witness. During her deposition, she had to explain to the grand jury that she had fired the gun to save her life, believing there was an intruder at her doorstep. Panic had set in, she said, as soon as she realized that she had mistakenly shot her husband.

Billy's friends eventually heard about her courtroom appearance and agreed that it was nothing more than a powerful performance. She had mentioned the prowler so often the evening of the party, she had seemed so agitated, or pretended to be. Had she truly been so afraid, or had she simply been establishing her pretext for her premeditated murder? Billy's friends could not help but remark on how refined her acting talents had become. It seemed to them that she'd rehearsed her story for just this performance.

The grand jury went on to listen to a total of nine and a half hours of testimony—a short amount of time considering there were more than thirty witnesses on the stand and large mounds of evidence to delve through. Still, the verdict turned out to be unanimous: the jurors voted not to indict her. Alfred T. Allen, foreman for the jury, spoke for all of them when he said, "She shot thinking she was defending herself and her family."

District Attorney Frank Gullotta was not happy with the results, but he went on to tell the reporters gathered outside, "The grand jury has found no evidence of culpability in the Woodward homicide."

Journalists tried once again to elicit a comment from Ann as she left the courtroom. They asked her how she was feeling now that she had been vindicated. Dressed in black and never taking off her sunglasses, her voice trailed off as she replied, "I'll never recover."

NINETEEN

⌒⁂⌒

For a scandal-loving society, the outcome of the official inquest didn't really matter. Ann Woodward was guilty, or so those who knew her said, during lunches, dinners, parties, squash matches, horse races, christenings, and fancy teas. Lacking the satisfaction of criminal charges or conviction, Ann Woodward's world set out to punish her in its own way. The rumor mill went to work, and soon she was banished from the very circles into which she had fought so hard to gain entry. There was no pity for the "self-made widow," as the newspapers came to call her, and in a storm of scorn, New York quickly shunned her. Having been barely tolerated when she married Billy Woodward as an outsider, having been considered a gold digger and social climber and not one of their own, now, after Billy's death, as a widow and possibly a killer, Ann found herself more alone than ever before. To be ostracized was achingly painful.

Those who knew Billy Woodward also remembered his recent trip to Kansas. He had seemed more excited about what he had learned about his wife than the purchase of the plane. A friend, Spitwood

White, now recalled asking him over drinks the day after his return why he had actually gone to Kansas, because during the conversation he hadn't even mentioned the plane. "Why, to get dirt on my wife," Billy had replied. To White, the answer had seemed unremarkable at the time, almost humorous, but after the shooting the conversation appeared to hold greater meaning. Billy must have gone there to compile evidence on his wife, White told the police, in order to get a divorce and gain custody of the children. It seemed like a plausible explanation, many now admitted, and it may have led to his murder.

The sordid innuendos gained even more traction when people began to talk about Ann Woodward's previous life with renewed attention and vigor. Some whispered about her not having been a showgirl at all but possibly a prostitute. Others heard rumors that she had been married before, and that her first marriage had not been legally dissolved before she married Billy, and that Billy had learned that legal detail during his trip to Kansas, which was why she had killed him. Many others discovered the truth about her father, that Jesse-Claude Crowell was not the late Colonel Crowell, as the marriage announcement had declared and as Ann recounted when she was asked, but instead that he was alive and living in Detroit, a destitute drunk who hadn't seen his daughter in years and had come to believe that she had made herself into the Hollywood actress Eve Arden.

Ann Woodward was unable to combat either the speculations or the truths that now arose around her. People would not pause to understand that she had concocted those versions of her life to impress them. They did not comprehend that she had done it for them as well as for herself. A pariah within a world to which she had once belonged—even if only by the sufferance of marriage—Ann intended to do all she could to remain within its members' good graces. Her mother-in-law, Elsie Woodward, had other plans for her.

Soon after the funeral, the Woodward children were shipped off to the boarding school in Switzerland. Elsie Woodward suggested that it would be best for Ann to go mourn her husband elsewhere, specifically in Europe, for a period of no fewer than four years. Her income as a widow was more than adequate to fund her exile, she told her daughter-in-law. More than ever, Elsie wanted her out of sight. Her suggestion was an ultimatum. Elsie threatened to remove her name from the children's trust fund if she didn't do as told. Ann had no choice but to agree. Now, in New York, Elsie would be the only Mrs. Woodward.

❧

For Ann Woodward, seeking solace in traveling was like a return to the old days with her mother, when she and Ethel fled their various homes in Kansas and in Kansas City for new prospects. As she packed her trunks and suitcases, Ann hoped to avoid notoriety and persecution in Europe. As soon as she set foot in England, she realized that it would not be so. Going out on the first morning after her arrival, she ducked her head beneath a black umbrella and even donned dark sunglasses, but she was recognized anyway, her photograph having been splashed across the pages of the international papers soon after the murder. She was no longer greeted by international society as one of its own. She would not be glamorized on the best-dressed lists or in the society pages. Suspected of being a murderess, her company would no longer be sought, but avoided.

Over the next decades, she became lonely abroad, living in modest luxury but in low-grade, persistent misery, taking comfort in other men, as well as finding refuge in drugs and alcohol. There was no meaning in a life that now lacked family, husband, home, and vocation. She longed to confide in someone all that she had endured, all she was still enduring, but there was no one; her mother was dead, she had never been close to her aunts, and she did not know whether her father was dead or still alive, nor did she want to find out. In the United States she had only acquaintances, not real friends, most of whom would view her joylessness as poetic justice.

Whenever she returned to New York to visit, she relearned that the murder had not faded from society's memory, thanks in part to Elsie's weekly soirees attended by society figures, entertainers, publishers, writers, and even athletes. These lunches and afternoon drinks were gossipy—sometimes just frothy, but often pointedly critical. The topic of Ann Woodward generally came up; it was nearly impossible to ignore, as her guests would whisper about it. Elsie Woodward also kept framed pictures of her son all over the house. In death, Billy Woodward was elevated to sainthood while in life he had been anything but.

Then, in 1975, the story of the murder gained a second wind.

∽

Truman Capote had by then become one of the most famous literary figures, thanks to his books *Breakfast at Tiffany's*, which had become a popular movie starring Audrey Hepburn, and *In Cold Blood*, the best-selling "nonfiction novel" that had also been made into a movie. He leveraged his literary prominence into cultural celebrity. Much like Ann, he had ingratiated himself into New York society. Whether its social figures were as infatuated with Truman as he was with them was hard to say. But clearly, they were flattered by his attentions and entertained by his droll persona. He was on everyone's guest list, and when Truman Capote attended a party, a celebration, or a glamorous opening of any sort, it was sure to be a success. The Black and White Ball he threw at the Plaza Hotel in 1966 was a triumphant social and media event and made him not just a guest in society but also, on occasion, an arbiter and host.

Truman had long been collecting gossip about the women and men navigating the complex lanes of Manhattan's social order. He knew that their stories—flirty, fun, gossipy, bitchy, personal, heartbreaking, intimate, and, most of all, what they believed to be private—would be the foundation for his next book, which would explore this milieu that was so extraordinary to him. Truman didn't intend to blackmail anybody with the things he knew and learned. But he was a writer, after all. Given the opportunity to use some of what he gathered, he intended to do just that. And there was one subject above all that had sparked his imagination: the Woodward murder. It was such a sordid, lurid tale, yet so delicious. The initial idea to use Ann Woodward as a main character for a book had started to germinate in Truman's mind as soon as the shooting occurred and stories about it appeared in the newspapers. Although the story was now twenty years old, it remained fodder for gossip within Truman's own circle of friends. Like a ravenous bird, he listened, hoarding their anecdotes, later jotting down all the details into his notebooks: about Ann, about Billy, Elsie, and the gossip that swirled around them. What had really happened that chilly, foggy night in October 1955? And who knew what? He was especially intrigued by Ann Woodward herself, so much so that he underlined Ann's name several times throughout the pages of his notebooks.

Truman Capote was fascinated by people like Ann Woodward, people who schemed their way into society, much as his mother had done, the strivers who devoted their lives to associating with and winning acceptance from the "right people." Truman had done the same thing himself. No one appeared to point out the incongruity to him, that he was the son of a woman similar to Ann Woodward and was, as a gay literary man from the South, a version of her. Truthfully, many of his friends, mostly society figures, had followed a similar path.

Truman had a connection to the Woodward family through some friends of his, and likely he could solicit insider knowledge on what had truly transpired. Furthermore, whatever information on the investigation he couldn't glean, he would simply make up, as was his habit. Besides, he did not intend this book to be a straightforward nonfiction account, with Ann Woodward as its sole protagonist, but a combination of genres involving several of his high-society friends. So he took notes on the story, outlining the text of a book that he believed would be the longest and best of his career, and the most provocative one he had ever written.

He engaged several friends to help him gather information beyond what he would learn from intimate chats. His friend C. Z. Guest had not only been a friend of Billy Woodward's but also attended the Bakers' party the evening Ann shot him. Brought up in Boston with a background similar to Billy's, Guest had followed Billy's early path until she too decided to resist her family's expectations. Instead of attending elite schools, marrying a man chosen by her family, having children who would in turn follow the path she had followed, all of which seemed very boring to her, she had rebelled against convention by dropping out of those schools, becoming a showgirl, and posing naked for Diego Rivera. But unlike Billy, she had eventually married and settled down with Winston Guest, a polo great who had made a respectable socialite out of her, introducing her to a different kind of crowd.

After having learned that CZ had been at the Bakers' party the night of the murder, and that CZ had remained connected to the outcast Ann Woodward, Truman immediately thought he could exploit this sliver of information for his benefit. He also had a friend who worked at the Nassau County Police Department. Truman hired him to copy all the reports regarding the burglaries in Oyster Bay Cove and the murder itself, which were now stored in the police archives. He read them with relish, particularly those detailing Billy's affairs and his other illicit exploits.

∽

Truman believed this was going to be a big novel, the one that was to transform him from a writer of small, evocative works to an author of novels of social mores on broad canvases, in the matter of such great novelists as Jane Austen, Anthony Trollope, and Henry James. Over the next years, his novel's scheme broadened to include other characters as central protagonists, many of whom were also fashioned from the lives of his famous friends. He already had the title for this novel in progress, *Answered Prayers*, taken from a famous quote by Saint Teresa of Ávila: "More tears are shed over answered prayers than unanswered ones." He thought the quote described Ann Woodward and her life, as well as the lives of others with whom he was intimately acquainted. Truman imagined the book to be a large and sprawling epic, one that spanned three decades and moved across several continents. His only limits, he felt, were those imposed by his imagination.

Since the 1950s, Truman had wanted to write a novel that would rival Marcel Proust's *In Search of Lost Time*. His subjects would be rich Americans, particularly rich American women, and he would do for American aristocracy what Proust had done for the French. "I always felt he was kind of a secret friend," Truman said of Proust. It was true that both writers shared some similarities. They were homosexual and they enjoyed the company and the confidences of women in high society, reciprocating by telling them intimacies of their own. Truman, much like Proust, had unusual working habits, which included writing well into the night while reclining in his bed with a notepad propped up on his knees, expending hours searching for a line or a word that would complete a sentence. And while both writers mingled freely among elite society, both were privately scornful of its excess and hypocrisy. In 1920 Proust had opined that women, at their core, were shallow. He said, "In most women's lives, everything, even the greatest sorrow, comes down to a question of 'I haven't got a thing to wear.'" That Truman felt an affinity to Proust, who thought so little of women, said as much about his own feelings toward the socialites surrounding him as it did about his decision to write about them.

In the summer of 1958, while on a holiday in Greece, Truman watched the calm azure seas stretching out before him and allowed his mind to wander. He felt inspired and able to write even more deftly, as well as to think ahead to projects he had in mind. The warm sun, the calm waters, the lovely scent that could be found only in that part of the world, always permitted him to relax and, at the same time, to contemplate his creative endeavors with a little more depth: where he wished his writing to go and what form he wanted his stories to take. And soon a sketch began to take shape. He already had its main character in the form of a New York socialite who had killed her wealthy husband, but now the story expanded, widening to include other protagonists and further ideas.

In a letter to his Random House publisher, Bennett Cerf, Truman described this new work as "a large novel, my magnum opus." In addition, it would be "a book which I must be very silent, so as not to alarm my 'sitters,' and which I think will really arouse you when I outline it (only you must never mention it to a soul). The novel is called 'Answered Prayers,' and if all goes well, I think it will answer mine." There were reasons why he was keeping so mum about the work. He was using as inspiration his friends in high places, modeling his protagonists after such people as his friends William and Babe Paley, Slim Keith, Gloria Vanderbilt, and all those who had shared a secret with him, or perhaps told him a story about themselves or anyone else they had in common. The only problem was that these people didn't know they were being used; nor had they given him permission to become models for his work. Thus, Truman assumed that it would be best to keep the details about *Answered Prayers* quiet for a while, secret, at least until his book was well underway.

At that time, his own expectations were high. He already had in mind eight long chapters that would span close to eight hundred pages. But as the months passed and as Truman began to write, the length shortened to six hundred pages. Eventually he spoke of four hundred pages, and then just three hundred.

Truman's ambitions for the novel soon became part of its burden. This was not just a book anymore. He had taken on a monumental task that somehow was not coalescing, despite his best intentions. His faltering efforts were due not just to the scale of his novel but also to the inner demons who increasingly bothered him.

❧

Despite the commitment to his Proustian epic, Truman found other, ultimately more manageable projects to entice his attention. On Monday, November 16, 1959, while having coffee in his Brooklyn Heights apartment, Truman opened the *New York Times* and on page 39 saw a short article that would change his life and American literary history. The headline read, "Wealthy Farmer, 3 of Family Slain." The crime had taken place in Holcomb, Kansas, the previous day. "A wealthy wheat farmer, his wife and their two young children were found shot to death today in their home," the story began. "They had been killed by shotgun blasts at close range after being bound and gagged." All four members of the Clutter family has been murdered.

The murders fascinated Truman, as did the words of Sheriff Earl

Robinson quoted in the same *New York Times* article: "This is apparently the case of a psychopathic killer." The subjects and themes seemed to have been plucked from a novel already: the setting—a middle-American town, quiet and pastoral, somewhere where no one would think an atrocity like this could be carried out. A typical fall day and an eerie moonlit night. A good, solid, wealthy family taken prisoner in their own home and murdered by someone without any moral compunctions. There was such a randomness to the killings. Truman was looking for something on which to sharpen his nonfiction skills even further, besides the articles he already wrote. Perhaps he could expand this story into something that would have greater impact than a simple true crime story. True, he was still mulling over *Answered Prayers*, but now the murder in Holcomb fascinated him even more than the killing of Billy Woodward.

He was intrigued by the victims themselves, who were part of a close-knit and religious family, not only loved by those members of the family who were away when the murders occurred, but also admired by everyone in town. Stranger still, the investigation would later reveal that the victims had not fought with the intruders. The fact that Herb Clutter hadn't appeared to resist or sought to save his family said something, although the investigators didn't know what yet.

What Truman had in mind wasn't simply a summary of the case, but a series of articles depicting how the inhabitants of Holcomb, a town of just three hundred in western Kansas, reacted to the murders, and how the remaining children, who had not been living at home, were coping with the deaths of their parents and siblings. At this point, the identity of the killer or killers did not matter to him; finding a perpetrator and winning criminal justice was not the true purpose of the story. When later he was asked why he had decided to write about the murders, he responded, "After reading the story it suddenly struck me that a crime, the study of one such, might provide the broad scope I needed to write the kind of book I wanted to write. Moreover, the human heart being what it is, murder was a theme not likely to darken and yellow with time."

He pitched the idea of articles on the murder to the editors of *The New Yorker*, who agreed to let him write about it. Later, he would broker a deal with Random House, who would publish the story in book form shortly after the articles appeared. It was a publishing deal that would lead to the kind of major national recognition Truman Capote had always craved; it would also provide him with the financial freedom he had fantasized about. Truman set aside *Answered Prayers* and Ann Woodward and embarked on the course that would lead him to the blockbuster *In Cold Blood*.

TWENTY

꧁꧂

Although Kansas was unfamiliar territory to him, Truman was eager and even excited to begin this new journey. He had initially asked his old friend Andrew Lyndon to accompany him to Kansas; but Andrew was too busy. He then invited his friend from Monroeville, Nelle Harper Lee, to go with him as he reported the story. The murders had not been solved yet, and he suspected that the people of Holcomb would be afraid and suspicious of those around them, including each other. Truman knew that the reporters arriving in the aftermath of the crime would only add to that sense of mistrust. This was in part why he had asked Lee to join him. She was kind to people, had her way of putting them at ease, and they would view her as less peculiar than they would see him. As it happened, Lee's own novel, *To Kill a Mockingbird*, was finished but hadn't been published yet, so she was free to join him. In mid-December, not a month after the Clutter murders, the two boarded a train from New York and headed to Kansas.

This was not the first time he had somehow become involved in a tale of murder. He had once crossed paths with a killer, when he was ten and visiting relatives in Monroeville. At the time, a sixteen-year-old girl named Martha had arrived in the area to vacation with her relatives. Martha had taken a liking to Truman, and the two had ended up spending many languid summer hours together. At a certain point, Martha had even convinced him to run away with her, although she hadn't told him where; the two made it just a few miles out from Monroeville before they were caught and he was returned to his relatives, while Martha was sent back north to her family.

A dozen or so years later, Truman heard the name of his childhood runaway partner once again, when Martha Jule Beck and her accomplice, Raymond Martinez Fernandez, were accused of committing a string of murders, as many as twenty, the authorities theorized. They were known as "the Lonely Hearts Killers," as they met their victims through the lonely hearts ads in the newspapers.

❦

While Truman had already anticipated the possibility that people might be hesitant to speak to him upon his arrival, he hadn't thought that the inhabitants would decline to speak to him at all. There was, first of all, the natural midwestern reserve that was difficult to crack, along with the fear that came from the fact the killer or killers were still at large. But second, and at least as important, was the fact that it was Truman Capote asking the questions. It didn't take him long to realize that his charms would not be appreciated there as they were in Manhattan. Indeed, some of the things that rendered him amusing and notorious elsewhere were anathema in Kansas.

Truman was a gay man with a presentation that people of the era would label as flamboyant. He was forthrightly effeminate and possessed a direct interrogatory style, but he hadn't altered anything about his looks and mannerisms to adapt to the more traditional habits of western Kansas. Kansans looked on him as they might have the fragments of an asteroid landing on their doorstep.

Although he did not look like a professional reporter, he did have the traits required of one: he was patient and asked carefully worded questions that others might have found too delicate to articulate. And with Nelle Harper Lee's help, he managed to gain the confidence of two very important people: the lead investigator into the case, Alvin Dewey, and his wife, Marie Dewey. The Deweys had been married for seventeen years and were parents to two young boys. Truman learned that he had something in common with Marie Dewey, a former FBI stenographer—like Truman, she had been born and raised in Louisiana and was still fond of the foods of her childhood. This helped forge a kinship among the small group that eventually morphed into a friendship that would last for years after the case was over.

When the rest of Holcomb's inhabitants noticed the friendliness developing among the Deweys, Truman, and Lee, they warmed up to the interlopers. It became easier for Truman to speak with those he needed to question in order to complete his article. While in New York he had mingled with the upper class, the reality was that Truman had a fondness for people who were more of the class he had grown up with. He enjoyed hearing about their lives. Truman was comfortable with Marie. The southern lilt in her voice reminded him of home.

As Truman began his work, the killers of the Clutters, Perry Smith and Richard "Dick" Hickock, were on their way to Mexico. They were ex-convicts who had heard of Herb Clutter from a fellow inmate, Floyd Wells, who had concocted the tale in order to beguile his cellmate, Hickock. Wells had mentioned to Hickock that he had once worked for Herb Clutter, a wealthy man who kept a safe hidden in his house, located at the outskirts of Holcomb. Wells said that Clutter typically kept a stash of some ten thousand dollars in cash. It was one of those stories that inmates tell each other to pass the time, much as southerners tell tales on their porches. As with those tales, this story was untrue.

Richard Hickock believed every word of the story and decided that as soon as he got out of prison, he would drive to Holcomb and rob Herb Clutter. But he could not do so on his own. His cellmate before Floyd Wells had been a younger man named Perry Smith, who was already outside on parole. Hickock planned to convince Perry Smith to join him in robbing Herb Clutter. And when the time came, Smith readily agreed.

On the evening they had set for the robbery, Hickock and Smith brought along with them shotguns, knives, rope, and some tape. Several of the items they had bought while driving to Holcomb; the rest they already owned. Their plan was to quietly and quickly enter the house, find the safe, empty it, and make sure they'd leave no witnesses behind who could place them at the scene. Hickock kept telling Smith that they didn't want witnesses, and while he anticipated there would be four, probably six people in the house, he informed Smith he should be ready to deal with up to a dozen, possibly. Hickock assured Smith that this was going to be a brisk job, and simple. However, once inside the house, it didn't take long for them to realize that there was no safe anywhere, nor was there any money hidden in any other portion of the house. But there were four witnesses. A false story that had been shared between two prison convicts to pass the time turned into the hideous murder of four people. And a talented and ambitious writer reading about it in New York would then get his hands on that narrative, seemingly spun for his purposes.

❧

As the robbers—now turned killers—hopped into their car and drove into the cool Kansas night, they counted their pitiful spoils: nearly

forty dollars in cash, a pair of binoculars, and a portable radio be-
longing to the now-dead fifteen-year-old boy in the family. Heading
to eastern Kansas, they buried what remained of the length of rope
and bindings, as well as Hickock's twelve-gauge shotgun shell cas-
ings. They were keenly aware that they needed to be careful, for if
they were caught by the police, their actions would be grounds for the
death penalty.

The Clutters were well known in Holcomb and its vicinity. Most
people also were aware that they did not keep much money in their
home. Thus, agents from the Kansas Bureau of Investigation (KBI)
speculated that the murders had to have been committed by someone from out of town, someone who was not mindful of the Clutters'
habits and proclivities, who was not cognizant of the fact that Herb
Clutter preferred to pay everything by check. Herb Clutter himself
was a respected farmer who did business not only in Holcomb but also
throughout Kansas. Farmers and ranchers who dealt with him thought
him fair and knowledgeable, one who had gained an education not
only working the lands hard, but also at one of the state's premier
institutions, Kansas State University, succeeding in their agricultural
department. He had also become an agricultural agent, advising other
farmers and ranchers about using innovative technologies to improve
their own businesses. He then put this knowledge back into practice
for himself, building his own farm and a home, planting Chinese elms
that flanked the driveway leading toward the main house. He was
proud of his property, located at the southwest edge of town, and of
his reputation as a decent midwestern man.

News of a possible reward in the case had reached the ears of
Floyd Wells, Richard Hickock's former cellmate, who was still im-
prisoned at the Kansas State Penitentiary. When he heard what had
happened, he suspected that his old friend had indeed believed the

tale he had concocted and actually gone ahead and killed Clutter and his family. Wells requested the one-thousand-dollar reward offered by the *Hutchinson News,* a Kansas paper, for himself, in exchange for giving the Kansas Bureau of Investigation the tip it needed to proceed. And it was that tip that put officials finally on the right track toward apprehending the killers.

After spending time in Mexico, which was the first plan they'd come up with, Hickock and Smith returned to the United States when their money ran out, and when they failed to find jobs that gave them enough to live the high life they wanted. Their return gave detectives the opportunity to catch them. Hickock and Smith were arrested in Las Vegas by a police officer who recognized their stolen car parked in front of a post office, where the two were picking up a parcel of Smith's belongings he had shipped to himself from Mexico. The KBI were notified of the arrests, and soon agents were on their way to Nevada to retrieve Hickock and Smith. Neither were notified as to why they were being arrested. Las Vegas officers had simply told them they were being seized for a parole violation. The officers had been warned by KBI agents not to mention the murders back in Kansas until the agents showed up.

The KBI agents immediately separated the two suspects, so that they would not be able to speak to each other and discuss what to tell them. But by the time Hickock and Smith were arrested, the two suspects had been on the run for weeks; they had had plenty of time to hash out the story they might have to tell the authorities should they ever be brought back to Kansas on murder charges.

Following some mundane conversation, KBI agents eased each man into discussing the Clutter murders. Even as the two were driven back to their home state in separate cars, they were reluctant to talk, until Richard Hickock blurted out that Perry Smith had committed all four killings. Smith also revealed his part in the murders, though initially he blamed Hickock for shooting the two women. On January 6, 1960, the caravan returned to Kansas, arriving in Garden City. A crowd had gathered in front of the courthouse. Within the throng stood Truman Capote and Harper Lee, huddling deep within their coats, shielding themselves from the cold.

Truman soon realized that his story had expanded tremendously. It was no longer just a chronicle of a small midwestern town reckoning with murder. Instead, he had on his hands a rich narrative involving the people who had committed those crimes, their motives, other characters who had been caught in the saga; the lawmen who had worked to bring the killers to justice; the aftereffects of the murders, and the moral complexities of the judicial system.

Once he was able to gain the confidences of Hitchcock and Smith, something curious happened: townspeople came to believe that Truman won access to them through a little bribery. And that he had used this bribery not only with the accused killers, but also with those men who were in charge of watching over them. Perhaps it was true, in some small way, anyway. He offered all of those involved, criminals and lawmen alike, little gifts of magazines and cigarettes, which they craved and enjoyed. He made the accused killers feel as if they had more to say beyond their confessions, as if they were people who owned a personal history and an interesting life to explore, not one defined only by the recent acts they had committed. Truman wanted to know all about their childhoods, and all about the circumstances that had led them to the home of Herb Clutter. Slowly the two killers began to trust him, looked forward to his visits, and went so far as to think of him as a close friend who could help them beat their convictions.

The accused killers' memories were uncanny, Hickock's in particular; he was able to give Truman the kind of details he could only dream about, the type of material that would eventually profoundly shape his work. Both men recalled particulars of their trip to Mexico, the road signs they had passed, the hotel rooms they had stayed in—the minutiae so vivid that it transported Truman to the places they had been. The weight of the killers' words began to feel heavy on Truman's psyche. And Perry Smith, with his flair for the artistic, aside from tangible specifics, provided Truman with poetic imagery and symbolism for the actions he and Hickock had engaged in.

Hickock and Smith were kept in separate cells, so Truman had the opportunity to talk and work separately with each of them. He pitted their stories against each other for accuracy, establishing a timeline, comparing travel routes along the various Kansas roads on their way to Mexico. And, most of all, Truman compared both of their stories against the official sequence of the murders. Truman had managed to get copies of the confessions they had given to the KBI agents, but, in addition, Hickock and Smith had also confessed to him, so he was able to place the two confessions side by side and check for accuracy. At times he felt elated and overwhelmed all at once—it was such a stunning coup to have those two men speak to him so freely about their motivations. There developed a strong friendship between them, especially between Truman Capote and Perry Smith. Truman felt a deep sense of compassion for the killers.

Truman began to see several parallels between his life and that of Perry Smith. There was a physical resemblance between the two, both men being small and somewhat effeminate, attributes for which they had been bullied and disparaged while growing up. Both had also suffered the pangs of parental abandonment, always yearning to be loved and seen by their mothers, women who were more interested in showing their affection to strange men than to their children. They had also grown up with a need to express themselves artistically that very few people around them had understood. In Truman's case, that need had turned him into a successful writer. In Smith's case, somewhere along the way he had taken a wrong turn that had caused him to seek out Hickock's company. He was now held in a state penitentiary as an alleged killer, being interviewed by a man Smith likely envied for having achieved the kind of life he had failed to earn.

To a certain degree, Truman must have understood Smith's yearnings, even his anger. And he also must have understood that at some level, luck had played a role in the fact that his life had turned out differently. Perry Smith was a disturbed and disturbing mirror image of himself.

Truman Capote was not the only one to notice this uncanny similarity to Perry Smith. Alvin Dewey, a keen observer of human nature, remarked, "Truman saw himself in Perry Smith, not in being deadly, of course, but in their childhood. Their childhood was more or less the same."

Smith's and Hickock's trial moved quickly. It started on March 22, 1960, and they were found guilty on March 29, a little more than a week later. Barring any delays, their execution would happen on May 13, 1960. Truman Capote felt confident that he would spend about a year writing In Cold Blood, what he now called his Big Book, and then he would be able to move on to his next project, Answered Prayers. He hadn't forgotten about Answered Prayers, or about Ann and Billy Woodward. However, the judicial system moved at its own pace. Smith and Hickock quickly received a stay of execution from the Kansas Supreme Court; then another one followed. The book Truman had anticipated wouldn't take more than a year to finish would now take longer, as Smith and Hickock remained on death row for the next five years.

In the meantime, Truman Capote kept in touch with Alvin Dewey, writing several letters in order to keep updated about the case. In one he asked, "Will H. & S. live to a ripe and happy old age?" Then, he continued on, "Or will they swing and make a lot of other folks very happy indeed?"

During this period, Truman Capote lived two separate lives. He spent most of his time abroad, writing all that he could of *In Cold Blood*, without the actual ending. In July 1960, while living in Spain's Costa Brava, he wrote to his former lover Newton Arvin, "I will be here until October, then going elsewhere, maybe Switzerland." Then he went on to explain why: "Because I don't want to go home until I have finished my Kansas book, as it is very long (I should think 150–200 thousand words) that may take another year or more. I don't care—it has to be perfect, for I am excited about it, totally dedicated, and believe, if I am patient, it could be a kind of masterpiece: God knows I have wonderful material, and lots of it. . . . Sometimes, when I think how good it could be, I can barely breathe. Well, the whole thing was the most interesting experience of my life, and indeed has changed my life, altered my point of view about almost everything—it is a Big Work, believe me, and if I fail, I still will have succeeded."

He often returned to New York and partied with his friends, especially with William and Babe Paley. William Paley was the head of the Columbia Broadcasting System (CBS) and Babe his socialite wife and the woman Truman considered his best friend. Truman indulged in extravagant vacations on the coast of Spain and in Italy with them, and part of the spring and summer in other spots around the Mediterranean by himself.

After five years, no more stays were granted to Perry Smith and Richard Hickock, and their executions were scheduled for April 14, 1965. Finally, Truman could write "The End" on this manuscript.

The two murderers asked him to be present at the execution. Truman traveled to Kansas, accompanied by Joseph Fox, his Random House editor. Truman lost his nerve at the last moment, and instead of visiting Perry Smith and Richard Hickock in their respective cells, he saw them for just a few minutes right before they were led toward the gallows, handing them a few cigarettes while engaging in some meaningless small chatter before they were led away. He then joined the rest of those present assembled to view the execution.

When it was all over, and Capote and Fox were on a plane heading back to New York, Truman cried the entire flight. It was true that now he could finish his book; it was also true that Perry Smith and Richard Hickock had killed four members of the Clutter family. Nonetheless, there was also no denying the fact that what Truman Capote had just experienced was life-changing, the epilogue to a dark predicament in which he had found himself caught up for years. And now it was all over.

He had made many friends in Kansas, especially Alvin and Marie Dewey. And Kansas itself had started to feel almost like a second home for him. But in returning to New York he realized that it was time to shake off what he had experienced. But before he did that, there was one last duty he had to attend to. Aware that no one else was going to fulfill the task, he took it on himself to order gravestones for Perry Smith and Richard Hickock. For Truman Capote, ordering the headstones was likely not just a kindness. It marked the end of an era. He was literally done with them.

Settling those affairs, Truman Capote got to work, quickly finishing *In Cold Blood* in the two months after Perry Smith and Richard Hickock were executed. After proofreading, changing a few things, and rereading the manuscript, he was finally satisfied—it was good. He gave the manuscript to Joseph Fox at Random House. Now he could turn back to *Answered Prayers*.

TWENTY-ONE

❧

Most of *In Cold Blood* was written during Truman Capote's frequent stays in Europe. At the time, he felt that placing physical distance between himself and Kansas would give him some perspective on his work. Then he could also deal with the sense of duty that was compelling him to write the book. "I suppose it sounds pretentious," he wrote to Donald Windham, "but I feel a great obligation to write it, even though the material leaves me increasingly limp and numb and, well, horrified—I have such awful dreams every night."

At the end of 1965, *The New Yorker* published *In Cold Blood* in four separate articles, giving Random House, which would publish the entire book in early 1966, only a hint of its future success. Unlike the lyrical reflections of his earlier works, Truman's style in *In Cold Blood* turned more somber. Gone were his poetic musings and gothic reveries. In its stead readers found spare prose and a rigorous if evocative style of reportage that would capture readers with its stark illustrations of what had happened in Holcomb, Kansas. The movie rights were quickly sold to Twentieth Century Fox, and because of the staggering book sales, money began flowing toward Truman steadily, a novelty he was unaccustomed to.

The opening lines of the book itself instantly became etched in literary history: "The village of Holcomb stands on the high wheat plains of western Kansas, a lonesome area that other Kansans call 'out there.'" Novelistic in style, the book gave rise to a string of nonfiction crime books and would eventually be the foundation for a trend. *"In Cold Blood* may have been written like a novel," Truman said, "but it is accurate to the smallest detail—'immaculately factual.'" Perhaps that was true according to his version of events, but many readers had started to wonder about certain portions of the book, such as the deeds committed by the killers and the sequence of how the investigation had progressed. Even a handful of the detectives on the case found a few faulty passages in the narrative.

The writer John Richardson, who knew Capote, said, "Truman had absolutely no respect for the truth. He felt that as a fiction writer he had license to say whatever came into his head as long as it had a surprising point or shape to it, or an unexpected twist to its tail." Others felt similarly about Truman's propensity to reshape factual events. Gore Vidal wasn't as impressed with *In Cold Blood* as the rest of the world seemed to be. In a 1972 interview, he stated, "Capote had a reputation for rearranging facts to suit his fancy or his needs." The writer and screenwriter Wyatt Cooper, who was also familiar with Truman, added, "He improves . . . God's own imagination." "His view of reality and mine are very different," Donald Windham agreed.

But Truman wasn't bothered by the allegations. In an interview with *Cosmopolitan* magazine soon after the book's release, he said, "I just call it making something 'come alive.' In other words, a form of art. Art and truth are not necessarily compatible bedfellows."

He quickly settled into his new life of means. Nonetheless, he could not so easily shake off the emotional burden that *In Cold Blood* had brought on him. "No one will ever know what *In Cold Blood* took out of me," he told a friend. "It stripped me right down to the marrow of my bones." As a result, the discipline he had always displayed earlier in his life began to waver. Whether he still felt tired from the deep researching and intensive writing of the book, or because he hadn't completely overcome the experience of seeing the killers die, he could not tell. But he felt a sort of heaviness settle on him. He tried to blunt it with alcohol.

Initially, Truman Capote enjoyed himself, reveling in all the success that was coming his way with the publication of *In Cold Blood*, even if there were those who believed that he was partying too much. "He looks like a tycoon, thickset, well-dressed, no longer the little gnome of *Other Voices*," said his friend Cecil Beaton, increasingly concerned as to how fame was changing Truman. "I feel T. is in a bad state and may not last long." Nelle Harper Lee felt somewhat similarly. In a rare interview, which she gave to *Newsweek*, she said, "Truman is happy. But there's only one thing worse than promises unkept, that's promises kept." It appeared that she had her own version of Saint Terese's quote.

He was luxuriating in his newfound status and security, Truman explained to his lover, Jack Dunphy. But Dunphy had always approached life with a certain amount of skepticism, which was often at odds with Truman's personality. He was known around New York as an unsociable and rather sulky man, the exact opposite of Truman. "All parties are bad, so far as I'm concerned," Dunphy once said. "I don't believe in social life for a reason: it doesn't do anything for you." To Dunphy, Truman seemed to be cultivating his celebrity status more than his literary career, and he was repulsed by all this glitz and glamour that brought nothing to his character. There was no substance to the people Truman spent most of his time with, Dunphy insisted, and they were going to keep him from his true literary endeavors. Dunphy maintained that the company Truman kept, most especially the company of his socialite women, would diminish the expression of his talent. But Truman adamantly disagreed. He was simply coasting on the success of *In Cold Blood*; in time, he assured Dunphy, he would find his way back to his work.

Truman still relished reading the reviews that came in for *In Cold Blood*. The *New York Times* called it "a modern day masterpiece," while the *Charlotte Observer* was more effusive, opining that he had created "a book that claws its way into your very being and stays." *The New Republic*, on the other hand, called Truman the "most outrageously overrated stylist of our time," while the *San Francisco Chronicle* deemed *In Cold Blood* "as powerless and empty of significance as a dead snake."

It didn't matter, as Truman Capote continued doing his part to make sure that his book, and himself, stayed in the limelight. "A boy has to hustle his book," he told *Newsweek*. And hustle he did, giving as many interviews as he could, appearing on countless television programs, and attending as many parties as was humanly possible, running himself dry. Not surprisingly, while traveling to Switzerland, he was hospitalized with a virus he was unable to shake off. And there were times in New York when, feeling overwhelmed, he simply hopped into his green Jaguar and took off for a long drive, sometimes wandering for hours, often landing at a motel where he would sink into an anonymous and cheerless bed. It was one of those things he enjoyed most in life, he confided once to his friend Cecil Beaton. Those lonely trips became more frequent after the publication of *In Cold Blood*.

He needed a new project to concentrate on. He desired a return to his life of creativity, to a routine in which blank pages were quickly filled with script and then steadily accumulated on his desk. For the past few years, he had dedicated himself to solving a riddle. *In Cold Blood* had taken over his life, given him purpose. But now the killers were dead, and his book was finished and published. He spent some time writing a movie script that was repeatedly rejected, and a television show for which he had great hopes but that was never produced. To dull the sting of those rejections, he wrote more arduously than ever, and he continued to indulge in drugs and alcohol, whether alone or with company.

∽

Maybe a party. Even Truman was aware that to throw himself a party to celebrate the success of *In Cold Blood* was a little tacky. What he needed, Truman quickly realized, was to find someone within his community who could serve as a guest of honor, a person he could use as a subject of celebration, thus deflecting the attention away from himself. That said, he acknowledged that most people would still understand that the party was in reality all about him.

Searching for the perfect guest of honor, he went down the list of appropriate personages. He didn't want to select anybody from among his most famous lady friends, those lights of New York society: they were all marvelous in their own way but could also be bluntly petty and jealous of one another, and they didn't have independent identities and power in the larger world. Also, he didn't want to explain to them why he had chosen one woman over the other, why one would receive such vast attention while the other would be bypassed. While a squabble among them was always a lot of fun to watch, Truman knew that a feud with him would not be. And so, he settled on Katharine Graham.

Kay Graham was the publisher of the *Washington Post*, and had been introduced to Truman Capote by Babe Paley only recently. She and Truman had vacationed together when he had invited her on a sailing trip along the coast of Turkey, on Marella and Gianni Agnelli's boat. Kay Graham hadn't been thrilled about the prospect of the trip. She knew that all those who would be participating were permanent features on the social scene and on best-dressed lists; they paid special attention to the latest fashions coming out of Europe and made use of the latest cosmetic trends and hair styles. In comparing herself with them, Kay Graham felt she came across a little outdated, even homely. But Truman insisted that she go. She would feel better, he told her, wanting to get her out of her occasional dark moods; she was still mourning her husband, Philip Graham, who had died by suicide. And so, after some nudging, she had agreed to accompany him.

Surprisingly, Graham later admitted that Truman had been correct all along. She had indeed enjoyed herself, as a pattern had been established as soon as they'd arrived on the boat. She had read Truman's books, and the two of them spent their time discussing literature and exchanging philosophical ideas, talking well into the night. It made for a memorable time.

By early October 1966, Truman Capote had sent out 540 invitations to his Monday, November 28, Black and White Ball, which he had started referring to as the "best goddam party" anybody would ever attend. This was not going to be just any old party, but a reverberating social event, he often mused, where individuals from a variety of backgrounds and creative endeavors would have a chance to mingle and make an evening that would be talked about for years.

Truman held on tightly to every aspect of the preparations, convinced that its many details needed to remain secret, unless he wished to reveal anything himself—everything from the guest list to who was invited to the smaller individual parties held before the main event, and who was arriving with whom as their date. Of course, when reporters plied him for little nuggets of information, he'd wave a hand and try to sound nonchalant about the whole occasion. With his usual casual attitude, he would state, "They don't understand. This is purely and simply a party for my friends." Of course, it was hard to believe him. While he had become friendly with many people in high places, it was difficult to imagine that his intimates included the likes of Rose Kennedy and the Baron and Baroness Guy de Rothschild.

On November 28, 1966, madness overwhelmed what the journalist Tom Wolfe would call the beautiful people who had made the list of invitees to Truman's masquerade Black and White Ball. Despite the inclement weather, many dozens of onlookers lingered outside the Plaza Hotel, hoping to catch a glimpse of the assembling celebrities.

A *Washington Post* reporter who wrote about the party, and about Truman himself, said, "His name, coupled with a guest-list that reads like a who's who of the world, has escalated his party to a social happening of history-making proportions." The journalist was correct; the guest list comprised Hollywood glamour, Washington's powerhouses, and New York's elites, along with several friends Truman had made in Kansas and who had helped him in the research of *In Cold Blood*. Of course, his New York society friends and their partners were there too, along with the elite from the worlds of publishing, entertainment, and the theater.

Truman Capote prepared for the party in his hotel room at the Plaza. The experience could, perhaps, help him forget the memory of an earlier hotel room, a much shabbier one to which his mother had brought him and left him to fend for himself for a period of hours, while she disappeared into the city to party and look for men. He had been only a small child then, three or four years old, and the room had seemed so big, so dark, so empty to him. He often spoke of that moment to reporters, describing it as a pivotal episode in his life, one when something had broken inside.

All the guests were due to arrive at ten in the evening, but photographers and reporters had been setting up for hours before, and the gawkers had been amassing all day. Truman Capote already viewed the evening as a success. Months before, simply mentioning the idea of the party had started people talking. Furthermore, letting it slip that he planned on inviting only a finite number of people to the affair had put everyone on edge. Now Truman looked at the scene before him in stunned silence. He and Katharine Graham had taken their spots to receive their guests, Truman wearing a classic tuxedo and a thirty-nine-cent mask purchased at FAO Schwarz, while Graham wore a white wool ball gown and matching wool crepe jeweled mask.

However, not all partygoers were impressed. As the guests streamed inside, the writer and editor Leo Lerman, who was attending not only as a friend of Truman's but also as a writer from *Mademoiselle*, had this to say: "The guestbook reads like an international list for the guillotine." With the Black and White Ball, Truman Capote had achieved the highest possible apex of his fame. But, as it turned out, it was also at this moment that his descent began.

TWENTY-TWO

～✦～

Rather than beginning a new book, Truman decided to return to *Answered Prayers*, the Proust-influenced text that had taken so much of his time prior to the discovery of the news article that had led to *In Cold Blood*. Finally, he could go back to it without interruptions. "Oh, how easy it'll be by comparison!" he said to a reporter. "It's all in my head."

He realized once again that the 1955 killing of Billy Woodward at the hands of his wife, Ann Woodward, had everything he could wish for in a story: secret pasts, social climbing, glamour, sex, transgression, an enthralling crime. Not to mention the fact that a part of him wanted to exact revenge on Ann Woodward for her insult when the two had clashed briefly in Saint Moritz in 1956, shortly after the Billy Woodward murder case had been closed and she had become embroiled in an affair with Claus von Bülow. Truman still had not forgotten the fact that she had called him a "fag," and later on, "a little toad."

~⁓

On January 5, 1966, Truman Capote had signed a contract with Random House for *Answered Prayers*. He would be working again with the editor Joseph Fox, just as he had with *In Cold Blood*, which would be published just days later and had already garnered much advance buzz. Truman would make sure to report that *Answered Prayers* was going to be nothing like the books he had written before, most especially nothing like *In Cold Blood*. His publisher echoed his grand ambition that *Answered Prayers* would be "a contemporary equivalent to Proust's masterpiece *Remembrance of Things Past*."

He fed some delicious but innocuous items about this forthcoming new book to the press, but then remained tight lipped, happy at the anticipation and consternation the book was inciting. But in spite of his bravado, many of his friends had an inkling that there was nothing there—that in fact, after *In Cold Blood*, he was having a difficult time writing. The book was more public performance than product.

As it turned out, the delivery date for the manuscript of *Answered Prayers* came and went without any sign of the manuscript. There was an unspoken understanding within his publishing house that Truman had been mentally and physically drained by the development of *In Cold Blood*—the book had taken nearly six years of research and writing—and the emotional stress inflicted on him had been overwhelming. Editors at Random House understood and accepted that perhaps he needed more time to return to his disciplined way of life.

But the reality was that while he constantly talked about *Answered Prayers*, he had written only a handful of chapters, which at most were only individual stories. Consequently, in 1969 Random House canceled the original contract and offered him an entirely new one. This actually was a more advantageous arrangement for the author: a three-book deal with a higher advance, with the first book, *Answered Prayers*, to be delivered in January 1973. But when January 1973 arrived, the deadline was once more postponed to January 1974, which was later changed to September 1974. While none of the new manuscript ever appeared, Capote did publish some material during this time, although these were works he had written during the 1940s and 1950s. The only new writing was contained in *Music for Chameleons*, which would be published in 1980.

He wrote about this period of his life in the introduction to *Music for Chameleons*, as a sort of explanation:

> *For four years, roughly from 1968 through 1972, I spent most of my time rewriting and selecting, rewriting and indexing my own letters, other people's letters, my diaries and journals (which contain detailed accounts of hundreds of scenes and conversations) for the years 1943 through 1965. I intended to use much of this material in a book I had long been planning: a variation on the nonfiction novel. . . . In 1972 I began work on this book by writing the last chapter first (it's always good to know where one's going). Then I wrote the first chapter, "Unspoiled Monsters." Then the fifth, "A Severe Insult to the Brain." Then the seventh, "La Côte Basque." I went on in this manner, writing different chapters out of sequence. I was able to do this only because the plot—or rather plots—was true, and all the characters were real: it wasn't difficult to keep it all in mind, for I hadn't invented anything.*

But other than that, there was nothing one could call a book. And his editors and fans waited.

TWENTY-THREE

"**B**eautiful people have something more. . . . It's a level of taste and freedom. I think that's what always attracted me. The freedom to pursue an aesthetic quality in life is an extra dimension like being able to fly where others walk. It's marvelous to appreciate paintings, but why not have them? Why not create a whole aesthetic ambiance? Be your own living work of art? It has a good deal to do with money, but that's not all of it by any means." Truman Capote felt that certain people were endowed with the necessary skills or, more appropriately, with the necessary pedigree to succeed in this stratum of society.

The rich had always fascinated him. But not just any rich. It was the New York rich whom he admired, the people who dazzled his mother, Nina Capote, when she encountered them on the fringes of her own circle, and those of European origins too, particularly the ones who held a title next to their names. People who moved about town with style and mystery and skeletons in their closets. He suspected that money somehow allowed them to bend the rules that everybody else had to live by. Their behavior wasn't guided by a moral compass, or by human laws.

Had they earned their wealth? Had they inherited it, or married into it? What did money allow them to do that others could not? Did it change their personalities? Unknown to him, his friends were also watching him for the same reasons, studying his behavior for changes as money began coming in from his books.

He knew that most of the women he befriended and was writing about had not been born into wealth but had married into it, struggling for a place of their own with no small amount of scheming and conniving. Ann Woodward was the showgirl version of the more middle- and upper-middle-class women who through beauty, manners, grace, luck, and pluck had shouldered their way into the inner realm of position and privilege. They were, he often proclaimed, self-made creatures, not unlike himself. In their own way, each of them was an artist "whose sole creation is her perishable self."

The beautiful, well-known, and socially connected ladies who were his friends became famously known as his swans. In dining rooms, restaurants, cafés, and clubs, at charity functions and private parties, they chatted and ranted, plotted against others, bickered and criticized, made up and drank champagne. They were witty, funny, and sometimes vitriolic; their cattiness could be truly viperous, and they could make and ruin reputations. And Truman Capote, in the middle of it all, was equally as funny, acute, generous, or gossipy. He christened each of them with his own chosen nickname to make them all feel even more special.

Babe Paley was Truman's favorite swan. She was already a style icon born to prominent parents in Boston, and part of the so-called Fabulous Cushing Sisters, the three sisters who went on to marry very powerful and wealthy men. Slim Keith ranked second on Truman's list of favorites. She was also a socialite and well known for her fashion sense. Sharp, witty, and a friend to Babe Paley, Slim was born to humble parentage in Salinas, California, before making advantageous marriages that propelled her up on the social ladder. Lee Radziwill entered the swan circle later than most. Known as Princess Lee Radziwill for having married Prince Stanislaw Albrecht Radziwill, she was the younger sister of First Lady Jacqueline Kennedy and a struggling actress whom Truman believed always disliked living in her sister's shadow. Gloria Guinness was considered by the press to be one of the most beautiful women of the times, although Truman didn't agree with the assessment; he thought Babe Paley deserved the title. Guinness was born in Mexico to poor parents but had achieved high-society status by marrying a series of wealthy and well-connected men. And the last woman, but certainly not the least, to round up the group was the bona fide Italian princess Marella Agnelli, wife of the Italian Fiat chairman and womanizer Gianni Agnelli, and the only woman in the circle who was not as enamored with Truman as the others were.

Truman had come across a passage in a nineteenth-century journal by Patrick Conway, who wrote about observing "a gathering of swans, an aloof armada . . . their feathers floating away over the water like the trailing hems of snowy ball-gowns." Truman was immediately reminded of his circle of female friends. He even quoted some of those words in an introduction to Richard Avedon's book *Observations*, listing the attributes that a swan—a woman-swan, that is—should possess.

"Of first importance is voice, its timbre, how and what it pronounces," Truman began. They should possess a certain measure of cleverness, although "dumbness seldom diminishes masculine respect." Most important, of course, was money. "Authentic swans," Truman continued, "are almost never women that nature and the world have deprived. God gave them good bones; some lesser personage, a father, a husband, blessed them with that best of beauty emollients, a splendid bank account. Being a great beauty, and *remaining* one, is, at the altitude flown here, expensive." Of course, money alone wasn't enough—a lot of women had money. A woman also needed a discriminating personal style to know what to do with the money.

A splendid gathering of swans, their long necks straight and ornamented with expensive pearls and jewels, their faces painted and lips rouged in the most fashionable colors, their hair expertly coifed, their figures finely dressed and styled; nothing was ever out of place, and nothing was left to chance. The newspapers were full of articles depicting the doings of society women and girls, from debutante balls to charity galas to nights out dancing at popular clubs where commoners were not allowed to enter, to languorous lunches at expensive restaurants that lasted well into the afternoon, to vacations abroad in places most people couldn't even find on a map. And Truman had been admitted into this circle and made not only a part of it, but the leader of the flock. He revered his swans the same way he had admired his mother, longing for acceptance, desiring to be a part of their world.

In return Truman brought a wit and excitement to the lives of these women that other men, including their spouses, always seemed to lack. They missed him deeply when he was not in their presence. He had developed a strategy to get them talking. Never shy, he revealed a small secret about himself, which forged a sort of intimacy between them, and then allowed the swans to confess something about themselves that up until that moment had been hidden. The only difference was that when he spoke, he did so for a brief moment, while they talked for hours.

In an interview with Gloria Steinem in 1967, the feminist writer wondered if there was "something of the voyeur in every writer." And

Truman replied, "Well, there certainly is in me!" Then he thought a moment longer. "I love listening to other people's conversations, no matter how dull they are. I can be mesmerized, as long as they have the quality of being overheard. In fact, if I could have one wish granted, it would be to become the Invisible Man. I really have thoughts about that. I would drink a magic potion, walk around, and watch everything that people are doing and saying; then drink this other little potion and I'd be visible again."

Truman didn't have the swans' money, but he had his talents and charm. He always held court like a king, a glass of liquor in one hand and a cigarette in the other, clad in his usual attire—dark glasses, a vibrant scarf tied around his neck, and a colorful sweater that on someone else would have looked tacky but on him was stylish. He knew how to be bubbly, charming, sarcastic, and honest. He was the best friend one could ever hope for, as well as the worst enemy anyone could ever encounter. That he was openly gay never bothered the women, and their husbands never saw him as a sexual threat. In fact, the men tolerated Capote because he was entertaining and did not challenge their own masculinity. "Most men of the era," said Louise Greenwald, "were homophobic—very homophobic. But Truman was their exception, because he was so amusing. Nobody came into their houses that their husbands didn't approve of. In a way, Truman could be very seductive, and he was a good listener. He was sympathetic. He seduced both the men and the women." This was indeed a peculiar relationship that he had with the women. In his company, they lost their inhibitions and found the freedom to speak candidly, their gossip becoming an art form.

He was the man they confessed their sins to, and the one who listened to them without reproach; the one they turned to when they found out who had slept with their maids; when they heard rumors of who had sought an abortion; or of secrets they were trying to bury with money. And Truman knew just what to offer in return. Flattery when they needed it, or consolation when it was appropriate. Advice on their love affairs or perfect silence when that was all they needed. And while many believed him caring and loving, others realized that he was quite the opposite: shrewd, able to parlay a little bit of knowledge to his great advantage. Either way, there was always some sort of amusement with him around, and the conversation never dragged. He also had the power to offend with a smile on his lips and a twinkle in his eyes, while several of them smiled back, thinking it a joke.

He enjoyed watching as photographers and reporters posted themselves outside such restaurants as La Côte Basque to watch not only celebrities, but also the celebrated socialites and their companions. Their lunch dates had become notorious, and as Maury Paul had once said, "Nobody gives a damn who you sleep with. In this world, it's who you're seen dining with that counts."

Nonetheless, as time went on, several of Capote's swans detected a touch of spitefulness and maliciousness in his words, something that made his gossip seem less fun and more bitter. "I can break up anybody in New York I want to," Truman once told Slim Keith, with a certain amount of pride. She did not like hearing that, as the breakup of a marriage seemed like a sport to him. As it turned out, her own marital problems would be a major topic of Truman's gossip when the time came.

Truman had always warned his friends against angering him. If they weren't careful, he'd say, he would write them into his books. For some reason, people never took him seriously. Instead, those around him tended to drop their guard. And he, with sharp ears and shrewd eyes, always remembered all the useful snippets they would reveal. That they would come to regret their liberties never crossed the swans' minds.

TWENTY-FOUR

❧

For years Truman teased and threatened his friends with *Answered Prayers*. Marella Agnelli recalled Truman boasting endlessly about the unfinished book. He had always compared himself to Proust, telling her that his still incomplete book was "going to do for America what Proust had done for France." Somehow, Marella doubted it. Toward the end of 1974 and the beginning of 1975, Truman approached Joseph Fox, his editor, to say he was going to publish several selections drawn from the unfinished book in various magazines. These included "La Côte Basque," "Mojave," "Kate McCloud," and "Unspoiled Monsters." Fox was not thrilled with Truman's decision. By publishing the stories before the actual book came out or was even scheduled for publication, Truman was revealing too much about the entire narrative. But Truman would not listen. This was just a bit of publicity on his part to entice the audience before publication, Truman said. It would leave readers wanting more, he assured Fox.

In May 1974 *Esquire* published "Unspoiled Monsters," which was long enough to be called a novella. In it, Truman Capote introduced the main narrator, P. B. Jones, a bisexual hustler living in a room at the YMCA, struggling to write a novel called *Answered Prayers*. P. B. Jones sounded suspiciously like Truman Capote himself, which readers of course pointed out. When asked about the similarities, Truman often replied: "P.B. isn't me, but on the other hand he isn't *not* me. I'm not P.B. but I know him very well." For the story's publication, Truman appeared on the cover posing as a very sharp-looking assassin, holding not a gun but a stiletto heel. When the issue came out, editors at the journal *Women's Wear Daily* nicknamed him "the Tiny Terror." The moniker would stick.

On certain occasions, at parties or galas, Truman enjoyed telling the story of visiting his doctor, who recommended that his patient find himself a healthy hobby. Couldn't he think of anything else outside of writing that he enjoyed doing, the doctor asked, to which Truman replied, "Yes, murder." The doctor laughed, and Truman laughed too, he told his listeners—but Truman wasn't laughing at all. While retelling the story to another friend he said, "Some people kill with swords and some people kill with words."

The book he had been ruminating about for so many years was a sort of a pistol with which he could commit a murder, or many murders—a book of killings. Maybe that was what he had been planning to do for so very long, commit murder with his pen, aiming it toward his friends and enemies, those who had knowingly and unknowingly hurt him. Maybe he would even gain retribution for the death of his mother, who, like her son, had never belonged to the world she ached to enter.

The excerpt, and the cover itself, caused a ruckus, readers clamoring for more pages and wondering when the whole book would be published. In the meantime, in a subsequent interview with *People* magazine, he was asked to describe the upcoming *Answered Prayers*, and not so shockingly, he compared it to a gun: "There's the handle, the trigger, the barrel, and, finally, the bullet. And when the bullet is fired from the gun, it's going to come out with the speed and power like you've never seen—wham!"

∾

While *In Cold Blood* had proven relatively effortless to write—despite the cruelty and brutality of its subject—*Answered Prayers* seemed to have a mind of its own. Although he felt destined to write this book, Truman told friends and reporters, he appeared unable to find the fortitude to engage in another long project.

However, in spite of all his distractions, from fame to alcohol to his own deep traumas, he was able to write fragments of what he hoped would become his masterpiece. And with the notorious Ann Woodward returning for another, longer visit to the United States in 1975, Truman knew the time was right to pitch a story to *Ladies' Home Journal*. "La Côte Basque, 1965" was supposed to be the seventh chapter of *Answered Prayers*. The title referred to Henri Soulé's restaurant on East Fifty-Fifth Street, and the story's protagonist was a woman named Ann Hopkins, obviously based on Ann Woodward.

Truman Capote was writing of an extraordinary incident that shocked America's upper crust. The narrative had everything a writer, and in turn a reader, might possibly desire: it reeked of power and oozed with razzle-dazzle. It also featured a very attractive couple moving seamlessly among New York's wealthiest. And it highlighted a treacherous murder. However, the chapter proved to be a bit too provocative for *Ladies' Home Journal*, given that it described the main character, Ann Hopkins, as not only possessing very flexible morals, but also being known around France as "Madame Marma-lade," a nickname given to her by the boys populating the Riviera because of a "trick she did using her tongue and jam." Thus, Truman looked to place "La Côte Basque" elsewhere. *Esquire*, it seemed, had no qualms.

TWENTY-FIVE

⌒※⌒

In early September 1975, acquaintances of Ann Woodward's telephoned her with the news that Truman Capote had sold his story to *Esquire*, and that publication was expected in early November. Before the magazine hit the newsstands in November, someone sent her an advance copy of it. Whether this was done to warn her or hurt her, she didn't know. But Ann was troubled by the news, and then by the story itself.

Ann Hopkins, the protagonist of Truman's story, was a wealthy New Yorker from the Midwest who shot her husband and got away with it by confessing to the police that she had mistaken him for a burglar—though the man had been naked, as he had recently come out of the shower. This Ann Hopkins from Truman's story came across as a vicious, trigger-happy gold digger who killed her husband because he had asked her for a divorce; it appeared that he had taken a trip to her hometown, where he had learned that her first marriage hadn't been annulled. Rather, she was still married to her first lover and had engaged in a bigamous relationship with her second.

In unsparing language, Truman Capote described his Ann Hopkins as "always a tramp," one who had been raised in a "country-slum way" where she had become nothing more than a "white-trash slut."

Ann Woodward didn't know why Truman Capote hated her so much. She barely remembered meeting him in Europe nearly twenty years earlier, at the restaurant in Saint Moritz, and she may well have forgotten their very public spat. Nonetheless, it seemed he had not. Or maybe she knew that as a woman who had had a public role in society and had caused a scandal, she had left herself open to being a character in a roman à clef. Her story didn't belong to her anymore; it belonged to anyone who would write about it. She had lost agency over her own character.

Even before its publication, people were talking about "La Côte Basque, 1965." Much of New York society—and there were many who were privy to an advance copy of the magazine—knew that it was a barely disguised retelling of the Billy Woodward murder. Ann Woodward felt her world constricting around her, she told her few acquaintances. She had tried, with only a measure of success, to put the death of her husband behind her, and to make a semblance of a new life for herself. But her efforts appeared to have been useless. She knew the date of the upcoming publication, then noted, "I must be far away," as if a bomb were about to explode. However, as the date approached, she made no effort to return to Europe, or to run somewhere else where she would not be privy to public snark. Her anxieties simply multiplied.

As the days counted down before the magazine went on sale, Ann Woodward grew more and more frenzied. She took medications, read the papers, sought out information from the few people who had remained in her life, but overall, she dreaded waking in the morning. One day in late October, she donned her favorite dress, painted her face in a thick layer of base, mascara, and lipstick, ingested a fistful of pills, and climbed into bed. The pills Ann Woodward swallowed were Seconal, the same drug that had killed Truman Capote's mother.

When she heard the news of Ann's suicide, Elsie Woodward, Ann's mother-in-law, had just one thing to say: "That's that. She shot my son, and Truman just murdered her."

Capote didn't seem to feel any guilt about what happened to Ann Woodward, or about the accusations pointed in his direction that "La Côte Basque, 1965" had caused Ann Woodward to take her own life. He once said to a friend, "I think the only person a writer has an obligation to is himself."

※

Those who knew her wondered if, with her death, the scandal that was Billy Woodward and Ann Woodward's marriage and their life together would finally be put to rest. But they also asked about their children, and how they would lead their lives going forward. The answer to that was soon to come. James, the youngest and always the more sensitive of the two boys, eventually had enlisted in Vietnam and was left so traumatized by what he saw—and likely by what he had endured after the killing of his father—that upon his return became a drug user and was often in and out of mental institutions. Ann, before her death, did her best to seek out doctors who could help him, both in the United States and Europe. In 1972, he jumped from a balcony but survived. But in 1976, not a year after his mother's death, he succeeded in killing himself.

Billy and Ann's older son, William, sought to put what was now referred to as the family's curse behind him. He became a journalist and in the late 1960s even ran for public office. He followed the family's banking tradition in a way and served as the New York State deputy superintendent of banks. He married and had a daughter, and for a time lived a quiet life. But his marriage began to unravel, and the old ghosts of his family's past returned. Friends began to comment on how depressed and despondent he seemed. Then, in 1999, he stepped through the window of his apartment's kitchen and jumped fourteen stories to his death. Those who knew him were not entirely surprised. They blamed his depression, and in no small part, a family history. They could also have blamed Truman Capote.

TWENTY-SIX

❧

When *Esquire* hit the stands, "La Côte Basque, 1965" became like an underground tremor winding its way beneath the most exclusive buildings and penthouses in the city, jarring awake everyone living there.

Apart from Ann Woodward, the rest of the characters in "La Côte Basque, 1965," were also based on the very famous and powerful friends with whom Truman had held court: celebrities, tycoons, and, most of all, the wives of important business leaders, such as Babe Paley. The stories they had shared with him in the privacy of salons and restaurants, during lunches, dinner dates, and afternoon teas had now suddenly become very titillating bits for anyone to feast on. There was a snarky, operatic quality to the story, at once intimate and mocking. Those who read it didn't know if it was the true story itself that was deplorable, or if their anger should be directed toward Truman Capote for writing it. It was possible they felt a combination of the two—and the reality was that certain readers couldn't tolerate either one. "La Côte Basque" left nothing to the imagination. It was a thinly concealed and tawdry chapter of his novel in progress depicting the sordid lives of those he knew and airing out all their squalid dirty laundry. Rather than a conventional tale, what unfolded in "La Côte Basque, 1965" was more of a long and gossipy conversation, precisely what Truman Capote was accustomed to enjoying in real life, within a milieu he now knew so well.

"Have you seen *Esquire*?" The question was on everyone's lips. It wasn't only because readers were curious to read what supposedly had driven Ann Woodward to the murder of her husband and eventually to take her own life. Truman Capote had unleashed his venom on other socialites too, those who were, or had been, his closest friends. And even before the *Esquire* story was read by all, frantic telephone calls were exchanged among the women who had taken center stage in Capote's life and now naughty tale. In particular, Slim Keith was left open-mouthed by the narrative. She felt betrayed.

∽

Nancy "Slim" Gross Keith was born on July 15, 1917, in Salinas, California, a place that would be immortalized by John Steinbeck in *East of Eden*. Slim savored her childhood in the West, where she learned to enjoy solitary adventures on the beach. She made very few friends, even though the area was populated by families with children around her age. Slim's father owned a handful of fish canneries.

Much like her future friend Truman Capote, Slim grew up with a very active imagination, leaning on her creativity to compensate for the lack of real playmates and companionship. She shared the house with not only her parents, but also an older sister, a younger brother, and her grandmother—her mother's mother, whom her father despised. In her autobiography, Slim wrote, "My family was something else. We were sheltered and insular, and almost thoroughly isolated."

Her father, a racist, obtuse, unpopular man, supposed that most people were plotting against him in some fashion or another, and returned to them the venom he thought they aimed at him.

One winter night when Slim's father was away on business, there was a fire roaring in the hearth, and the rest of the family were in the living room reading or preparing for bed. No one noticed when at some point her eight-year-old brother, Buddy, got closer to the fire to warm up. The boy's flannel pajama top caught fire. Slim's mother pushed him down to the floor to put out the flames. For the rest of her life, Slim could hear Buddy's screams as the fire scorched his skin, and her mother's anguished cries as she tried to help her son. They called her father to return home, as well as a doctor to rush to the house, who suggested the boy undergo a blood transfusion. Slim's father volunteered, insisting that no one else should touch his son. However, overcome by his injuries, Buddy died. The family broke apart thereafter. After the death of her grandmother, Slim persuaded her mother, who no longer had any attachment to Carmel or Salinas, to sell everything and move to Los Angeles with her. Moving to Los Angeles would give Slim a new life—and ultimately lead her to resettle in New York City.

❧

Slim met Howard Hawks on August 30, 1938, at the Cedar Club, a small and exclusive gambling establishment in Los Angeles. She had gone there with Bruce Cabot, an actor, who had invited her to go and watch a boxing match with him. She had agreed, looking forward to the dancing and drinking that would come later. The Cedar Club had become the place to see and be seen, where all the popular people attended the after-hours soirees. Although Slim didn't know Hawks personally, she was aware of him by reputation; he was one of the most prominent movie directors in Hollywood. Aside from being successful, he was also tall, good-looking, and charming. Slim was surprised when Hawks showed interest in her, because he was already married and a father. She learned those facts when she visited him the following day at his house. Hawks admitted that his wife was sick and hardly ever home. She was, as he conceded, "emotionally disturbed."

This seemed to be a very popular excuse used by married men of the time who could not so easily disengage themselves from their wives but were eager to begin a new relationship with another woman. Hawks made it clear that for the moment their own relationship could be only an illicit one. Slim understood. However, she was still young, and while it was improper and clandestine, being desired by the likes of Howard Hawks seemed as exciting as it was scandalous.

It took Hawks three years, but finally he managed to distance himself from his wife and win a divorce. He and Slim were married on December 11, 1941, in Pasadena, California, just days after the bombing in Pearl Harbor. While the bombing put Americans in mourning, Slim couldn't help but be excited about her wedding and the idea of starting a new life with this extraordinary man.

A year after the wedding she came to a shocking realization. The legend that was Howard Hawks was one of his own making, constructed like one of his movies. There was nothing truthful about him, nothing that wasn't fabricated like one of his film plots. Howard had begun cheating on her soon after they were married. He believed no woman could resist him and tried very hard to prove his assertion right. Now Slim found herself to be the wife being cheated on. There were so many other women in his life that the tally Slim kept in her head grew too long to manage accurately. When she became pregnant, it quickly became clear Howard was not interested in another child, as he already had children by his previous wife. On February 11, 1946, when Slim woke up after the delivery, it was her doctor who greeted her and complimented her on a beautiful and healthy baby girl, Kitty Steven Hawks. Howard Hawks was occupied on a movie set.

Just months later, in July, Slim met the talent agent Leland Hayward at a party given by mutual friends. Both were guests at the event without their respective spouses, and after the party was over Leland drove Slim home. Their romance blossomed for months as they tried to see each other privately. He even asked her to marry him when they were both free of their spouses, and she agreed. He was practically divorced, he told her. He lived in Los Angeles, almost always by himself, as his wife, who suffered from depression, spent most of her time with their children cocooned in their house in Connecticut. Slim should have recognized the similarities between Hayward's marital story and Hawks's, but Hayward turned out to be a better husband. They would be together for the next twelve years. In her letters and autobiography, Slim described those years as the best in her life. He became a lifelong confidant, a friend, a lover, a supporter, her business partner, and someone she knew she could turn to for all of her emotional needs. He was kind to her, talented, and charming.

Together with Slim's daughter, Kitty, Slim and Leland moved to New York, where they set up house at 13 Sutton Place. This was 1948. Then, on June 10, 1949, as their divorces became final, Slim and Leland finally got married, the ceremony taking place on Long Island's Gold Coast at the home of William and Babe Paley.

༄

Slim met Truman Capote in the early 1950s during a dinner party at the home of Diana Vreeland, the legendary editor of *Vogue*. She was not entirely surprised to find him there. Since the publication of *Other*

Voices, Other Rooms in 1948, Truman Capote had become the darling of the New York social scene, and Slim found herself warming to his charm.

"Anyone with a little time on her hands would have done the same," Slim later wrote in her autobiography. "This funny looking dwarfish figure with the fiery southern accent was, you quickly learned, no oddity to be collected casually and then discarded; in any social situation he was a tremendous asset."

Sharing a keen interest in literature, the two immediately bonded. Truman Capote, Slim learned, was also a fascinating conversationalist, as well as an amusing and engaging dinner guest; one could not help but be beguiled by him and the tales he told. That night at Diana Vreeland's party, the two vowed to follow up with a lunch date, and a few days later Truman called to invite her to tea. Slim accepted, and before long they were seeing each other very often. These visits occurred most often in the city, for when on Long Island Truman stayed with Babe Paley, whom he considered a more personal friend. Truman himself thought of the two women as his two best friends. Although Babe and Slim were similar in many respects, they differed in ways that made them interesting. That is why Truman enjoyed their company, because there was a darker side to their friendship that often emerged, a jealousy and pettiness that often appeared. Truman, as was his fashion, often did his best to incite a confrontation between the women.

Truman and Slim's friendship was cemented in 1958, when the film producer Sam Spiegel, an intimate of Slim and Leland, invited Truman, along with the actor Cary Grant, to accompany him to the Soviet Union. The Soviets had proposed that Spiegel visit to showcase several of his films, and in return they would promote a handful of their own. During the 1950s, few Americans ever visited Russia. Truman invited Slim, who accepted. Afterward, from Moscow, Spiegel and Grant flew to Leningrad on their own, while Slim and Truman opted to travel via the Red Arrow, a slow overnight train from Moscow. It was crowded, and a tediously long trip, but Truman and Slim enjoyed each other's company, thanks to Truman's wit. As they ate and drank vodka, the Russian night passed by, bonding their friendship.

Following the visit to Leningrad, they went to Copenhagen. By now Slim and Truman had spent nearly three weeks traveling together, the trip more amusing than either one had anticipated. On their last night in Copenhagen, following their dinner, Truman accompanied Slim to her room and waited until she got into bed. Slim felt no shame performing her nightly routine in front of him, removing her makeup, donning her nightgown. "I felt as though I was getting undressed in front of my daughter," Slim later wrote. She would remember their conversation years later. Before leaving for his own room, Truman had said to her, "Sleep well, because I love you very, very much."

Slim replied, "I love you too, Truman."

Truman stared at her for a few seconds. "No, you don't," he replied.

"Don't say that—Of course I do!"

"No, no, no, you don't. No one loves me. I'm a freak. You don't think I know that? I know how difficult it is for people to adjust to what I look like and how I sound when they first see me. It's one of the reasons that I'm so outrageous. I don't think anyone has ever loved me—maybe Jack . . . But not many other people. I'm an *object*. I'm a centerpiece, not a figure of love, and I miss that. There's not an awful lot to love."

Slim was taken aback by such a surprising declaration, she later wrote. "That's nonsense," she told him. "You love whom you love."

Truman smiled and shook his head. "Sometimes, Big Mama, imagine what it's like to be me. When I walk into a roomful of people who don't know me, I always do something silly instead of walking into a room straight. If I just walk in, I'm this funny, sewed-off fellow with a high voice, and it's hard for people to accept me. But if I come in and say, 'I don't want to sit with the boys, I want to sit with the girls,' everybody giggles and everybody's more comfortable. I do that on purpose to make it easier for people to be around me because then I'm easier and the whole thing is better."

Slim didn't know how to respond. Deep down, she knew Truman was accurate. Hadn't she herself called him a funny dwarfish thing, especially when she had first met him? An odd little creature? And he was very much aware of what other people thought of him, how they reacted to him. To try to deny it now, or to say otherwise, would be futile and hypocritical on her part. She obviously cared for him and felt no small amount of pity. Or perhaps it was compassion.

And while it was true that she did love him, it was also true that she never really trusted him. And he knew as much.

"You never confide in me, Big Mama," he'd often chastised her.

"That's right, honey," Slim would always reply. "I don't because I don't trust you." She had easily figured out that if he gossiped with her about other people, telling her things their mutual friends had revealed to him in confidence, chances were high that, in turn, he would repeat to other people those things she shared with him privately. She already knew that he was a tattletale and, moreover, that he was a writer. The two were a terrible combination. Her concerns would be eventually solidified when she read "La Côte Basque," in which she became the mouthpiece for the story, Lady Coolbirth, a middle-aged American and "big breezy peppy broad" who revealed everyone's secrets during a boozy lunch with Jones, the story's protagonist and Truman's stand-in. There, a drunken Lady Coolbirth not only gossips about the rest of the swans, who come in and out of the restaurant in stages, but reveals their dirty deeds and familial secrets previously thought private. Slim Keith would not take to having a guest spot in Truman Capote's story. It was a breach of their friendship—one she intended to make Truman pay for.

TWENTY-SEVEN

❧

Babe Paley picked up the telephone in November 1975 and called Slim. In a hurried and somewhat panting voice she asked her if she had seen *Esquire*. Slim answered that she had not. Babe insisted that Slim go out and get herself a copy, and then that she'd call her back right away. Not an hour later, Slim was finished reading, and she knew that she had been used. She could not comprehend why Truman Capote had done such a despicable thing. Everything she and Truman had ever talked about, all the conversations and bits of gossip they had ever shared in private—or what she had come to believe had been a measure of privacy—all that had passed between them, was splashed on the pages of *Esquire* for anyone to read.

The ladies had assumed that there had been an understanding, that everything they shared with Truman would stay within their circle—confidential. But this must have been a one-sided agreement, something they had envisaged on their own, likely after the publication of "La Côte Basque," because Truman Capote had never made such promises, nor had any of them ever tried to elicit such pledges from him. And certainly, they had always known that he was a chatterer, a gossiper with them, and about them with others.

It did not take long for word to reach Capote that his swans were not happy with him, especially Slim, who was so furious she declared that she would never see or speak to him again. And to insult him even further, she went so far as to suggest to friends that "La Côte Basque" wasn't even a well-written piece of prose. In return, he tried calling her, but she was not feeling very generous toward him and never answered. He attempted to have mutual friends approach her on his behalf, but she always refused to acknowledge his pursuits in any way. When all else failed, he became angry. Who were these women to hold a grudge against him? What did they think—that he was some sort of silly adornment they could simply pass around when it pleased them, then discard? Talk to him only when it was convenient to them, then ignore?

Years after the fact, Slim Keith told a writer, "I read it and I was absolutely horrified, because there I was. My character is simply the person he's lunching with. All of the stuff—the story about Ann Woodward . . . was told by me, a person called Lady Coolbirth. . . . It was like looking into a mirror. Very odd experience," Slim admitted. Then she continued, "I really felt bereft. I guessed, having lost a very nice, good part of my life. I never would take it back under any circumstances. What I don't understand, to this day, is what sort of thinking brings a person to that point and to do something like that."

During the later years of his life, when Truman had become essentially idle, Slim wrote. "Add idleness and boredom to heartbreak, in Truman Capote you got viciousness." And later still, she noted, "I knew he was a troublemaker, I knew he was a snoop, but, like everyone else, I thought he was armed with nothing more than a penknife. In fact, it was a dagger."

She had once scolded him, as she would have done a small child. It wasn't nice to spread rumors, she told him; they generated trouble where there was none. He'd smirked at her, saying, "Never mind, Big Mama. You just wait and see. And if you wait long enough, it all comes true." Oddly enough, and to her surprise, he was usually right.

Rather than enjoying the publication of his story and all the recognition he was receiving, Truman Capote felt frustrated, unable to accept the idea that his swans were now rejecting him. As the holidays approached, he wired Slim, who was in Australia for Christmas. In a move that was as bold as it was pathetic, he attempted to reenter her life. "Merry Christmas, Big Mama. I've decided to forgive you. Love Truman," he wrote. Slim didn't respond. She had already spoken to an attorney, inquiring as to whether or not suing Truman Capote for libel was an option.

In an interview she gave some time later, she said, "I had adored him, and I was appalled by the use of friendship and my own bad judgment . . . after *La Côte Basque* I looked on Truman as a friend who had died, and we never spoke again. I took the cleaver and chopped him out of my life. And that was it."

"When Truman died on August 25, 1984, I felt nothing," she said following his death. "For me, he had died nine years before."

❧

Each swan had her own enticements, but he was particularly beguiled by Marella Agnelli. That she was actual nobility made her that much more fascinating to Truman. That she seemed somewhat put off by him made him want to know her even more.

Every time he saw her, Truman was struck by Agnelli's strong Italian features, her staring at him with those eyes that were intelligent, almost accusatory, seemingly saying, "I know what you are doing."

While most women Truman knew acted as if they were royalty, Marella Agnelli was true Italian aristocracy. She was born Princess Donna Marella Caracciolo dei Principi di Castagneto in Naples, in 1927 to an Italian father and an American mother from the Midwest. The combination of their influences gave Marella old-world refinement coupled with new world spontaneity.

Her family had made their home in Rome, in the Trastevere area, where the Agnelli family also had a residence. Marella was familiar with the Agnelli family, which founded Fiat, and while she had never met the wildest member of the clan, Gianni, his reputation was well known not only in Italy, but also abroad. Gianni managed to keep busy with indulgences and no small number of lovers, including Pamela Churchill, the divorced wife of Randolph Churchill, son of Winston Churchill. Marella kept occupied with modeling and a number of beauty pageants, winning or placing in several of them.

Although Gianni Agnelli's affair with Pamela Churchill had ended, his 1953 marriage to Marella did not bring about a sudden end to his philandering. In marrying, he was merely looking for a measure of respectability. Marella also quickly provided him with a son, Edoardo, to continue the family legacy, granting Gianni Agnelli the heir he had desired.

In the meantime, as Marella raised the family and took care of their homes, Gianni entertained women he took to calling his "tarts" all throughout Europe. Marella knew all about the women. She pursued a life separate from his, following several passions that included photography and gardening, which she was able to enjoy in her many homes, including a villa and palazzo in Turin.

Even as Marella grew older, she was still endowed "with a tall, slender body and a perfectly swan-like neck rumored to be the longest and most graceful in Europe," according to a newspaper report.

There was something about her remoteness that intrigued Truman Capote. While Babe Paley seemed to open up like a flower to him, Marella Agnelli kept to herself. He once took the time to compare Marella Agnelli with Babe Paley, and said, "If they were both in Tiffany's window, Marella would be more expensive." In his story, Lady Coolbirth revealed Marella's life of decadence, along with all of Marella's husband's indiscretions and the fact that she looked the other way in order to keep up her status in society.

In 1962 Truman Capote boasted of a new swan joining his flock: Lee Bouvier Canfield Radziwill, the sister of First Lady Jacqueline Bouvier Kennedy. Truman had often socialized with Jackie Kennedy and bragged about that relationship. But he found Lee Radziwill a bit more fun than Jackie. Lee was also a bona fide princess, a title bestowed on her through her marriage to Prince Stanislaw Albrecht Radziwill of Poland, which in Truman's eyes, as in the eyes of many others, rendered her more attractive.

However, by 1962 that marriage appeared to be on the rocks. Truman wrote a letter to his friend the photographer Cecil Beaton about meeting Lee Radziwill. "Had lunch one day with a new friend Princess Lee (Radziwill)," he told Beaton. He then added some gossip, as was his practice, and even on the page Truman appeared to be gloating. "(My God, how jealous she is of Jackie: I never knew); understand her marriage is all but finito."

For her part, Lee Radziwill became just as enamored with Truman as the other women were, if not more. "He's my closest friend. More than anyone else. I can discuss the most serious things about life and emotional questions. I miss him terribly when I'm away from him," she admitted soon enough. "I trust him implicitly. He's the most loyal friend I've ever had and the best company I've ever known." Even after "La Côte Basque" came out, Lee Radziwill would continue to stand by Truman's side. Unlike the rest of the swans, she was not gossiped about mercilessly but described only as jealous of her sister and struggling to find her own way.

But the swan Truman loved most of all was Barbara "Babe" Paley.

Babe loved him too. Only Truman Capote had ever come close to guessing the depths of her desolation and disappointments, or so she proclaimed. While all could see that Babe was enamored with Truman, Slim Keith warned her to be careful. It was a mistake to tell him everything, Slim once told her. Babe didn't, or couldn't, listen.

TWENTY-EIGHT

In his private notes Truman wrote of Babe Paley, "Mrs. P. had only one fault: she was perfect; otherwise, she was perfect." Truman considered her the ultimate swan.

She was invariably meticulously dressed and made up. Her perfume was subtle or strong, depending on the situation. She was five feet, eight inches tall, thin, with perfect posture and an unending supply of grace. She spoke in a low voice that just begged the listener to lean in and take even further notice of her. She was known to be a little reticent, cool, which Truman soon learned was her way of covering up her loneliness and insecurities. In time, she warmed up to him. "She had an icy exterior," he wrote, "but once you got behind that fine enamel outside, she was very warm and very young."

While Truman was dazzled by her, his boyfriend Jack Dunphy was less impressed. He once said, "It wasn't the Cushing family in Boston that made her. It was Bill. She would have been nothing if she hadn't married him, and Truman wouldn't have had much to do with her, either. Whether he admitted it or not, he was attracted to money and power."

Babe Paley was celebrated for her style, for her beauty, and for her class, none of which come without hard work. She was an image, a vision, and could not afford a day off from herself. That had always been her job, and her fate, and she was always agonized about it.

∾

Babe Paley was born Barbara Cushing on July 5, 1915, in Boston, the daughter of Harvey Cushing, the illustrious American doctor known as the father of brain surgery, and the formidable socialite Katharine "Kate" Cushing.

Her father was always busy at work, never at home to spend his time with her or the rest of the family. Nonetheless, Dr. Cushing was adored by his children. When she was eight, Babe wrote her father a note, begging him to "stay at home with me and don't go earning money. We'll just do something funny. I'll give you my pennies and I'll give you my shiny buckle. I'll arrange all for you." Arranging things became part of her nature, and she would still be doing so years later, most especially for her husband.

Kate Cushing once admitted to a friend, who happened to be a gossip columnist in New York, that she expected each of her daughters "to marry into the highest level of European nobility or into America's moneyed aristocracy." Word got out.

Millicent Fenwick, a socialite and ultimately a congresswoman who knew the Cushings well, said, "Each of the girls and especially Babe entered the world convinced that they were the most attractive young women in the world, combining both beauty and brains." Betsey Cushing was the first of the three sisters to marry, in June 1930, to the handsome James Roosevelt, the oldest son of Eleanor and Franklin

Delano Roosevelt. The marriage attracted the kind of attention Kate Cushing had always told her girls they were deserving of.

Of the three very striking Cushing sisters, Babe was celebrated as the most beautiful. She had very dark eyes that matched her raven-like hair, and a personality that was gracious, generous, and nurturing. She later graduated from the Westover School in 1933, and the following year made her debut.

In early 1934, on Long Island, she was involved in a serious car accident. Her nearly perfect face was shattered almost beyond recognition, her teeth completely knocked out. Recuperation required dozens of surgeries and months of rehabilitation, which her father, Dr. Cushing, supervised. Although she had to wear dentures for the rest of her life, she remained as beautiful as ever, even if life might seem more fragile to her in the accident's aftermath.

As a young woman she moved to New York and began working for *Glamour* magazine, eventually becoming an editor for Condé Nast's *Vogue*. Millicent Fenwick said, "Babe was a wonderfully warm human being, genuinely interested in people, not just family and friends but also coworkers. The most lowly employee at *Conde Nast* was a recipient of her kindness. Babe was like a stove, a furnace, she generated so much warmth to everyone she came in contact with."

Babe resided at the Saint Regis Hotel with her companion Serge Obolensky. Obolensky was a character himself. A Russian prince who had married a princess before escaping to the United States with a price on his head, he was also an adventurer, an American commando who later parachuted into Nazi Germany, and a well-known socialite who had made himself at home at the Saint Regis. Given Babe's family's strict rules of etiquette, when asked about this out-of-the-ordinary arrangement, an anonymous friend responded, "Morality is for the middle class."

꧁

Years later, when she met William Paley, Babe's first marriage to Stanley Grafton Mortimer Jr. had produced two children and then ended. Of Stanley, people mostly remarked on his excessive good looks. He was "absolutely one of the handsomest men I had ever seen," a Newport socialite recalled. The grandson of one of the founders of Standard Oil, Stanley could also count as one of his ancestors John Jay, the first chief justice of the United States Supreme Court. Mortimer Jr. was a New York socialite and a member of the Tuxedo Park community. Babe Cushing married Mortimer Jr. on September 21, 1940, and divorced in May 1946. A quick first marriage to use as a test run, some people suggested, just what a socialite needed to do in order to climb higher and faster on the social ladder.

William Samuel Paley was the son of a Russian Jewish immigrant who in the United States started a cigarette manufacturing company. After graduating from the Wharton School of Finance, William Paley joined the family business, later becoming responsible for a small, struggling radio network his father had also purchased. William Paley was only twenty-six years old at the time he took over the radio station. However, due to his tenacity, intelligence, creativity, and eye for business, in ten short years he guided the radio network into becoming the Columbia Broadcasting System, or CBS, directly challenging NBC for supremacy over the airways.

William Paley was charming, wealthy, and extraordinarily talented. That he was Jewish didn't bother Babe, even if it did bother her mother, albeit only slightly. But William Paley was married to Dorothy Hart Hearst, with whom he had adopted two children, and he was also renowned for his extramarital affairs. Nevertheless, he and Babe began seeing each other and planning a life together, assuming that his divorce would eventually become final.

It was the New York *Daily News* that broke the story, on July 23, 1947, from Reno, Nevada: "This rough and ready divorce capital gasped tonight when it learned that William S. Paley, president of Columbia Broadcasting System, had given his wife a check for $1,500,000 settlement in the divorce she obtained today. Verification of the payment, the largest ever made in this mecca of parting couples, came from those who saw photostatic copies of the check. . . . Mrs. Paley, so far as is known, has no further matrimonial plans, but CBS president is reportedly planning to marry Mrs. Barbara (Babe) Mortimer, willowy socialite eyeful from Boston." They married five days later, on July 28, 1947.

∽

Truman Capote arrived into the Paleys' life by sheer misunderstanding. In January 1955, the movie producer David Selznick and his wife, the actress Jennifer Jones, were slated to fly to Jamaica with William and Babe Paley to be guests at their house. The couples had been friends for several years. David Selznick asked William Paley if they might bring along their friend Truman. Bill and Babe agreed, thinking it an honor to host the former president of the United States Harry Truman.

Despite the confusion, Truman managed to impress the Paleys even before the plane took off, especially Babe, whose desire for an intimate friend was suddenly realized in the shape of a diminutive, southern, witty young man. Jennifer Jones was not surprised that he managed to make himself likable right away, especially to Babe. "Babe looked at him and Truman looked at her, and they fell instantly in love," Jones said later, not without a touch of jealousy.

Babe could find a refuge in Truman, she soon realized, as the reality was that even with her new husband, her life had not turned out the way she had expected. In her former life, she had spent her days working at a magazine. However, now her time was taken over with having to care for William Paley. He was fastidious, and Babe had to make certain she had on hand everything he needed, including her decorative presence. It was not easy for her to express any resentment. Her own mother had taught Babe to suppress her feelings; and that's what she often did regarding her husband. On occasion, though, she couldn't allow her opinions to fester any longer, and eventually in Truman she found a willing listener for anything she dared to say, at any time she decided to unburden herself. Babe adored him. "There is great beauty in his face," she told a family friend, "especially in his eyes just after he takes his specs off. They look so vulnerable."

Through the 1960s as his fame grew and he wrote less and less, Truman's own lax tongue had become even more undisciplined. Babe's dependency on him grew. She revealed nearly everything to him. Nothing about her life, it seemed, was sacred, including the most intimate details about her sexual life, or the lack of it; her sisters and their husbands' infidelities or what they preferred in bed, usually with others. Despite the fact that she was still a young woman—only past forty—and still considered one of the most beautiful, stylish, and vibrant women in the country, her husband had moved on from her, discovering a younger crop of women to sexually satisfy him.

This part of her life she certainly believed to be private, revealed only to her sisters, her mother, and Truman Capote. However, Truman often disclosed her revelations to friends of his—or hers—who were dismayed. Nevertheless, none of them advised Babe to keep quiet; nor did Babe ever indicate that she knew anything about the privileged information he revealed to her about their mutual friends.

For the next two decades, wherever the Paleys went, one was likely to find Truman Capote tagging along. "We were a great little trio!" he once said. While initially Truman came to revere only Babe, it didn't take long for him to grow to admire William Paley as well. William was a powerful man fifteen years Babe's senior, and Truman was flattered to have an open invitation to the Paleys' inner court, to the villa in Jamaica, and especially to their home on Long Island, Kiluna Farm, which was Babe's domain.

Back in New York, while William Paley returned to his job in the offices of CBS, Truman Capote and Babe Paley lunched at Quo Vadis or La Côte Basque. Truman was once witness to an event that in his mind started a fashion trend. He and Babe were leaving a restaurant when she found herself overheated. She was wearing a Hermès scarf tied around her neck, which she suddenly removed and cinched around the handle of the bag clutched next to her. It was a practical move prompted by the weather. Still, it started a trend all over the United States, with women fastening their own scarves around their own purses. Truman was fascinated by the power people like Babe held over the lives of others. That a single action caught by the camera could ignite a connection with those who read the papers seemed to him remarkable.

Throughout her life, Babe had shared her innermost secrets with her sisters, Minnie and Betsey, and with her mother, Kate. Once her mother was gone, Babe and her sisters became even closer and created a tighter circle, impossible to breach. But when Truman Capote came along, it seemed as if another sibling had nudged his way into their innermost sanctum.

"She was the most important person in my life, and I was the most important person in hers," Truman once said of Babe. "I was her one real friend, the one real relationship she ever had. We were like lovers; she loved me and I loved her. The only person I was ever truly in love with was her. She once joked that her analyst said she loved me more than anyone else, more than Bill or her children, and he thought she should have an affair with me."

But not everyone was as fond of Truman as Babe was. In fact, several acquaintances felt that he had become simply an annoying appendage. Sibylla Clark, a friend of the Paleys who witnessed their relationship with Truman, said, "Babe was very attentive to Bill. He liked to have attractive people around. There was always lots of superb food around (he loved lots of food). The flowers were always incredible. Babe's life was spent with houses, travel, parties, and gardening . . . I saw the Paleys both in New York and Nassau. And remember Truman Capote well. Found Truman to be silly. I mean, that voice! The others liked him. He was always making some sort of little wisecrack at somebody's expense."

While there was no doubt that he could understand her, or pretended to, the fact remained that she was confessing her private confidences to the most notorious gossip in New York, who was also a writer, no less, one who felt energized and rejuvenated by knowing other people's intimate secrets. Most people who knew Truman Capote were aware of his tendency for tattling, and most of those who met him quickly picked up on that propensity. Babe Paley, it seemed, overlooked it. Until "La Côte Basque" came out. In the *Answered Prayers* excerpt, Truman revealed a one-night stand between Sidney Dillon, obviously a caricature of William Paley, and the wife of a New York governor, likely based on Mary, Nelson Rockefeller's first wife. The story revealed how the two flirted at a party before consummating the encounter at an apartment owned by Dillon.

After the story was published, Babe suspected the character of Sidney Dillon was based on her husband and asked Slim Keith about it. While Slim denied it to Babe, she was indeed aware that the character was a thinly veiled portrait of William Paley, as Truman had been chatting about the details of this encounter with Keith for months.

Babe Paley knew the truth, despite Slim Keith's brush-off. She was hurt and humiliated. She decided to put family first and never speak to Truman again, horrified she had befriended him to begin with.

TWENTY-NINE

~✦~

With "La Côte Basque," Truman had hoped this chapter from *Answered Prayers* would be a bombshell, and indeed it was. However, no one could have prepared him for the violent, vitriolic reactions he received, most especially from his friends, who immediately recognized themselves. It was obvious to them that Capote had considered everything they'd talked about to be suitable material to use. That he had meant to keep nothing private. And that his swans and muses should have been aware that everything they told him was up for grabs.

Babe Paley had become ill with terminal cancer before the *Esquire* publication, and Truman had visited her often, which had brought her a lot of pleasure. He had never mentioned his upcoming story, keeping the publication details to himself. When her health permitted, she had also visited him at his apartment, which gave them the opportunity for further intimate conversation. But then *Esquire* came out. Truman had chosen to publish the story while Babe was dying.

Of course, the women had known that he was working on a new book. Truman had been talking about it for years, to the point where friends had become almost exasperated hearing about *Answered Prayers*. He had often received calls from his swans asking whether or not certain people would be featured in the book, and his answer could either frighten the callers or flatter them. Either way, he had never heard, seen, or even received any suggestion that he not use anything they said in his book.

In interviews, whether printed or on television, he always spoke of the incredible stories he was going to reveal, salacious and scandalous, all the plots he was fabricating. But he was often drunk in public, and there were times when he made a fool of himself. Maybe seeing him in that condition made people stop taking him seriously, believing there were no books left in him at all. Perhaps they did not think that he had any vigor left to embark on another long book, much less to bring it to publication. That it was simply just a lot of smoke he was blowing in the air. That there was no *Answered Prayers*.

⁂

As the brouhaha over "La Côte Basque, 1965" took on a life of its own, Clay Felker, the editor of *New York* magazine, asked the journalist Liz Smith to interview Truman, who was then in California. Initially, Capote seemed thrilled by the prospect, and Smith flew to Los Angeles to meet him. But while on the telephone he had sounded excited by the idea of chatting about his sensational story, Smith saw that in person Truman was actually quite perturbed by all that was happening. "He was the most surprised and shocked person you can imagine, and he would call to ask me—torment me—about what people in New York had said about him," Smith recalled. "After *La Côte Basque* he was never happy again."

The article Smith wrote, "Truman Capote in Hot Water," was published in February 1976 in *New York* magazine. "Society's sacred monsters at the top have been in a state of shock," Smith declared. "Never have you heard such gnashing of teeth, such cries of revenge, such shouts of betrayal and screams of outrage." And for those who were still trying to figure out who the women in Truman's story were, Smith went ahead and revealed the real names of his swans. "It's one thing to tell the meanest story in the world to all your fifty best friends," Smith continued. "It's another to see it set down in cold, century expanded type."

Truman was astonished that all his former friends had now become such prudes. He said to Liz Smith, "As for my personal life, I don't care what anybody says or writes about me personally. I have been a public exhibit all my life. So, let them go ahead and make me a monster. I was a beautiful little boy, you know, and everybody had me—men, women, boys and fire hydrants. I did it with everybody. I didn't slow down until I was nineteen, and then became very circumspect. But everybody knows where everybody is sexually. There are no secrets, and that's why I can't understand the shocked response to 'La Côte Basque 1965'! What is all this business? Are all these people living in some other mediaeval century? I'd never sue anyone for anything that I've been lied about my whole life. I'm just surprised they don't hire a hitman."

While initially he was distressed by the fact that many of his swans no longer spoke to him, eventually he began to shrug, claiming that he didn't care, as everything he had done was for his love of literature and for the sake of his art. "The artist is a dangerous person because he's out of control," he said. "He's controlled only by his art." To Diana Vreeland he remarked, "Oh, honey! It's Proust! It's beautiful!" as if that explained everything.

~

While Truman's fame had come because of his earlier books and was later followed by the rocketing success of *In Cold Blood*, it was also true that many of his women felt they were partially responsible for Truman's success, given that they had shared with him their limelight, social connections, and money. It wasn't true, and it bothered him that they believed it so. He was an artist who had accomplished everything on his own, he felt, not a mere hanger-on who needed socialites to advance his career.

He had hoped to shine a spotlight on the rich, their defects and infidelities, their murders and crimes, and their various dirty deeds, but what he had really done was turn the shotgun on himself. By exposing their sins, he had committed literary and social suicide.

But why was his work so vicious? What did he hope to accomplish? Why would he write a book that would cause him to be virtually blacklisted and contribute so profoundly to his mental and physical downfall? In 1973 he told *Rolling Stone* magazine, "[*Answered Prayers*] will kill my last chances in the world of ever winning anything—except, perhaps, twenty years in jail." Jail never happened, but what followed was almost as dire.

The life Truman Capote had built, and the friendships he had cultivated, dissolved in less than a New York minute. Much like Ann Woodward, he never recovered from being pushed out of their rarified circle. Whether he realized it or not, he would now suffer the same anguish Ann Woodward had suffered at the hands of her detractors.

Just as Ann Woodward had been on the receiving end of society's wrath upon the death of her husband, Billy Woodward, Truman Capote now found himself the target of retribution from the very same people he had spent years courting. Truman Capote, the darling of the literary society, a small-town boy who had been accepted into a world he had yearned to be a part of, pampered as if born into it, allowed to hear its members' deepest secrets and privy to their most intimate dreams and desires—was nothing but a traitor, doomed to exile.

THIRTY

〜❈〜

It stunned Truman just how quickly his women dismissed him. He lamented to his friend Joanne Carson, ex-wife of the famed entertainer Johnny Carson, how these women had never understood him. "They know I'm a writer. I don't understand it."

The swans believed Truman Capote had exposed himself for the fraud that he truly was. He had never loved them, they said; he had pried into their lives only for information to use in his stories. But the same could be said for them, Truman's supporters fired back, including C. Z. Guest. They had never cared for him either. They had used him as nothing more than some sort of decorative object, a willing ear, a sounding board and mirror. He was, essentially, in service to them, a butler to their sentiments. Why should he not take what he'd been given and make a story of it?

Now, to his bafflement, his former friends sharpened their claws and fought back in the only way they knew how: they ignored him. Society shut and locked its doors. Staying away from Truman Capote became the thing to do. In a 1980 *Playboy* interview he said, "In the

271

long run, the rich run together, no matter what," and smiled wistfully, almost sadly. He then added, "They will cling, until they feel it's safe to be disloyal, then no one can be more so."

Truman Capote's literary idol, Marcel Proust, once remarked, "In society a great friendship does not amount to much." Truman likely would agree. Even the man he considered one of his best friends, Cecil Beaton, followed the events happening in New York from England and aligned himself with those who loathed Truman. Much like Capote, Beaton's appetite for gossip was insatiable, and he had spent many days and nights chatting with Truman about mutual friends and acquaintances while in England and in the United States. Beaton had always been complimentary of Truman's works to friends and during interviews. And Truman was kind in hosting him when the time called for it. But now all that was forgotten. Friends of both agreed that this was not occurring as suddenly as most believed. The reality was that Cecil Beaton had been steaming with jealousy for almost a decade, ever since the publication and immediate success of Truman's *In Cold Blood*. In fact, in his diary he wrote, "The triumph of Truman is salt in one's wound." Watching Truman implode must have worked like a salve to soothe that wound. He wrote to a friend, "I hate the idea of Truman," then added, "How low can he sink?"

Truman Capote had underestimated his swans, most especially Babe Paley, who was loyal first to her family and worked frantically to keep any sort of scandal under wraps, much as Elsie Woodward had done when Billy Woodward was shot. Babe immediately regretted ever bringing Truman into her life. She had been conned, she thought, even as she was dying. She refused to speak to him or to listen to any of his excuses. Truman wrote telegrams and called her house, but Babe Paley would never speak with him again.

Marella Agnelli said in an interview, "I got so intimate with Truman because he had a very special quality. He would observe people and see their soft spots; he became their father confessor. I found myself telling him things I never dreamed of telling him. Absolutely. He was waiting like a falcon. He created a very deep sort of intimacy. Very deep, very tender." She reminisced, "He called us swans. In a way, I was a little disillusioned. Too many swans. Some of the swans I didn't like so much, at all. For some I had an enormous admiration, so on one side I was flattered, but on the other, there were too many. My relationship with him was enormously personal, unique and special. . . . The intimacy, the laughs, the giggles: I thought it was a special relationship between Truman and me. I didn't think he was giggling and laughing with Babe and Gloria or Slim. . . . I must tell you frankly that he did not adore us for ourselves, though he made us believe he did. We always think when the intimacy comes it is because of ourselves. But with Truman, it was the situation in which we lived that interested him. . . . We only had one common denominator—the kind of life we lived."

Marella Agnelli had started distancing herself from Truman before the *Esquire* story hit the stands, when, on one occasion, "he began saying these horrors to me about someone I cared for a lot, passing them off as little asides. . . . It was a nightmare . . . suddenly I looked at him and saw my enemy . . . the man is dangerous, you should run away. Suddenly I connected. I thought that only somebody very strange or mad could have a very intimate, kind, warm relationship and at the same time stab," Agnelli said. "Three days later I asked Truman why he had said what he did. 'I thought it was better that you knew,' he told me. 'Everybody knew and you didn't.' And then, talking about somebody else, he said, 'Some people kill with their swords and some with their words.' I did not know how long it took, but one day I realized that I didn't care for Truman. He was out. I was not even curious, not about his books, nor his life. I knew this man would stab me."

Lee Radziwill was one of the few women who did not ostracize him. It was true that her role in "La Côte Basque" was minor and she was not depicted poorly by Truman, despite some negative statements she had made in the past about his sexuality. However, she had always liked him for the interesting man that he was. And when the *Esquire* debacle ensued, she stayed by his side. She went on to declare in several interviews that it was not Truman who had taken advantage of the women, but that instead he had been used by the swans.

"He was in absolute shock," she recalled in an interview. "He'd hear of another monument falling, and he'd say, 'But I'm a journalist—everybody knows that I'm a journalist!' I just don't think he realized what he was doing, because, God, did he pay for it. That's what put him back to serious drinking. And then, of course, the terrible fear that he could never write another word again. It was all downhill from there."

Radziwill watched as he eroded. He started to carry with him a sort of black doctor's bag stuffed with pills, always washed down with a glass of liquor, much as his mother had done. Radziwill went on, "He needed to take tranquilizers because he was an extremely nervous person . . . much more tense than people realized, or that he appeared to be when he was trying to amuse everyone. I think his life was a strain every day."

But eventually his drinking drove even Lee Radziwill away. They "drifted apart because of his drinking," she said. "We just forgot about one another. I mean, I never forgot about him, but we didn't see each other, because he wasn't making any sense whatsoever. It was pitiful, because there was nothing you could do. He really wanted to kill himself. It was a slow and pitiful suicide."

Many friends, including fellow literary figures, were not just alarmed but surprised that Truman was displaying such poor judgment. The writer Tennessee Williams said, "This story Capote has written is shockingly repugnant and thoroughly libelous. Capote's a monster of the first order, a cold-blooded murderer at heart. He's a liar, and everybody knows he is." Williams appeared in the story as a common john, so it was not surprisingly that he felt that way.

William Styron described the act of publishing the story as self-sabotage. "It was disastrous. And to me, inexplicable. Writers don't have to destroy their friendships with people in order to write. It seemed to me an act of willful destruction."

Truman's friend George Page agreed. "It dawned on me that his publishing those excerpts was a very self-destructive act and that I think he knew it. When he was sober, he took a sort of impish glee in what was about to happen. I really believe that he knew he had thrown a bombshell that was going to change his life. . . . It knocked him for the most part right off his extraordinary social pedestal."

The writer Norman Mailer, with whom Truman did not have a friendly relationship, said, "He had to feel that his social life was swallowing him. Because the warmth, the entertainment, the humor, the creativity he brought to his relations with all these people had to have its reverse side, which is that he'd seriously get to hate them more and more because they swallowed his talent."

Mailer also suspected that Truman, despite running in the same circles as the women he wrote about did, hardly got what they were about. "He didn't understand the true social force of New York," Mailer said, "that certain things he wrote could not be forgiven. But then he also misjudged his own resources. He did not have the stuff left to say, 'A plague in your house,' and write the book he could write. That book had probably died in him ten years earlier."

On reading the story, some were surprised that those who were portrayed felt so betrayed. Didn't they know better than to share their most intimate secrets with him? C. Z. Guest did not snub him, as many pushed her to do. She revealed to a reporter what she believed should have been apparent to everybody else too. "Everybody knew the man's a professional, and they told him those things anyway. He's a dear friend of mine, but I wouldn't discuss very private matters with him. I don't even know who those factual people are."

He had other supporters. The writer Dotson Rader considered "La Côte Basque, 1965" simply perfect. "Marvelous, beautiful writing. It's unimportant whether it's true or not since it is presented as fiction. Truman was always treated by those people as a kind of curiosity, expected to do his act. That was humiliating coming from people who had no qualifications other than being rich and social. Everybody in the world has been telling Truman their deepest confidences for years and he never said he wouldn't use them."

THIRTY-ONE

⟡

When Ann Woodward shot her husband, Billy Woodward, in 1955, she was shunned by those who knew her and criticized by millions who didn't. She was called a parasite who killed her spouse in order to gain his money. The members of high society whom Ann had tried so hard to befriend turned their backs on her, and years later, when she returned from Europe, they still would not acknowledge her. Now, after Ann's suicide, no doubt in anticipation of Truman Capote's damning article, she was even pitied, if only just a little. And what to say of those poor sons of hers?

Elsie Woodward watched from a distance as Truman Capote self-destructed and imploded. Patrick O'Higgins, an intimate friend of Elsie's, had this to say about the entire "La Côte Basque" wreck: "He'd gone downhill. People think, 'What a shame that a great talent should be reduced to writing gossip.' Some people are really hurt because they've been kind to him. The Paleys were always so fond of him. But Elsie hasn't been hurt. She didn't even read the piece. She couldn't care less. All she'll say is, '*Se ne le comes pas*'—isn't that perfect?"

277

Truman claimed that he didn't care. In an interview, he said, "I never think about it. I have a way of blocking things completely out of my mind and I have since I was a child, because I've had a lot of things to block out of my mind. Things that create anxiety and apprehension and what no . . . It's just as though I took some kind of magical pill." When people began to attack him following the publication of "La Côte Basque, 1965," he added, "They can accuse me of mass murder, and it wouldn't make my pulse skip a beat. I don't care about anything. You should never let them sense a weakness in you, because then they'll go for you like sharks."

He tried to appear unaffected by the backlash. In repeated conversations, whether private or public, as well as in newspapers and magazine articles and interviews, not to mention on television appearances, he made sure to leave the impression that the subjects of his fiction should not have been at all surprised. In one interview, shortly after the story appeared in *Esquire*, he said, "I've been seriously writing this for three and a half years. I told everybody what I was doing. I discussed it on TV. Why did it come as such a surprise? This thing was only a chapter. My God, what will happen when 'Unspoiled Monsters' comes out. . . . Lord, I have a lot to say, baby! I haven't even begun to say it, though the book is eighty percent written."

But the publication of the entire book was always delayed. His remaining friends speculated he was done with the rest of the chapters and refused to have them published. Perhaps the reception to the *Esquire* story hurt him more deeply than he cared to admit. Perhaps he did not want to lose the handful of acquaintances who still lingered by his side by publishing the rest. But if that was truly the case, what did he do with the remaining chapters? Did he burn them in a sort of sacrificial pyre? Did he store them somewhere where a researcher would one day find them, when they could no longer hurt anyone? Did he give them to a trusted friend with the promise never to read them? And if so, who was that friend?

But as much as he boasted he was immune to his being ostracized, the reality was different. Kate Harrington, the daughter of one of his lovers, said that he took the rebukes like a death in the family. "He went into a colossal depression," along with indulging in heavy drinking and drugging to try to blunt his feelings. "He wouldn't get out of bed and the days would turn into nights; he never opened the blinds and I'd sit and we'd talk. He was so upset he'd cry." The house was silent, because his telephone had stopped ringing, the past and the present seemed to blend together. He had imagined that people's anger would eventually abate, but it never did. "He was staggered by that," said Kate Harrington. "For two years he sort of went on, but it was never the same."

Suffering intense psychological pressure, Truman Capote turned to cocaine. Studio 54 became a place of refuge. "The nightclub of the future," he called it. "It's very democratic. Boys with boys, girls with girls, girls with boys, blacks and whites, capitalists and Marxists, Chinese and everything else—all one big mix." Several stints in rehab didn't work, and his relationships with his lovers faltered.

Truman's new lifestyle played havoc not only with his mind but also with his body. He grew corpulent. His manner turned grotesque, some of his former friends said; simply a parody of his younger self. "Long before Truman died," the writer John Richardson remembered, "I saw a sort of bag lady with two enormous bags wandering around the corner of Lexington and 73rd, where I lived then. And suddenly, I realized, Christ! It's Truman! I said, 'Come by and have a cup of tea.'" Back at the apartment, Richardson stepped into the kitchen to prepare the tea, leaving Truman alone for a few minutes. By the time Richardson returned and joined Truman again, "half-a-bottle of vodka or scotch or whatever it was—was gone. I had to take him outside and gently put him in a cab."

He suffered various falls and even endured a seizure. Blood clots formed on his lungs. His health issues, coupled with his alcoholism, caused him to turn away from society at large. To those few he saw, he claimed that he was still working on *Answered Prayers*, but the reality was that his writing had slowed, if not stopped. He was an American icon tumbling toward his own ruin.

⁊

By 1984 Truman Capote was exhausted in every sense. His reservoir of talent appeared depleted, and most of the friendships he had cultivated throughout his life had disappeared. There were those who had decided to stand by him despite all that was happening, but those were few indeed. One was Joanne Carson. He went to visit her in California. In one of the last interviews he gave before leaving, he gave one final reiteration of his defense: "I can't understand why everybody's so upset. What do they think they had around them, a court jester? They had a writer."

On August 25, 1984, Joanne Carson entered his room to find that Truman Capote had died. He was a month away from his sixtieth birthday. When learning of his death, the writer Gore Vidal, no friend or fan of his, called his passing "a wise career move." His friends and editors, and eventually scholars, searched for the remaining pages of *Answered Prayers*, as he always suggested there were hundreds more to share. None were ever found. A former lover, John O'Shea, was said to have seen the complete manuscript, but he must have been the only one who ever did. Friends, including his editor, suggested he had stashed it away in the locker of a bus station. But still others feared that Capote had burned the remaining pages, likely prior to flying off to California. Either way, it appears that he took the mystery of *Answered Prayers* with him.

EPILOGUE

⁓⁂⁓

Following Truman Capote's death on August 25, 1984, Gerald Clarke, his friend and later biographer; Joseph Fox, his editor at Random House; and Alan Schwartz, his lawyer and literary executor, searched for the remaining chapters of *Answered Prayers*. But they found nothing. They went through his apartment at the UN Plaza, purchased with the royalties from *In Cold Blood*, which at the time had been the It place to live. And they turned the beach house in Sag Harbor inside out. But the remaining chapters did not surface. Was there anything to actually find?

Joanne Carson said there was. She maintained that Truman had kept a little writing spot at her house, where he had worked relentlessly on the manuscript. "I saw them," she said. "He had many, many pages of manuscript, and he started to read them. They were very, very good. He read one chapter, but then someone called, and when I went back, he just put them aside and said, 'I'll read them after dinner.' But he never did—you know how that happens."

She eventually told reporters that Truman Capote had given her a key to a safe deposit box the day before he died, claiming the box contained the pages of *Answered Prayers*. But he didn't tell her where the box was located.

In Sag Harbor, Myron Clement was happy to look for the missing pages too. Truman Capote had been a good friend and neighbor to him and Joe Petrocik. "Truman would talk to us about all these things that were going into *Answered Prayers*," Clement said. "I remember I was at the other end of his couch, and he'd be reading all this from a manuscript. . . . And then it occurred to me, later, just before I nodded off to sleep, maybe he made the whole thing up. He was such a wonderful, wonderful actor."

Joe Petrocik didn't think he had made anything up. He recalled one occasion when, driving back from Manhattan to Long Island, Truman "handed me the manuscript to read on the way. I actually had it in my hands."

That said, no pages were ever found. Even today, decades after the publication of those few chapters meant to be included in the finished book, questions remain as to what happened to the rest of *Answered Prayers*, whether he trashed the pages, burned them, lost them in a move, or, as some researchers have come to believe, never wrote them at all.

Jack Dunphy, Truman's longtime friend and lover, believed that after the intense firestorm that erupted following the publication of "La Côte Basque," he simply went on to pretend that he was still writing *Answered Prayers*. In reality, his creative output dedicated to the novel had stalled to a glacial trickle, and he simply did not have the guts to admit it to his readers or to his fellow writers. Eventually, his editor Joseph Fox came to realize that perhaps he had written many more pages to the book, maybe even completing it, although when he was done he ended up being so unhappy with the results that he got rid of it, likely burning it while "incoherent because of drugs or alcohol or both." If Fox's theory is to be believed, it would explain why some people got the chance to see pages of the manuscript, while others never did. The writer John Knowles also admitted to having seen several pages, although he later agreed with Joseph Fox that Truman probably got rid of the rest.

However, not all were fond of this theory. The director Frank Perry recalled an episode with Truman that gave another spin to the enduring saga of *Answered Prayers*. "I asked him how everything was going, and he said, 'It's wonderful. . . . Look at that, finished pages, two and a half inches. It's wonderful.'" Perry then went on, "Later, being a cynic, I drifted off to ruffle through the manuscript. It turned out to be a Missouri bankroll, which is to say, the top three pages had typewriting on them and the rest were blank."

Alan Schwartz was also surprised not to find any additional chapters, considering how pushy Truman Capote had been toward Random House about getting the rest of his advance, and his position that the book was almost done. Nonetheless, it was not unusual for Truman to misrepresent the truth just a little.

Truman Capote had also once blamed his onetime lover John O'Shea for his inability to deliver *Answered Prayers*, insisting that O'Shea had stolen the only copy of the manuscript and driven to Florida with it. After asking Alan Schwartz to file a lawsuit against O'Shea in order to retrieve the manuscript, Truman told his friends a story of having gone down to Florida himself, whereupon he had rescued *Answered Prayers* from O'Shea's car before blowing up the car. "One day little Johnny went downstairs, and his car wasn't there," Truman was thrilled to say. "Instead there was a big puddle where a car used to be." It was a fun story he liked to pass as true, but one that no one believed. Later still, he also insisted that he had stashed the manuscript in a locker at the Los Angeles Greyhound station. However, that station was moved in 1991, and none of the old lockers were kept; if there was a manuscript there, it was lost. That said, the likelihood of the only copy of *Answered Prayers* being hidden in a bus station's locker is not very high. Just as with many of Truman Capote's tales, this one could have belonged to the fictional world.

Despite all the fascinating recollections people had related to *Answered Prayers*, the most likely truth remains that Capote never finished the book, and that whatever pages he had written and accumulated up to a certain point, he finally decided to destroy, spending his remaining years in a slow deterioration hastened by the publication of "La Côte Basque."

That is why questions over "La Côte Basque" itself, that infamous, raunchy little story, remain as well. Why had he decided to publish it before the whole book came out? What had he hoped to accomplish? A smart, intuitive man, he must have been aware, at some level, of what the response from his circle of friends would be—despite his denials to the contrary. Why would he be so eager to engage in a public spat with the very same people he had spent countless hours and years courting?

"I wonder whether he wasn't testing the love of his friends, to see what he could get away with. We had Truman around because he paid for his supper," John Richardson said, "by being the great storyteller in the marketplace of Marrakech. Truman was a brilliant recounter."

Truman didn't like the idea of being used for his talents, or of being kept around for entertainment only, like a circus monkey. "I was never that," he maintained. He was better than that. However, he needed to know for sure. And was there a better way to learn if his friends were devoted to him or his art than by using that very art against them?

But the publication of "La Côte Basque," while fierce, was nothing compared with the malevolence he received in return. He was snubbed by those he had fought so hard to befriend. And he must have realized how fleeting those relationships had been to begin with, how unimportant he truly was in their lives, if it was so easy for them to cut him out. Afterward, his downfall was swift and tragic, much like Ann Woodward's had been.

Overwhelmed by the burden of their own notoriety—Ann Woodward for shooting her husband, Billy Woodward, and Truman Capote for writing the successful *In Cold Blood*, the unfinished *Answered Prayers*, and the infamous "La Côte Basque," among others—they both struggled with alcoholism, addiction, and depression. In addition, in Capote's case there was the added burden of writer's block and the need for perfection, which made moving forward with his craft nearly impossible.

Ann and Truman were surprisingly modern, considering the times they lived in. And what they sought, eventually found, endured, and lost—all while in the public eye—speaks to today's culture with surprising freshness and clarity—a culture of celebrity dishing and hypocrisy, of the savagery of gossip that at the time was cultivated around lunch tables and dinner parties, while today can be served cold on various Internet sites, where anybody can be both judge and jury.

In "La Côte Basque," Truman Capote turned out to be judge and jury himself. While prior to its publication no one knew his innermost feelings about the women who surrounded him, though they might have guessed, they certainly figured them out after the story was published. It was an unusually mean, vindictive, spiteful, catty tale. However, that he unleashed most of his venom on Ann Woodward was not surprising. He never liked her, and the passing years had not mollified his stand. That she killed herself shortly after learning about the story never bothered him. What surprised Truman and bothered him the most was that he became socially shunned, ending up like Ann Woodward. After all, Ann had committed murder; he had not.

Although their culpability differed, the truth remains that Ann Woodward had shot and killed her husband with a gun, while Truman Capote had used his pen to drive her to suicide. In an indirect way, he had caused her death, whether he liked to admit it or not. What he also seemed unable to grasp was the fact that in turning the pen against his friends and enemies, he also turned it against himself. Doing so, he began his inevitable slide toward becoming a social pariah, just like Ann Woodward herself.

ACKNOWLEDGMENTS

～✳～

Writing a nonfiction book during the start of a worldwide pandemic is challenging, to say the least. Places you planned on visiting suddenly shut down, with no immediate date on when or if they'll open up again. People begin working from home, adjusting to new schedules and ways of living, and coping with stressors unheard of before, be it professional, financial, personal, or familial, or all of them. That said, with grit, passion, graciousness, tolerance, an unending supply of patience, tenacity, and a love of one's job, the work always gets done.

And that is what I found out. Librarians, archivists, and researchers, most especially, always get the job done.

In writing this book, I have dozens of people to thank, for favors and tips and leads of where to look for information big and small, but several stand out: Meredith Mann, librarian at the Brooke Russell Astor Reading Room for Rare Books and Manuscripts at the New York Public Library, the biggest repository of Truman Capote material a researcher can be lucky to find. Steve Hammond, the head of reference at the Oyster Bay–East Norwich Public Library, where, of course, Ann Woodward's life and Billy Woodward's death are amply covered. Denice Evans-Sheppard, the executive director at the Oyster Bay Historical Society, who, aside from providing information on Ann Woodward and Billy Woodward, as well as the entire Woodward clan, assisted with material on the social climate of the area at the time the Woodwards resided there. Jonathan M. Alley, curator of the Long Island Museum, provided some captivating material that related to not only the Woodwards, but Truman Capote as well. Mary Faldich, senior assistant district attorney, Appeals Bureau, Nassau County District Attorney's Office, patiently answered my questions on Billy Woodward's murder and led me down the correct path in order to find the material and files I needed. In that regard, Karen Matuza, of the Nassau County Police Department homicide squad, was incomparable. I connected to her thanks to Ms. Faldich, and in relating what my needs were, she explained what I could legally get my hands on. When one day thousands of files arrived at my home, it was like Christmas—a morbid sort of Christmas, but a holiday nonetheless. The details of the murder were there, as were the profiles of everyone involved. The book could not have been completed without this material. Dennis Wilson provided files regarding the bombing and sinking of the USS *Liscome Bay* and Billy Woodward's role and feelings on it. Kerriann Flanagan Brosky has written extensively about crimes on Long Island, and she was kind enough to speak to me about the Woodwards and their role in the society they inhabited.

In addition, I would like to thank Trish Todd, my editor at Atria, who was excited about this book from the very start, when it came to her in the proposal stage. Getting to know her and working with her has been not only a joy, but a privilege. She is funny, kind, and professional, and the book has only gotten better because of her masterful touch. Rob Weisbach, superb agent and friend with a discriminating taste, is able to see the good in a story, and its flaws, and is always, always capable of making me feel better when things are not working precisely as they should. We have worked together for many years, and hopefully this is the latest book of many more to come. David Groff read the manuscript toward its final stages, and his comments and suggestions certainly opened up my eyes to things I hadn't been able to consider, even after spending years with Ann and Truman. I am grateful he spent so much time working with me, and looking over the manuscript, for it is better for having been the beneficiary of his time. David Ebershoff also read over the drama that is *Deliberate Cruelty*. His opinion on the lives of Ann Woodward and Truman Capote were incomparable, and I am thankful that he took time to go over the manuscript.

I am grateful that my mom, Celeste, and my sister, Francesca, didn't get too bored listening to me rattle on about my latest finds about Truman Capote and Ann Woodward. Actually, they were quite riveted. I am grateful for their support, as I always am while working on a book. As well as for the support of friends, who also had to hear talks about Ann, Truman, the swans, and the fancy parties and dinners they engaged in. While our get-togethers were less fancy and not quite as catty, they were fun as well.

BIBLIOGRAPHY

NOTES

PROLOGUE

Ann Woodward and Truman Capote's spat while meeting in Europe is depicted in Gerald Clarke's impressive *Capote: A Biography*, George Plimpton's *Truman Capote: In Which Various Friends, Enemies, Acquaintances, and Detractors Recall his Turbulent Career*, and Lawrence Grobel's *Conversations with Capote*.

CHAPTER 1

Most of the information on Ann and Billy's drive home from the Bakers' party comes from the Nassau County District Attorney's Office *Investigation into the Death of William Woodward, Jr.*, October 1955 (hereafter referred to as *Investigation* in these notes). This source comprises thousands of pages that detail the murder itself as well as testimonies from Ann Woodward and dozens of others who were at the party and knew both Ann and Billy. There, Ann Woodward details the argument she had with her husband before and after the party, as well as her version of events regarding the shooting.

Additional details on the Duchess of Windsor are found in such books as Charles Higham's *The Duchess of Windsor: The Secret Life* and Stephen Birmingham's *Duchess: The Story of Wallis Warfield Windsor*.

CHAPTER 2

William Woodward's life story can be found in William Ogden Wheeler's *John Ogden, the Pilgrim and his Descendants, Their History, Biography, and Gene-*

293

ology. Billy's own privilege, and by extension, that of his family, is also found there.

There are also some terrific books that talk about Kansas during Ann's birth and stay there, such as A. T. Andreas's *History of the State of Kansas*; Ray Allen Billington's *Westward Expansion: A History of the American Frontier*; Frank Blackmar's *Kansas*; Carroll D. Clark's *People of Kansas: A Demographic and Sociological Study*; Charles C. Howes's *This Place Called Kansas*; Robert W. Richmond's *Kansas: A Land of Contrasts*; and Joanna Stratton's *Pioneer Women: Voices from the Kansas Frontier*.

CHAPTER 3

Details on Ethel and Jesse-Claude come from such books as Andreas's *History of the State of Kansas*, Billington's *Westward Expansion*, Blackmar's *Kansas*, Clark's *People of Kansas*, Howes's *This Place Called Kansas*, Richmond's *Kansas: A Land of Contrasts*, and Stratton's *Pioneer Women*.

CHAPTER 4

Ann Woodward talks about her life in Kansas City in the Nassau County District Attorney's Office *Investigation*.

The history of nightclubs such as El Morocco and the Stork is always fun to read. To do so, search for the most famous such book, Ralph Blumenthal's *The Stork Club: America's Most Famous Nightspot and the Lost World of Café Society* (Boston: Little, Brown, 2000).

For a thorough biography of Joan Crawford, the woman who so inspired Ann Woodward and countless other women during the era, I recommend Bob Thomas's *Joan Crawford*.

Information on John Robert Powers, his modeling agency, and his models is available in John Robert Powers, *The Powers Girls*.

CHAPTER 5

Information on Lillie Mae Faulk and Arch Persons, Truman Capote's parents, can be found in such books as Clarke's massive *Capote* and Plimpton's *Truman Capote*.

Information on Monroeville itself can be found in Grobel's *Conversations with Capote* and Marie Rudisill and James C. Simmons's *Truman Capote: The Story of His Bizarre and Exotic Boyhood, by an Aunt Who Helped Raise Him*, along with details concerning the lives and influence of Jeannie, Callie, and Sook Faulk. Here, Nelle Harper Lee also begins to make an appearance.

CHAPTER 6

Again, Truman Capote's life in Monroeville can be found in such material as Clarke's *Capote*, Plimpton's *Truman Capote*, Grobel's *Conversations with Capote*, and Rudisill and Simmons's *Truman Capote*. The early life of his parents and other relatives is also depicted in those sources, as is Lillie Mae's move to New York City, her eventual divorce from Arch Persons, and her marriage to Joseph Garcia Capote.

Maury Paul's life and doings are depicted in the works of Eve Brown, especially her book *Champagne Cholly: The Life and Times of Maury Paul*. Brown also wrote another book called *The Plaza: Its Life and Times*, in which her own life is talked about.

CHAPTER 7

The socialites have made for good subjects in such works as Marylin Bender's *The Beautiful People*, Allen Churchill's *The Upper Crust: An Informal History of New York's Highest Society*, Charlotte Curtis's *The Rich and Other Atrocities*, and the 1963 *Celebrity Register*, edited by Cleveland Amory.

Ann Woodward speaks of her life in New York and her mother's illness in the Nassau County District Attorney's Office *Investigation*. There she also details her time at the Powers Agency and describes her thoughts on modeling in general.

Information on Joan Crawford can be found in Thomas's *Joan Crawford*. The Stork's history can be learned from Blumenthal's *The Stork Club*. And an introduction to William Woodward and his peculiarities, especially his love of horses, can be found in *Who's Who in Thoroughbred Racing*, edited by Ned Welch; Shirley Vlasak Baltz's *A Chronicle of Belair*; and Tom Ainslie's *Ainslie's Complete Guide to Thoroughbred Racing*.

CHAPTER 8

Because of his relevance, William Woodward Sr. was quite well known, and much was written about him at the time. As such, much can be learned from Welch's *Who's Who in Thoroughbred Racing*, Baltz's *Chronicle of Belair*, Ainslie's *Complete Guide to Thoroughbred Racing*, and W. S. Bosburg's *Cherished Portraits of Thoroughbred Horses*. In these texts, information about the Belair Stud and Farm and the horses, especially Nashua, can be found.

Elsie Cryder's history is recorded in Wheeler's *John Ogden*.

Long Island's colorful history has spawned quite a few history books, including Monica Randall's *The Mansions of Long Island's Gold Coast*.

CHAPTER 9

Ann Eden meeting Billy Woodward at Fefe's Monte Carlo is detailed in the Nassau County District Attorney's Office *Investigation*. There, Ann reveals how she and Billy met and discusses their date at the 21 Club, their trip to Saratoga, and many more intimacies, such as their wedding.

Billy Woodward's joining the navy and the subsequent accident is written about in great detail in USS *Liscome Bay (CVE56) Loss in Action Gilbert Islands, Central Pacific 24 November, 1943*, War Damage Report No. 45, and Eliot Samuel Morrison's *History of the United States Naval Operations in World War II*.

CHAPTER 10

Billy's accident in the Navy is discussed in USS *Liscome Bay (CVE56) Loss in Action Gilbert Islands, Central Pacific 24 November, 1943*, War Damage Report No. 45, and Samuel Eliot Morrison's *History of United States Naval Operations in World War II*.

Information on the birth and upbringing of Billy and Ann's children is detailed in the Nassau County District Attorney's Office *Investigation*. These files also contain Ann's detailing to Edward Robinson her dealings with New York's upper crust and her difficulties in acclimating into the family. Information on Billy's affair with Princess Marina Torlonia can be found there as well, along with information concerning Ann's efforts to hire investigators to follow them.

The death of William Woodward Sr. and Billy's takeover of the horses, including Nashua, is detailed in such books as Welch's *Who's Who in Thoroughbred Racing*, Baltz's *Chronicle of Belair*, Ainslie's *Complete Guide to Thoroughbred Racing*, and Bosburg's *Cherished Portraits of Thoroughbred Horses*.

CHAPTER 11

Relevant information on Joseph Garcia Capote's divorce and subsequent marriage to Lillie Mae/Nina and his adoption of Truman are discussed in great detail in such books as Clarke's *Capote*, Plimpton's *Truman Capote*, Grobel's *Conversations with Capote*, and Rudisill and Simmons's *Truman Capote*. Here, Truman's party in Monroeville before he left for New York is also discussed in fine detail, as is the Capotes' turbulent life in Brooklyn and Connecticut, Truman's relationship with his mother, her depression, and Joe's many affairs.

CHAPTER 12

Information on Truman Capote's life in New York City can be found in Clarke's *Capote*, Plimpton's *Truman Capote*, Grobel's *Conversations with Capote*, and Rudisill and Simmons's *Truman Capote*.

Anaïs Nin's opinion of Truman Capote is expressed in *The Diary of Anaïs Nin*.

The details of Capote's leaving the job at *The New Yorker* and heading south to his family to continue working on his novel in progress *Summer Crossing* and his eventual shelving of it in favor of starting *Other Voices, Other Rooms* can be found in Clarke's *Capote*, Clarke's *Too Brief a Treat: The Letters of Truman Capote*, and Thomas Inge's *Truman Capote: Conversations*.

For an intimate look at Truman's relationship with Jack Dunphy, a good read is Dunphy's own *Dear Genius: A Memoir of My Life with Truman Capote*.

For those wanting to learn about Nina's suicide, an excellent source is Clarke's *Capote*.

CHAPTER 13

The most reliable information on Ann and Billy attending the Bakers' party on the Halloween weekend of 1955 comes from the Nassau County District Attorney's Office *Investigation*. Information on Billy Woodward wanting to buy the Helio plane in Kansas comes from there too, as do the details concerning the arguments that ensued because of it.

Details on Ann and Billy preparing for the party in their Oyster Bay home, leaving for the party, and arriving at the party come from the Nassau County District Attorney's Office *Investigation*, as does the testimony of the maid Annie Schroeder, who gave all the details of the Woodwards' actions prior to leaving for the party, those of the children, and everyone's actions upon arrival at the home. Recollections of those who attended the party are also found there, as is the conversation Lee Principe had with Billy Woodward when the Woodwards arrived in Oyster Bay. These particular files also describe, on a step-by-step basis, Ann's trip to the drugstore to buy cosmetics, and they detail her general attitude and mood about going to the party and being there that evening. They also talk about the ride back home.

CHAPTER 14

The information on Billy removing a pistol from the glove compartment of his car, and then removing the shotguns from the gun case and handing one to Ann, comes from Ann's retelling to Edward Robinson found in the Nassau County District Attorney's Office *Investigation*. This file also includes details of Ann's movements while in her bedroom and information on her general feelings, the shooting itself, the telephone calls to the police and her lawyer, and her trip to the hospital.

CHAPTER 15

Information on the rumors swirling around Oyster Bay regarding the murder, where they came from and who was spreading them, comes from the Nassau County District Attorney's Office *Investigation*.

These reports also include the detectives' conversation with Walter C. Keir, the private investigator Ann Woodward hired to follow Billy Woodward; materials on Ann and Billy Woodward's several separations, and who knew about them; and a report that details Ann's feelings on Billy's flirtations with Brenda Frazier the evening of the Bakers' party.

There is also a file on the detectives' conversation with Elsie Woodward and her reaction to her son's death.

Information on Ann's doctor, John Prutting, is found in the Nassau County District Attorney's Office *Investigation*, as are the reports concerning all he did in order to move her to a private hospital.

Ann's lawyer, Sol Rosenblatt, worked hard to mount a good defense. His tactics are described in the Nassau County District Attorney's Office *Investigation*.

And of great interest is Russell Havenstrite's letter to Edward Robinson describing the trip to India to shoot tigers and Ann's desire to learn to shoot, which is also included in these files.

CHAPTER 16

Paul Wirths, his movements, motives, thoughts, and feelings on the Halloween weekend of 1955 and in the days prior and following it, are described in great detail in the Nassau County District Attorney's Office *Investigation*, as well as in the Nassau County Police Department's *Probation Report, Paul Wirths*, case #8149, individual #13553, March 1955.

CHAPTER 17

Ann's care in the hospital under the direction of Dr. Prutting and his wife is described in the Nassau County District Attorney's Office *Investigation*, which also contains material on Elsie Woodward's visit to Ann while in the hospital, their chat about Ann and Billy's children, and Ann's eventual decision to agree to her mother-in-law's terms.

CHAPTER 18

Details on Ann Woodward's visit on November 21, 1955, to Mineola to be questioned by Edward Robinson can be found in its entirety in the Nassau County District Attorney's Office *Investigation*, in which a great back-and-forth between herself and Edward Robinson ensues.

CHAPTER 19

Information on Ann Woodward's acquittal, the public's reaction to it, and Ann's move to Europe is available in the Nassau County District Attorney's Office *Investigation*.

Truman Capote's infatuation with socialites and people in high places began early. Good places to look for information about it are in Clarke's *Capote*, Plimpton's *Truman Capote*, and Grobel's *Conversations with Capote*.

Information on Capote's desire to write *Answered Prayers* can be found in the introduction to *Answered Prayers: The Unfinished Novel*, in which his editor, Joseph Fox, speaks of Capote's trouble with it. In the above books, a reader will also find details about Truman Capote finding the article about the 1959 Kansas murder that eventually spawned *In Cold Blood*.

CHAPTER 20

Many books have been written about the genesis of *In Cold Blood*. Information on Capote's arrival in Kansas, his relationship with Harper Lee, his relationship with the people of Kansas, and his ability to get to know Perry Smith and Richard Hickock can be found in Clarke's *Capote*, Plimpton's *Truman Capote*, Grobel's *Conversations with Capote*, Kim Powers's *Capote in Kansas: A Ghost Story*, Richmond's *Kansas*, and Charles Shields's *Mockingbird: A Portrait of Harper Lee*. Many details of the murders are found in these books, as is information on the murderers and the Clutters themselves. How Capote and the writing of his book was affected by the judicial system in Kansas is also detailed, as is his frustrations with it.

CHAPTER 21

Information on the publication of *In Cold Blood*, and critics' and readers' reactions to it, can be found in Clarke's *Capote*, Plimpton's *Truman Capote*, and Grobel's *Conversations with Capote*. There were detractors who believed some of the material described was not entirely true, and information on that entire episode is also included in those sources. Also included are some of the best descriptions of Capote's famous Black and White Ball.

CHAPTER 22

Details on why Capote returned to *Answered Prayers* are included in Clarke's *Capote*, Plimpton's *Truman Capote*, Grobel's *Conversations with Capote*, and *Answered Prayers: The Unfinished Novel*. The latter includes a section written by his editor, Joseph Fox, detailing Capote's contract with Random House, his promises of when it would be finished, and the lack of material. Fox's ideas of what happened to the rest of the manuscript are also included there.

CHAPTER 23

Capote's fascination with the rich is described in Clarke's *Capote*, Plimpton's *Truman Capote*, Grobel's *Conversations with Capote*, Curtis's *The Rich and Other*

Atrocities, Churchill's *The Upper Crust*, Bender's *The Beautiful People*, Michael and Ariane Batterberry's *On the Town in New York*, and Amory's *Celebrity Register*. Material on Babe Paley, Lee Radziwill, Marella Agnelli, and several other swans is also found those sources.

CHAPTER 24

Details of Capote's efforts to continue *Answered Prayers* are included in Clarke's *Capote*, Plimpton's *Truman Capote*, and Grobel's *Conversations with Capote*. *Answered Prayers: The Unfinished Novel* comes with a commentary from his editor, Joseph Fox, which discusses Capote's efforts to finish the novel, Fox's ideas of what happened to the rest of the manuscript, and why he did not want Capote to publish "La Côte Basque" in *Esquire*.

CHAPTER 25

Information on Ann Woodward learning of Truman Capote's publication can be found, in a broad sense, in Clarke's *Capote*.

The reaction of the swans to "La Côte Basque" can be read in Clarke's definitive *Capote*, Plimpton's *Truman Capote*, and Grobel's *Conversations with Capote*.

CHAPTER 26

The effect of "La Côte Basque" on Truman himself was also brutal. Read about it in Clarke's *Capote*, Plimpton's *Truman Capote*, and Grobel's *Conversations with Capote*. Here, Slim Keith's reaction to how Truman depicted her in "La Côte Basque" is revealed.

CHAPTER 27

Information on Babe Paley is available in Clarke's *Capote*, Plimpton's *Truman Capote*, Grobel's *Conversations with Capote*, Lewis J. Paper's *Empire: William S. Paley and the Making of CBS*, Russell Lynes's *The Tastemakers*, and Bender's *The Beautiful People*. In these texts, one can also find a wide variety of information on the life of Marella Agnelli, Lee Bouvier Radziwill, and information on Truman Capote's being blacklisted from the fine society he had courted.

CHAPTER 28

Information on Babe Paley can be found in Clarke's *Capote*, Plimpton's *Truman Capote*, and Paper's *Empire*. In these books, the relationship between Capote and the Paleys is also discussed.

CHAPTER 29

For further details on *Answered Prayers*, read Clarke's massive *Capote*, Plimpton's *Truman Capote*, and Grobel's *Conversations with Capote*.

In Capote's *Answered Prayers: An Unfinished Novel*, Joseph Fox, his editor, gives a long explanation as to why he believes Capote never finished the book.

Liz Smith's interview with Truman Capote is quoted in many books, including the ones mentioned above.

CHAPTER 30

On Capote being blacklisted and his reaction to it, read Clarke's *Capote*, Plimpton's *Truman Capote*, and Grobel's *Conversations with Capote*.

CHAPTER 31

On Capote's loneliness, read Clarke's *Capote*, Plimpton's *Truman Capote*, and Grobel's *Conversations with Capote*. These texts also include material on Capote's struggles with cocaine and alcohol, and his eventual death.

EPILOGUE

On the disappearance of *Answered Prayers*, read Capote's *Answered Prayers: The Unfinished Novel*. There, his editor, Joseph Fox, includes his thoughts, and those of others, as to what happened to the manuscript, and what steps were taken in order to find it.

ARCHIVAL MATERIAL

Truman Capote's letters and other relevant sources can be found scattered in libraries and personal collections located not only in the United States but also in England. The largest reservoir of this material is the New York Public Library, which holds a collection of Capote's letters to Alvin and Marie Dewey, Andrew Lyndon, Catherine Wood, Arch Persons, Jack Dunphy, and countless others.

Another collection is the Columbia University Library, which holds the Random House collection, full of Capote's letters to Robert Linscott, Bennett Cerf, and others.

Other material can be found at the Beinecke Rare Book and Manuscript Library at Yale University, the University of Delaware Library, and the Saint John's College Library at Cambridge University. In addition, the University of Texas at Austin, Duke University, Smith College, Radcliffe College, Washington University in Saint Louis, and the Henry E. Huntington Library in California also have smaller collections.

BIBLIOGRAPHY

BOOKS

Ainslie, Tom. *Ainslie's Complete Guide to Thoroughbred Racing*, revised and updated edition. New York: Simon & Schuster, 1979.

Amory, Cleveland. *The Last Resorts*. New York: Harper & Row, 1948.

———, ed. *Celebrity Register*. New York: Harper & Row, 1963.

Andreas, A. T. *History of the State of Kansas*. Chicago: A. T. Andreas, 1883.

Baldwin, Billy. *Billy Baldwin Remembers*. New York: Harcourt Brace Jovanovich, 1974.

Baldwin, Hanson W. *The Crucial Years, 1939–1941*. New York: Harper & Row, 1976.

Baltz, Shirley Vlasak. *A Chronicle of Belair*. Bowie, MD: Bowie Heritage Committee, 1984.

Batterberry, Michael, and Ariane Batterberry. *On the Town in New York*. New York: Routledge, 1999.

Beaton, Cecil. *The Wandering Years: Diaries, 1922–39*. Boston: Little, Brown, 1961.

Bender, Marylin. *The Beautiful People*. New York: Coward-McCann, 1967.

Bessie, Simon Michael. *Jazz Journalism: The Story of the Tabloid Newspapers*. New York: Russell & Russell, 1969.

Billington, Ray Allen. *Westward Expansion: A History of the American Frontier*, 4th edition. New York: MacMillan, 1974.

Birmingham, Stephen. *Duchess: The Story of Wallis Warfield Windsor*. Boston: Little, Brown, 1981.

Black, David. *The King of Fifth Avenue*. New York: Dial Press, 1981.

Blackmar, Frank W., ed. *Kansas*. 2 vols. Chicago: Standard Publishing, 1912.

Blumenthal, Ralph. *The Stork Club: America's Most Famous Nightspot and the Lost World of Café Society*. Boston: Little, Brown, 2001.

Bosburg, W. S. *Cherished Portraits of Thoroughbred Horses*. New York: Derrydale Press, 1929.

Brown, Angela. *When Battered Women Kill*. New York: Free Press, 1987.

Brown, Eve. *Champagne Cholly: The Life and Times of Maury Paul*. New York: E. P. Dutton, 1947.

———. *The Plaza: Its Life and Times*. New York: Meredith Press, 1967.

Capote, Truman. *Answered Prayers: The Unfinished Novel*. New York: Random House, 1987.

———. *In Cold Blood*. New York: Vintage/Random House, 1993.

———. *Other Voices, Other Rooms*. New York: Vintage/Alfred A. Knopf/Random House, 1948.

————. "Preface to *Music for Chameleons.*" *A Capote Reader.* New York: Penguin, 1987.

Churchill, Allen. *The Upper Crust: An Informal History of New York's Highest Society.* Englewood Cliffs, NJ: Prentice-Hall, 1970.

Clark, Carroll D., and Roy L. Roberts. *People of Kansas: A Demographic and Sociological Study.* Topeka: Kansas State Planning Board, 1936.

Clarke, Gerald. *Capote: A Biography.* New York: Simon & Schuster, 1988.

————, ed. *Too Brief a Treat: The Letters of Truman Capote.* New York: Vintage, 2004.

Curtis, Charlotte. *The Rich and Other Atrocities.* New York: Harper & Row, 1976.

Diliberto, Gioia. *Debutante: The Story of Brenda Frazier.* New York: Alfred A. Knopf, 1987.

Dunne, Dominick. *The Two Mrs. Greenvilles.* New York: Crown Publishers, 1985.

Dunphy, Jack. *Dear Genius: A Memoir of My Life with Truman Capote.* New York: McGraw-Hill, 1987.

Erenberg, Lewis A. *Steppin' Out: New York Nightlife and the Transformation of American Culture, 1890–1930.* Westport, CT: Greenwood Press, 1981.

Fitzgerald, F. Scott. *The Great Gatsby.* New York: Charles Scribner's Sons, 1925.

Galbraith, John Kenneth. *Money: Whence It Came, Where It Went.* Boston: Houghton Mifflin, 1975.

Grobel, Lawrence. *Conversations with Capote.* New York: New American Library, 1985.

Higham, Charles. *The Duchess of Windsor: The Secret Life.* New York: McGraw-Hill, 1988.

The History of Stevens County and Its People. Stevens County History Association. Hugoton, KS: Lowell Press, 1979.

Howes, Charles C. *This Place Called Kansas.* Norman: University of Oklahoma Press, 1952.

Inge, Thomas M., ed. *Truman Capote: Conversations.* Jackson: University Press of Mississippi, 1987.

Lee, Harper. *To Kill a Mockingbird.* New York: Lippincott, 1960.

Lynes, Russell. *The Tastemakers.* New York: Harper & Brothers, 1954.

Maxwell, Elsa. *How To Do It, or The Lively Art of Entertaining.* Boston: Little, Brown, 1957.

Morrison, Samuel Eliot. *History of the United States Naval Operations in World War II.* 15 vol. Boston: Little, Brown, 1968.

Nassau County District Attorney's Office. *Investigation into the Death of William Woodward, Jr.,* October 1955.

Nassau County Police Department. *Probation Report, Paul Wirths*, case #8149, individual #13553, March 1955.

Nin, Anaïs. *The Diary of Anaïs Nin*. Edited by Gunther Stuhlmann. New York: Harcourt Brace Jovanovich, 1971.

Paper, Lewis J. *Empire: William S. Paley and the Making of CBS*. New York: St. Martin's Press, 1987.

Plimpton, George. *Truman Capote: In Which Various Friends, Enemies, Acquaintances, and Detractors Recall His Turbulent Career*. New York: Doubleday, 1997.

Powers, John Robert. *The Powers Girls*. New York: E. P. Dutton, 1941.

Powers, Kim. *Capote in Kansas: A Ghost Story*. New York: Carroll & Graf, 2007.

Randall, Monica. *The Mansions of Long Island's Gold Coast*. New York: Hastings House, 1979.

Reddig, William M. *Tom's Town: Kansas City and the Pendergast Legend*. Philadelphia: J. B. Lippincott Company, 1947.

"The Residence of William Woodward, Esq., New York City, Delano & Aldrich Architects, New York." *The Architectural Record*, April 1919.

Richmond, Robert W. *Kansas: A Land of Contrasts*. Saint Charles, MO: Forum Press, 1974.

Rudisill, Marie, with James C. Simmons. *Truman Capote: The Story of His Bizarre and Exotic Boyhood by an Aunt Who Helped Raise Him*. New York: Morrow, 1983.

Shields, Charles. *Mockingbird: A Portrait of Harper Lee*. New York: Henry Holt, 2006.

Stratton, Joanna L. *Pioneer Women: Voices from the Kansas Frontier*. New York: Simon & Schuster, 1982.

Tappert, Annette, and Slim Keith. *Slim: Memories of a Rich and Imperfect Life*. New York: Simon & Schuster, 1990.

Thomas, Bob. *Joan Crawford*. New York: Simon & Schuster, 1978.

USS Liscome Bay (CVE56) Loss in Action, Gilbert Islands, Central Pacific 24 November, 1943, War Damage Report No. 45, Preliminary Design Section, Bureau of Ships, Department of the Navy. Washington, DC: US Hydrographic Office, March 10, 1944. https://www.history.navy.mil/research/library/online-reading-room/title-list-alphabetically/w/war-damage-reports/uss-liscome-bay-cve56-war-damage-report-no-45.html.

Vickers, Hugo, ed. *Beaton in the Sixties: The Cecil Beaton Diaries as He Wrote Them, 1965–1969*. New York: Alfred A. Knopf, 2004.

Welch, Ned., ed. *Who's Who in Thoroughbred Racing*. New York: Vantage Press, 1962.

Wheeler, William Ogden. *John Ogden, the Pilgrim and His Descendants, Their History, Biography, and Geneology.* Edited by Lawrence and Ogden Van Alstyne and Reverend Charles Burr. Philadelphia: J.B. Lippincott Company, 1907.

Windham, Donald. *Lost Friendship: A Memoir of Truman Capote, Tennessee Williams, and Others.* New York: Morrow, 1987.

ABOUT THE AUTHOR

Roseanne Montillo is an accomplished research librarian who earned her MFA from Emerson College and has taught creative writing at Emerson and Tufts. Her three previous books of narrative nonfiction, *Fire on the Track*, *The Wilderness of Ruin*, and *The Lady and Her Monsters*, were published to critical acclaim.